ROSE'S ICE CREAM BLISS

ROSE'S ICE CREAM BLISS

Rose Levy Beranbaum

Photography by Matthew Septimus

Houghton Mifflin Harcourt
Boston   New York   2020

Photography team RoseWood: food stylist Katie Wayne, photographer Matthew Septimus, me, Woody, and food stylist Erin Jeanne McDowell

hmhbooks.com

Library of Congress Cataloging-in-Publication Data

Names: Beranbaum, Rose Levy, author. | Septimus, Matthew, photographer.
Title: Rose's ice cream bliss / Rose Levy Beranbaum ; photography by Matthew Septimus.
Other titles: Ice cream bliss
Description: Boston : Houghton Mifflin Harcourt, 2020. | Includes index.
Identifiers: LCCN 2019033902 (print) | LCCN 2019033903 (ebook) | ISBN 9781328506627 | ISBN 9781328506689 (ebook)
Subjects: LCSH: Ice cream, ices, etc. | LCGFT: Cookbooks.
Classification: LCC TX795 .B467 2020 (print) | LCC TX795 (ebook) | DDC 641.86/2—dc23
LC record available at https://lccn.loc.gov/2019033902
LC ebook record available at https://lccn.loc.gov/2019033903

Book design by Tai Blanche

Food styling by Erin Jeanne McDowell

Printed in China

TOP 10 9 8 7 6 5 4 3 2 1

To Owen Eliot Daw,
who introduced me to
Turkish ice cream and the joys
of being a grandmother.

CONTENTS

FOREWORD

The first cake Rose and I baked together was the Perfect All-American Chocolate Butter Cake. Rose recommended a whipped chocolate ganache for the frosting. The result was a near-perfect cake, with a delicate fine crumb and light but luxurious icing.

Mind you, this was twenty years before I actually met Rose, but as anyone who has used her cookbooks knows, to read her recipes is to have Rose in the kitchen with you, encouraging, teaching, and cheering you on.

A few years ago, my friend Susannah Appelbaum invited me to come to Mohonk Mountain House in New Paltz, New York, for a cooking and wine event. "You can meet Rose Levy Beranbaum," she said blithely, as if the thought of meeting the Notorious RLB didn't instantly make me break out into a cold sweat. "I think you two will really get along."

After I watched Rose demonstrate her technique for making scones, Susannah pulled me up to meet her. Dry-mouthed, I tried to say something clever but opted for "Delicious!" and then offered up a fawning smile and shook her hand. Afterward I screwed up the courage to send her an email, and a correspondence and friendship instantly bloomed. A few emails and a few months later, I felt as if we'd known each other for years, because that's the kind of embracing person Rose is.

Shortly thereafter, I found myself in the basement kitchen at Rose's house in rural western New Jersey. All I could focus on was the shelf full of sprinkles. Just as a tailor shop has every color of thread, Rose's kitchen has every color of sprinkle. I could've spent hours looking through drawers and examining her well-labeled ingredients. My reward for tearing myself away from the kitchen was a slice of sunshine-yellow lemon curd tart, which managed to be both creamy and pucker-worthy, accompanied by an espresso to which Rose had added a demitasse spoon's worth of homemade dulce de leche.

And now, a few years later, she is like family, because that's how Rose is.

Rose never shows up empty-handed. There was a taco lunch at a restaurant where a slice of milk chocolate caramel tart magically appeared out of a small bag. I ate it as an appetizer. She showed up to my house with slices of milk bread she was testing. My kids glormed it up in seconds, but it wasn't quite good enough for Rose and she continued to work on the recipe. I may or may not have secreted away a few slices of chocolate babka—the first and only babka I ever wanted to eat more of. That was only outdone by a memorable single rugelach that came wrapped not just in plastic wrap, but also a layer of bubble wrap to keep it pristine on the ninety-minute journey to my house.

It's not just my family and I who have come to expect delicious surprises. My dog Bosco barks joyfully when he sees Rose and her collaborator, Woody, coming up the front walk. He recognizes the interlopers as purveyors of frozen bones that have been carefully saved for him from steak dinners.

I must be clear, however: There are terrible downsides to being Rose's friend. Especially during the testing phase of the ice cream book you're holding in your hands, I would more often than not find myself meandering my way through a half-wilted mediocre lunchtime salad when up would pop an email from Rose. It would contain nothing more than a photo of just-made blackberry ice cream or maybe grapefruit ice cream or a few chirpy thoughts about how wonderful her lunch of prune-Armagnac ice cream tasted.

My patience paid off on a stinking-hot August day. I drove out to her house to interview her for *Edible Jersey* magazine and was greeted with a homemade chocolate ice cream cone filled with a subtle and elegant hazelnut ice cream. Rose had even tucked one Piedmontese hazelnut at the bottom of the cone—a clever trick to keep the fast-melting ice cream from leaking out of the cone.

Let me reassure you that even if you never have the chance to meet Rose in person, her personality—her exuberance and meticulous attention to detail—is infused into the pages and recipes of all her cookbooks.

It shouldn't surprise anyone that the doyenne of cake baking now has an ice cream cookbook, for what better friend is there to cake than ice cream? The surprise, however, is that for a woman who has made her name with cakes and baking, her favorite dessert is actually ice cream. That love—nay, passion—is evident on every page of this book.

Of course this cookbook features recipes for stellar versions of basic ice cream flavors, such as vanilla and chocolate, but our Rose doesn't stop there. Among others, there is all-season apricot ice cream, dark brown sugar ice cream, and a "Bust my Bourbon Balls" ice cream, which churns her well-known boozy confections into vanilla ice cream.

I have the email correspondence to prove that Rose spent months trying out new and varied flavors for ice cream. The result is this glorious book, which will appeal to ice cream purists and adventurers alike.

Rose is a generous friend, an enthusiastic listener, and an engaging storyteller with a warm voice, lilting laugh, and sharp wit. The truth is, even if Rose never fed me another scoop of hazelnut ice cream, I would still be content to have the pleasure of being her friend.

Now, if anyone's looking for me, I'll be the one sitting contentedly eating raspberry butterscotch sauce by the spoonful, waiting hopefully for an email from Rose.

MARISSA ROTHKOPF BATES
Journalist and treasured friend

MY ICE CREAM

In my over 50 year career as a writer of baking books, I am known by many for cakes (*The Cake Bible*), am most proud of my flaky and tender cream cheese pie crust (*The Pie and Pastry Bible*), have the most fun making cookies (*Rose's Christmas Cookies*), and most enjoy making bread (*The Bread Bible*), but the sweet that I love most to eat is frozen, not baked—ICE CREAM—and that is why I have written this book.

My first memory of ice cream was the half-chocolate-half-vanilla Dixie cups of my childhood summers in the Catskills. They came with little wooden flat spoons attached to the lid, and the taste and feel of the wood against the cold creamy ice cream was as appealing as that of the cork that, in those days, lined the caps of green bottles of Coke. My love of ice cream could well be genetic. When my parents were in their 80s, my mother would call and report that "she and daddy had done something very naughty that night," which turned out to be that they had consumed an entire pint of ice cream. As a health addict devoted to low-cholesterol eating, this was a real sin she was confessing!

I've shared a few of my favorite ice cream recipes in some of my books before, but over the years I have improved them and streamlined my method as well. My favorite ice cream had remained my top choice over the years—caramel—until I created the Pomegranate Pride Ice Cream on page 110, which is now a close tie with the black raspberry ice cream on page 58.

Why make your own ice cream? For the same reason as baking or cooking—you can make it tailored to your own taste and texture. And it's fun, too.

My preference is for ice cream to be super creamy and totally free of iciness, therefore I make it with the highest level of butterfat desirable, at around 20%, using a high ratio of cream to milk and more egg yolk than most. I'd rather have a smaller scoop of what I call luxury ice cream than a larger one that is less rich. (Gelato, by comparison, usually contains about 10% butterfat and often does not contain egg, but is also denser with less air. Some machines, such as the Cuisinart, have an additional dasher that incorporates less air for making gelato. The increased density helps to compensate for the lower fat content, which would make it less creamy—see Equipment, page xxix.)

THE INGREDIENTS

Egg yolk, which contains lecithin, is an excellent emulsifier and thickener, and helps ensure a smooth and slower-melting texture, which in turn assures the best flavor and the creamiest, least icy texture for most ice creams without having to rely on added emulsifiers and stabilizers. The benefit of not using stabilizers is that you then do not have to heat most of the cream. This allows it to keep its flavor, and chills down the base quickly because it is added cold at the end. When other thickening ingredients, such as peanut butter, are added, the cream to milk ratio is much lower. For berries or other fruit I use one less egg yolk to avoid masking the fruit's flavor, but I do use a stabilizer such as cornstarch or nonfat dry milk to absorb some of the extra juice that would otherwise make the ice cream icy.

Heavy cream helps hold air, especially in a thinner mixture, and adds a delicious flavor. My preferred base for basic ice creams such as vanilla, by volume, is 3:1 cream to milk. Some ice creams, however, have added elements that would make such a high level of cream cloying, such as caramel, for which I use 2:1 cream to milk, and honey, for which I use only 1:1 cream to milk.

All my recipes were created with 40% butterfat cream (see below for how to determine the cream's butterfat content), but if only 36% is available, it works to approximate the fat content by adding some butter. **For every 2 cups/464 grams/473 ml 40% cream, if using 36% add 2 tablespoons/28 grams butter.** You can use double the butter if you desire a richer ice cream, as with the fruit curd ice creams, where there is enough of the acidic fruit juice to balance the extra butterfat.

Heavy cream, also referred to as heavy whipping cream, contains 56.6% water and 36% to 40% butterfat. "Whipping cream" has only 30% butterfat. To determine the butterfat content, if it is **40% butterfat cream**, it will be listed on the side of the container as **6 grams total fat**. Organic Valley and Stonyfield are two such brands. Cream that is 36% will be listed as 5 grams total fat.

My Basic Base

This formula yields about 1 quart/1 liter, or more if adding a significant quantity of a flavoring ingredient such as peanut butter or fruit purée.

Note: All recipes have the weight in grams, and the volume in measuring spoons, cups, and milliliters. The milliliters are an exact conversion from the cups and often are numbers that do not appear on metric measuring cups. Use the mark closest to it; for example, for 295 ml, use just slightly under 300 ml.

Cream: 50% (464 grams/2 cups/473 ml)

Milk: 17.2% (160 grams/⅔ cup/158 ml)

Sugar: 14.3% (133 grams/⅔ cup)

Egg yolk: 14%; 7 yolks (130 grams/½ cup/118 ml)

Glucose or reduced corn syrup (see page xxi): 4.5% (42 grams/ 2 tablespoons/30 ml)

Salt: a pinch (¹⁄₁₆ teaspoon)

Vanilla extract, if using: 5 grams/1 teaspoon/5 ml

These percentages will change when adding additional ingredients.

Making a Less Rich Ice Cream

If you prefer to make a less rich ice cream using fewer egg yolks and/or a higher proportion of milk to cream, the ice cream will be icy unless you use a stabilizer such as a cornstarch slurry (see page xxvi) or commercial stabilizer (see page xxii) and the more traditional method of making the base, which involves heating all the dairy, tempering the egg yolks, and cooling the base in an ice water bath.

MY METHOD

The traditional method of making custard-based ice creams is to heat all the dairy (cream and milk), and then to whisk a little of it into the beaten egg yolks (to heat them slightly, called tempering). The egg yolk mixture is then whisked back into the rest of the dairy. This laborious method is not necessary in most of my recipes. That is because the cream and milk available to most of us is ultra pasteurized, which means it has been heated to 275°F/135°C. There is therefore no need to reheat it. I mix and heat only the milk and part of the cream needed for heating the egg yolks to the proper temperature, and I reserve the rest of the cream to stir in cold. This brings down the temperature of the completed custard base, making it possible to refrigerate it without having to prepare an ice water bath (although you can chill it in an ice water bath to cool it more quickly). It also maintains more of the cream's flavor.

The egg yolks need to be heated to between 170° and 180°F/77° and 82°C to give the best texture to the frozen ice cream.

How Long to Chill the Ice Cream Base Before Churning

I almost always refrigerate the ice cream base overnight (at least 8 hours) or up to 2 days, but I have found that if the ice cream is refrigerated long enough to reach 35° to 43°F/2° to 6°C, the churned ice cream has just as good a texture as when chilled for 8 hours. You can also use an ice water bath to bring down the temperature more quickly, about 20 to 30 minutes. Simply add some ice cubes to a large bowl and pour in some water. Set the bowl with the ice cream into the ice water and stir often until it is chilled. To speed chilling even further, sprinkle the ice with a little salt, which will lower the temperature of the ice water.

Churning (or Spinning) the Ice Cream Base

Ice cream contains a high percentage of water, which becomes ice crystals when frozen. When calculating all the water contained in the ingredients of my basic vanilla ice cream, for example, it makes up more than half the weight of the entire mixture. Ice cream is made up of these tiny ice crystals, which are emulsified with fat and protein from milk and cream, and sugar, resulting in a sweet, creamy, smooth, and cold sensation on the tongue. Ice cream also contains air that is introduced during churning. The air increases the ice cream's volume (the technical term for this air and the ensuing increase in volume is overrun) and influences the texture: Ice cream with more air will be less dense, and subsequently perceived as less smooth and creamy. Most of my recipes fall between 20 and 30% overrun, with my basic vanilla at 27%, but the denser pumpkin has 19%, and the blackberry is much higher at 38%.

My favorite ice cream makers are the Breville Smart Scoop BC1600XL and the Cuisinart ICE-100. They have their own built in refrigerant compressors, and produce excellent ice cream. It is important not to exceed the recommended amount of ice cream base, to have the temperature of the ice cream base no higher than 43°F/6°C, and to prechill the machine for a minimum of 15 minutes before adding the ice cream base.

The Cuisinart ICE-100 recommends a maximum base of 5 cups/1.2 liters and the Breville Smart Scoop a maximum base of 3½ cups/830 ml. Most of the recipes in this book make about 4 cups/1 liter finished ice cream, some a generous quart/1 liter, and maximum 5 cups/1.2 liters of ice cream. However, I often prefer churning half my base at a time for the speediest freezing and smoothest, creamiest texture. A half base at a time will work in either machine.

Comparing the two machines, making a half batch, the Breville takes double the time but is slightly smoother and creamier. The ice cream is easier to remove because the temperature throughout is more uniform compared to when made in the Cuisinart's container, which freezes the ice cream hard on the bottom and sides. The Breville machine also has a useful read-out to let you know the progress of the churning and even a sound to let you know when to add mix-ins and when the ice cream is finished. But if making a full size base, the Cuisinart will produce much creamier ice cream.

Ice cream machines that contain coolant but not a compressor, such as the Donvier or other Cuisinart models, require chilling for a full 24 hours in a very cold freezer before churning the ice cream.

Storing Ice Cream

After churning and transferring to a storage container, ice cream needs to be frozen quickly to a lower temperature. My friend chef Robert Ellinger, who teaches ice cream making to professionals, explained that in industry they use a blast freezer after churning the ice cream. This fast freezing ensures the tiny ice crystals are imprisoned within the rest of the mixture. Slower freezing bursts the ice crystals so they lose their protective coating. The result is that they escape to form larger ice crystals, and even the small ones can be perceived as fragments of ice.

Since most people (including me) do not have a blast freezer at home, the biggest challenge is transferring the churned ice cream to a storage container before it starts to melt. In warmer weather, or if you do not have air conditioning, use a sturdy plastic scraper to move any ice cream that may have frozen harder against the sides to the center. Scrape the ice cream from the dasher into the machine's container, and leave it in the machine while transferring the ice cream to a well-chilled storage container, or set the ice cream container in the freezer for about 15 minutes before transferring it. If planning to soften the ice cream in a microwave when serving, be sure to store it in a microwavable container. (If microwaving, use only 9-second bursts so as not to melt the ice cream, which would form larger ice crystals on refreezing.)

Freezers vary in temperature, so my recipes indicate to chill the churned ice cream for at least 4 hours before serving. If you use a shallow container to store the ice cream, and your freezer is very cold, it will take a lot less time to reach a serving consistency. For soft serve, after transferring the ice cream to a storage container, I like to freeze it for 1 to 1½ hours, but if you like it softer you can eat it sooner. For all ice cream, before freezing, set plastic wrap directly on the surface to prevent the formation of ice crystals and then cover the container.

Set ice cream in the coldest part of your freezer. It also helps to surround it with cold packs (such as one designed for quick-chilling wine) to counteract the effects of freeze/thaw. If ice cream should become very icy or melted, it can be refrozen but will be denser than before. Ideally, ice cream without commercial stabilizers keeps for up to 3 days, after which the texture may become a little icy. Stabilizers bind the water so that during the thaw cycle, when some of the ice crystals melt, they will refreeze without becoming larger. If your ice cream becomes icy on longer storage, use it to make smoothies.

Sometimes ice cream that is made in a larger quantity than recommended, or in an alternative ice cream machine, may have a very slightly icy texture. I find that allowing it to soften before serving will completely eliminate any iciness.

I find the ideal temperature at which to eat any ice cream is 11° to 12°F/ −11°C. To soften ice cream, either transfer it to the refrigerator for 15 to 30 minutes, depending on the temperature of your refrigerator, or soften it in the microwave in 9-second bursts.

ICE CREAM STABILIZERS AND TEXTURIZERS

There are many ingredients, both commercial and commonly available, to help create and maintain a creamy texture in ice cream. Other than alcohol, most thicken the ice cream base, which helps trap more air when churning.

ALCOHOL My scientist husband once suggested that I add flavorless alcohol to my ice cream base because it would act as antifreeze and, when used judiciously, would keep the ice cream softer without it becoming too soft. The problem with adding alcohol is that the ice cream tends to melt faster when removed from the freezer. And too much alcohol would prevent the ice cream from getting firm enough. So, in recent years, I have turned to glucose, an invert sugar similar to corn syrup, which thickens rather than thins the ice cream base, to accomplish softening. Of course, when an ice cream benefits from the flavor of an alcohol or liqueur, such as Chambord in Pure Peanut Butter Ice Cream (page 145), or it is an intrinsic part of the recipe, such as Prunes and Armagnac Ice Cream (page 107) or Rum Raisin Ice Cream (page 105), it's a different story. In those cases it makes the fruit moister without making it icy and is mostly contained in the fruit so it doesn't over-soften the ice cream itself. Of course, you can always pour liqueur on top of the ice cream when serving it.

GLUCOSE AND CORN SYRUP Glucose, an invert sugar (formed through hydrolysis, or breakdown of sucrose), is an indispensable ingredient for minimizing ice crystals and keeping ice cream "scoopable," because it bonds more with water than does granulated sugar (sucrose), so less water is available to freeze into ice. Corn syrup can be substituted for glucose, but it is best to thicken it to the moisture level of glucose—easily done. If you just use it straight, it will not be as effective as glucose.

Years ago, when glucose was harder to find, I worked out the following substitution for liquid glucose for making rolled fondant in *The Cake Bible*. Glucose is now widely available in candy making and cake baking supply stores and online. But if you don't have any on hand, it is handy to have this technique:

To replace glucose with corn syrup, in a glass measure with a spout in a microwave, or in a small, preferably nonstick pan on the cooktop over medium-low heat, bring 80 grams/¼ cup/59 ml of light corn syrup to a full boil. Remove it from the heat source and stir in an equal weight or volume of corn syrup. This will result in the same consistency of glucose. Corn syrup weighs only 1 gram less per tablespoon than glucose, so it can be used in equal weight or measure but will not be quite as effective in preventing iciness.

I usually use 4.5% glucose in my recipes, or 5% if an ice cream freezes very hard; no more than 5% should be used.

MILK POWDER Milk powder is an excellent emulsifier. It bonds with both the liquid and the fat in the base, preventing ice crystals from forming when the ice cream is in the freezer. I use it in recipes that contain a high water content, to keep the ice cream from becoming icy. My formula is 2% of the weight of the base to simmer with 1 cup/237 ml of the dairy.

CORNSTARCH has the potential to transform ice cream from icy to smooth by bonding with some of the water in the ice cream base. It is a little more work as it requires two extra processes: cooking the dairy-cornstarch mixture, and making an ice water bath to cool down the ice cream base. I adapted this method from Dana Cree's award-winning book *Hello, My Name Is Ice Cream*.

Note: cornstarch does not do as good a job as a commercial stabilizer for longer storage of the frozen ice cream.

COMMERCIAL STABILIZERS Many professionals choose Cremodan 30 as their ice cream stabilizer, and I'm pleased to report it is now carried in small home-user size quantities at Kalustyan's, in New York City, and online. Commercial stabilizers are a blend of emulsifiers and stabilizers (mono- and diglycerides, sodium alginate, locust bean gum, carrageenan, guar gum, and sodium dioxide, added to prevent caking). This product will keep the ice cream smooth and creamy on freezing for longer than 3 days. It is easy to use because it just gets mixed into the sugar when making the base, but the cooked base mixture must reach 180°F/82°C, and the chilled base must be held for a minimum of 8 hours in the refrigerator before churning. The commercial recommended recipe amount is 3 grams/1 teaspoon per 1 quart/1 liter (0.3% of the base), but I prefer 2.5 grams/¾ teaspoon plus ¹⁄₁₆ teaspoon per 1 quart/1 liter (0.25% of the base). It still serves to prevent iciness, but has less of that slightly gummy and spongy consistency that I find undesirable.

THE BASIC TECHNIQUES OF MAKING ICE CREAM

The following methods are those that I like to use for my custard-based ice creams and that you will see in the recipes that follow. The specific instructions are given within each recipe, but this is a brief description of each method so you can see at a glance what is involved.

All methods for making custard-based ice cream require that the egg yolks be heated to between 170° and 180°F/77° and 82°C to give the best texture to the frozen ice cream. (This will also deactivate an enzyme in egg yolks called amylase, which would thin out the base during chilling prior to the freezing process.) If using commercial stabilizers such as Cremodan 30 (see page xxii), the temperature must reach 180°F/82°C.

The Simple Method

This method is used for ice creams that don't tend to get icy, such as my basic Vanilla Ice Cream (page 3). It does not use any stabilizers, so it is straightforward and fast, and does not require an ice water bath to cool down the ice cream base before chilling it.

1) Combine the egg yolks, milk, part of the cream, the sugar, glucose, and salt.

2) Heat the mixture to 170° to 180°F/77° to 82°C.

3) Strain the mixture.

4) Stir in the remaining cream to cool down the custard.

5) Stir in the vanilla, if using, and any remaining ingredients that don't get heated.

6) Chill until no warmer than 43°F/6°C before churning.

Combine the egg yolks, milk, part of the cream, the sugar, glucose, and salt.

Heat the mixture to 170° to 180°F/77° to 82°C.

Strain the mixture.

Scrape the mixture from the bottom of the strainer.

Stir in the remaining cold cream to cool down the mixture.

Stir in any remaining ingredients and chill.

Stabilizer Techniques

All three of the following techniques will require making an ice water bath to cool down the finished base before chilling it. Use a bowl that is larger than the bowl containing the finished ice cream base. Fill it with several handfuls of ice and add cold water. Set the bowl with the ice cream base into the ice water.

CORNSTARCH SLURRY METHOD

I use a small amount of cornstarch, mixed with a little of the milk, to make a slurry to thicken excess juices from fruit such as mango and banana, and also for berries. The slurry is added to the hot cream-milk mixture.

About ½ cup/118 ml of this hot mixture is whisked into the lightly beaten egg yolks to temper them. Then the egg yolk mixture is whisked into the rest of the hot mixture and brought to the usual temperature of 170° to 180°F/77° to 82°C, strained into a bowl, and cooled in an ice water bath before combining it with other ingredients such as a chilled purée or vanilla extract (ingredients that would dissipate if added to a hot mixture).

1) Make a slurry with the cornstarch and enough of the milk or cream to make it liquid. (An optional pinch of sugar will help keep the cornstarch from clumping.)

2) Bring all the cream, milk, sugar, glucose, and salt to a boil and simmer it for 2 to 3 minutes.

3) Cool for a few minutes to about 180°F/82°C so that the cornstarch does not clump when added.

4) Stir the slurry (cornstarch mixture) and whisk it into the hot mixture.

5) Bring the mixture back to a boil and simmer for 1 minute to activate the cornstarch.

6) Whisk about ½ cup/118 ml of this hot mixture into the lightly beaten egg yolks to temper them. Then use a whisk to stir the egg yolk mixture into the rest of the hot mixture.

7) Heat the mixture to 170° to 180°F/77° to 82°C.

8) Strain the mixture.

9) Cool the mixture in an ice water bath until no longer warm.

10) Stir in any remaining ingredients that don't get heated.

11) Chill until no warmer than 43°F/6°C before churning.

Make a cornstarch slurry with the milk or cream.

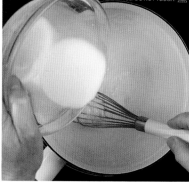

Add the slurry to the boiled dairy mixture.

Temper the yolks with a little of the hot mixture before adding them to the rest.

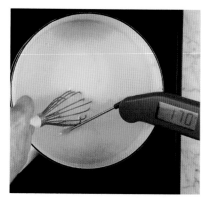

Heat the mixture to 170° to 180°F/ 77° to 82°C.

Strain the mixture.

Add the remaining ingredients and chill in an ice water bath.

NONFAT DRY MILK METHOD

The addition of dry milk is ideal for ice creams with high water content where the liquid can't be reduced and concentrated, such as red wine (which would lose flavor), or ice creams that just require a little stabilizer, such as coconut.

1) Stir together the dry milk, milk, half of the cream, the sugar, glucose, and salt and simmer it for 2 minutes.

2) Let the mixture cool slightly.

3) Whisk the milk mixture into the egg yolks.

4) Heat the mixture to 170° to 180°F/77° to 82°C.

5) Strain the mixture.

6) Stir in the remaining cream to help cool down the custard.

7) Cool the mixture in an ice water bath, if indicated, until no longer warm.

8) Stir in any remaining ingredients that don't get heated.

9) Chill until no warmer than 43°F/6°C before churning.

CREMODAN 30 (COMMERCIAL STABILIZER) METHOD

This type of stabilizer is especially useful to minimize the formation of ice crystals for ice cream that needs to be stored for longer than 3 days.

1) Whisk together the Cremodan and sugar.

2) Add all the remaining ingredients except for those that don't get heated.

3) Heat the mixture to 180°F/82°C.

4) Strain the mixture.

5) Cool the mixture in an ice water bath until no longer warm.

6) Stir in any remaining ingredients that don't get heated.

7) Chill for a minimum of 8 hours before churning.

EQUIPMENT AND INGREDIENTS

Please note that I am only listing brands and sources that have had a presence for many years. Of course, you can also search online for any particular equipment or ingredient.

EQUIPMENT

Ice Cream Machines

I loved my commercial brand Ugolini Minigel ice cream maker, which served me well for years, but found the fixed container a disadvantage when it came to washing or transferring the ice cream for storage, so I donated it to the very appreciative New York University food department (my alma mater). My Breville Smart Scoop and Cuisinart ICE-100, which also have their own built in refrigerating compressors, and have removable bowls, make just as good ice cream. They also come with either a second dasher or a setting designed to incorporate less air for making denser gelato-style ice cream. What I do miss is the windshield wiper attachment for the blades on the Minigel, which keeps the ice cream from freezing hard against the sides. For a comparison of the Breville and Cuisinart machines, see My Ice Cream on page xiv.

Ice cream makers with containers that have refrigerant but no compressor require 24 hours in the freezer to be cold enough to churn the ice cream completely. I have a large collection of Donvier hand-operated machines, from 1 quart/1 liter to 1 cup/237 ml for a single serving.

PACOJET I would be remiss not to mention the king of ice cream makers even though most of us, including me, would find it hard to justify spending several thousand dollars on this machine—even if you make at least one ice cream every day! The beauty of this ice cream maker is that its supersharp blades will turn any frozen mixture into a smooth, creamy consistency without the need for stabilizers.

Thermometers

The Thermapen instant-read thermometer is the most accurate and speedy of any I know. If using commercial stabilizers (see page xxiv), where the temperature of the base is required to reach 180°F/82°C, a superaccurate thermometer is an imperative. Alternatively, it is possible to judge the temperature of an ice cream base that doesn't use commercial stabilizers by assessing the thickness and consistency. But, of course, it is much more reliable to use a thermometer.

Scales

Using weight rather than volume for measuring ingredients makes the entire process faster, easier, and more accurate. I recommend the Escali Alimento digital scale. If you prefer to weigh very small amounts, it is necessary to have a scale that is accurate to at least 1 decimal place, such as the My Weigh i201, accurate to 0.01 gram up to 200 grams, or the Escali L600 High Precision, accurate to 0.1 gram up to 600 grams.

Plastic Squeeze Bottles

These are great for storing glucose and also for adding ribbons of mix-ins or drizzling toppings onto the finished ice cream. I store glucose in the refrigerator and either remove it several hours ahead or warm it in the microwave for about 9 seconds or in a pan of hot water. Glucose can ferment if contaminated, so when transferring it to a squeeze bottle, be sure to use a clean funnel.

Plastic Wrap

I recommend Stretch-Tite brand because it clings so tightly to the bowl or whatever else needs to be wrapped. Plastic wraps are not 100% impermeable, so for freezing baked goods and ice cream, it is best to use a couple of layers. Freeze-Tite, however, is designed for freezing and is double the thickness, and also wider (15 inches).

Reduction Spatula

Many of my berry and fruit recipes call for reducing the fruits' juices to concentrate and prevent iciness. I designed a small silicone spatula, called Rose's Reduction Spatula, with markings from 6 inches down to ½ inch to make it easier to determine when the liquid has reached the desired level. The spatula can be used to stir the pot either on the cooktop or in the microwave. I leave it in the microwavable container in the microwave while reducing the liquid, which prevents air bubbles from forming and bursting out of the container without needing to stir or swirl the liquid.

INGREDIENTS

The basic ingredients I use for ice cream are egg yolks, sugar, glucose, cream, and milk. Recommendations and references to types or specific brands of ingredients are given throughout the book, but here is a more detailed description and also several current sources that may be helpful.

Chocolate

When 60% to 62% cacao chocolate is specified, two of my favorites are Valrhona 61% Extra Bitter and Guittard 61%. Dark chocolate will keep for many months if well wrapped in plastic wrap and placed in an airtight container at cool room temperature, and away from humidity.

Citrus Fruit

The aromatic oils reside in the colored portion of the citrus fruit. If you are using citrus zest, use liquid dish detergent and a scrubby to remove any sprays from the fruit, which will be bitter, then rinse well and dry before zesting. When zesting, avoid removing the bitter white pith. A Microplane is the ideal tool to produce finely grated zest.

AVERAGE AMOUNT OF ZEST AND JUICE

	ZEST	JUICE
1 lemon	1¼ to 2 teaspoons	47 to 63 grams/3 tablespoons to ¼ cup/ 45 to 59 ml
1 orange	2 to 3 tablespoons	60 to 121 grams/¼ to ½ cup/59 to 118 ml
1 grapefruit	about 2 tablespoons	about 200 grams/¾ cup/188 ml

1 tablespoon of citrus zest, loosely packed, weighs 6 grams

Dairy

HEAVY CREAM Heavy cream, also referred to as heavy whipping cream, contains 56.6% water and 36% to 40% butterfat. "Whipping cream" has only 30% butterfat. To determine the butterfat content, if it is **40% butterfat cream**, it will be listed on the side of the container as **6 grams total fat**. Organic Valley and Stonyfield are two brands containing 40% butterfat. Cream that is 36% will list 5 grams total fat.

MILK Wherever milk is called for in a recipe, use whole milk.

Egg Yolks

The ratio of yolk to white in an egg can vary to such a degree that a recipe calling for 6 yolks may actually need as many as 9. Since the creamy texture of ice cream is so dependent on egg yolks, the ingredient charts list a range for the number of yolks needed to obtain the correct weight or volume.

Unbroken yolks, sprayed with nonstick cooking spray to prevent drying, will keep in an airtight container in the refrigerator for up to 3 days.

Egg whites will keep frozen for several months. They are great for making Lemon Ginger Ice Cream (page 117) and Fluffy Nougat Ice Cream (page 160), and the Angel Food Tunnel Cake (page 246).

Essences and Oils

Mandy Aftel, of Aftelier Perfumes, carries the most exquisite essences, such as peach, pear, and strawberry. Just a few drops make a dramatic enhancement of natural flavor. They keep indefinitely at room temperature. **Source: www.aftelier.com**

Boyajian citrus oils, such as lemon and orange, are extracted from the rind of the fresh fruit. They have a pure but intense flavor and are a world apart from citrus extracts. Citrus oils require refrigeration. **Source: www.boyajianinc.com**

Edible dried lavender (do not use non–food grade lavender, which has been sprayed by pesticides) is carried by Kalustyan's and Orchard View Lavender Farm. **Sources: www.kalustyans.com and www.orchardviewlavenderfarm.com**

Fruit Concentrates and Mango Pulp

Passion fruit, blood orange, and raspberry concentrates from the Perfect Purée of Napa Valley are available through mail order and are carried by Kalustyan's. Ratna is my favorite brand of Alphonso mango pulp and is also carried by Kalustyan's. **Sources: www.perfectpuree.com and www.kalustyans.com**

Food Color

Only four ice creams in this book suggest a few optional drops of food color: Back Road Wild Mint Chip (page 30), Royal Velvet Lavender (page 36), Pomegranate Pride (page 110), and Grapefruit (page 126). If you prefer a "natural" liquid food color, search out the 365 brand at Whole Foods or India Tree Nature's Colors. **Source: www.indiatree.com**

Nuts

Always taste nuts before adding them to a recipe because the oils they contain can become rancid. Store nuts in an airtight container in a cool place or in the freezer. Frozen, they will keep for over a year.

HAZELNUTS (FILBERTS) The most flavorful hazelnuts are from the Piedmont region of Italy. **Source: www.gustiamo.com**

Nut Pastes

PISTACHIO PASTE My favorite pistachio paste, Agrimontana, is made from 100% Sicilian pistachios, and usually available at Buon'Italia and Mercato. **Sources: www.buonitalia.com and www.mercato.com**

PRALINE PASTE Agrimontana also makes a 100% hazelnut praline paste which is 60% hazelnuts and 40% caramelized sugar, and is sometimes available at Buon'Italia. For more about praline paste, see Scoops (page 164). **Sources: www.buonitalia.com and www.mercato.com**

Salt

Fine sea salt contains no additives and is easiest to measure accurately and consistently.

Stabilizer

The commercial stabilizer Cremodan 30 is available in 1 pound/454 gram cans from Pastry Chef Central and also in very small packages referred to as Ice Cream Stabilizer from Kalustyan's. See page xxviii for more information on how to use it. **Sources: www.pastrychef.com and www.kalustyans.com**

Sugar

For ice creams calling for sugar, either superfine or fine granulated works well. The advantage of superfine is that it dissolves more quickly in the ice cream base.

For brown sugar, light or dark Muscovado sugar from India Tree has the most complex and delicious flavor. Light Muscovado is closest in molasses content to a combination of light and dark brown sugar, but it's fine to use dark brown sugar alone. **Source: www.indiatree.com**

GLUCOSE I use this invert sugar in almost all of my ice cream recipes. It is invaluable to make softer, creamier ice cream. I've created a method of heating light corn syrup to approximate the moisture content of glucose (see page xxi), but if you make a lot of ice cream, it's simpler and faster to purchase glucose. Always use a clean, dry spoon to portion it; a wet or dirty spoon can contaminate the glucose and cause it to spoil. If stored refrigerated and kept uncontaminated, it will keep for years. Glucose is available at candy and cake decorating supply stores such as NY Cake. **Source: www.nycake.com**

Vanilla

VANILLA EXTRACT My favorite brands of pure vanilla extract are Heilala, Nielsen-Massey, and the Vanilla Company.

VANILLA PASTE This excellent product contains the seeds of the vanilla bean combined with vanilla extract, natural gum thickeners, and sometimes a small amount of sugar (varying by manufacturer). Heilala suggests using it to replace one-third of the volume of their vanilla extract. Nielsen-Massey recommends using it to replace an equal volume of their vanilla extract. Patricia Rain, of the Vanilla Company, uses the entire bean (the pod as well as the pulp and seeds) to produce her vanilla bean paste, and suggests using only one-quarter of the volume of her extract. It is best to check the label for suggested amounts. And since vanilla is best added after chilling the base, I recommend adding it to taste. **Sources: www.heilalavanilla.com, www.nielsenmassey.com, and www.vanillaqueen.com**

INGREDIENTS SPECIFIC TO RECIPES IN THE ICE CREAM SOCIALS CHAPTER

Butter

Choose unsalted grade A or AA butter for the freshest flavor and texture. Lower quality butters will contain more water and less butterfat. My preference is Organic Valley's cultured butter.

Cocoa

Unsweetened cocoa powder is pulverized pure chocolate liquor with three-quarters of its cocoa butter removed. I prefer the flavor of Dutch processed, aka alkalized, cocoa. This refers to the process by which the cocoa powder has been treated with a mild alkali to mellow its flavor by neutralizing its acidity, which also makes it easier to dissolve.

Eggs

All my recipes use USDA grade A large eggs, which means that twelve eggs in the shell should weigh a minimum of 680 grams/24 ounces and a maximum of 850 grams/30 ounces. This does not mean, however, that each egg is the same size. The weights given for eggs on the recipe charts are without the shells.

Eggs, still in the shell, can be brought to room temperature by setting them in a bowl of hot tap water for 5 minutes.

Flour

My recommended all-purpose flour is General Mills bleached. (It is important to use a national brand, as protein content varies widely with regional ones.) When I specify cake flour, you will get vastly superior results using bleached cake flour.

Sugar

Superfine is specified in recipes where it is needed, such as for cookies (for a smoother texture) or meringue (because it dissolves more effectively in the egg white). Fine granulated sugar is coarser, but can be processed in a food processor to simulate superfine. The two most common brands of superfine sugar available are C&H and Domino. C&H is slightly finer. India Tree, labeled as caster sugar, is the finest of all. **Source: www.indiatree.com**

FLAVORFUL ICE CREAMS

This chapter includes most of the basic, best-loved ice creams, such as vanilla, caramel, dulce de leche, and mint chip. You may also be tempted by some unusual flavors, such as honey, brown sugar, red wine, and stretchy Turkish ice creams.

VANILLA ICE CREAM

Makes: About 1 quart/1 liter

America's favorite flavor, and when using vanilla beans and this recipe, one of my top favorites as well! The larger proportion than usual of cream to milk, the high amount of egg yolk, and the choice of my favorite vanilla beans make this my ultimate expression of vanilla ice cream.

ICE CREAM BASE

sugar	125 grams	½ cup plus 2 tablespoons
1 Tahitian vanilla bean (or 2 Madagascar vanilla beans), cut lengthwise (see Scoops)	.	OR 2 teaspoons (10 ml) pure vanilla extract
heavy cream or crème fraîche	464 grams	2 cups (473 ml), *divided*
7 (to 11) large egg yolks (see page xxxii)	130 grams	½ cup (118 ml)
milk	160 grams	⅔ cup (158 ml)
glucose or reduced corn syrup (see page xxi)	63 grams	3 tablespoons (45 ml)
fine sea salt	.	a pinch
pure vanilla extract	.	1 teaspoon (5 ml)

✣ Have ready a fine-mesh strainer suspended over a medium bowl.

1) In a medium saucepan, place the sugar and vanilla bean. Use your fingers to rub the seeds from the center of the vanilla bean into the sugar. Remove the pod and set it in a 2 cup/473 ml glass measure with a spout. Add 348 grams/1½ cups/355 ml of the cream. Cover and refrigerate.

2) Add the egg yolks, milk, and the remaining cream (116 grams/½ cup/118 ml) to the sugar mixture and, with a silicone spatula, stir them together. Stir in the glucose and salt until well blended.

3) Heat the mixture on medium-low, stirring constantly, until slightly thicker than heavy cream. When a finger is run across the back of the spatula, it will

Continued

leave a well-defined track. An instant-read thermometer should read 170° to 180°F/77° to 82°C.

4) Immediately pour the mixture into the strainer, scraping up the thickened mixture that has settled on the bottom of the pan. Press it through the strainer and scrape any mixture clinging to the underside into the bowl.

5) Stir the refrigerated cream with the vanilla pod and the vanilla extract into the custard mixture. Cover and refrigerate for a minimum of 8 hours or until no warmer than 43°F/6°C. (Alternatively, cool in an ice water bath.) Set a covered storage container in the freezer.

6) Remove the vanilla bean pod and rinse and dry it for future use. Churn the vanilla custard in a prechilled ice cream maker. Transfer the ice cream to the chilled container. Press a piece of plastic wrap on the surface of the ice cream, cover the container, and allow the ice cream to firm in the freezer for at least 4 hours before serving.

SCOOPS

❉ If using a Tahitian vanilla bean and it is soft and pulpy, you will need to process the seeds with the sugar in a food processor.

❉ If using vanilla extract to replace the vanilla bean, whisk it in with the 1 teaspoon/5 ml vanilla after adding the cream in Step 5.

VARIATIONS

CINNAMON ICE CREAM
Cinnamon ice cream is an excellent accompaniment to apple or peach pie.

Omit the vanilla bean. Add 9 grams/4 teaspoons of ground cinnamon and use only ½ teaspoon/2.5 ml of pure vanilla extract in Step 5. (I prefer Korintje for its robust flavor; if using a milder cinnamon, add more to taste.) Use an immersion blender or countertop blender to incorporate the cinnamon fully.

FIRE-AND-ICE ICE CREAM
I created this recipe in 1981 for an importer of pink peppercorns. The peppercorns add a sweet burst of heat and lovely color.

Use only half the vanilla bean. Add 2 teaspoons/3 grams of crushed pink peppercorns and only ½ teaspoon/2.5 ml of pure vanilla extract when adding the cream in Step 5.

Continued

Candy Cane Peppermint Ice Cream, page 7

Bust My Bourbon
Balls Ice Cream

CANDY CANE PEPPERMINT ICE CREAM

My friend Susannah Appelbaum adds crushed candy canes to vanilla ice cream every year after Christmas, saying that using the candy canes that decorated the tree keeps her and the children from being sad when the Christmas tree is taken down. This inspired me to create this delicious variation. The crushed candy canes are crunchy but also a little chewy, which provides a satisfying texture. The ice cream is a perfect delight just as it is, but if you are inclined to gild the lily, a touch of ganache topping would be the way to do it. Alternatively, you can add chocolate curls or thickly grated chocolate flakes (see Back Road Wild Mint Chip Ice Cream, page 30).

You will need about 156 grams/1 cup of crushed candy canes and 4 teaspoons/20 ml of pure peppermint extract to replace the vanilla bean and all of the vanilla extract. Add the peppermint extract after adding the cream in Step 5. Add the crushed candy canes during churning, after the ice cream has reached soft serve consistency.

To crush the candy canes, place them in a reclosable freezer-weight bag and set them in the freezer for at least 30 minutes. Set the bag on a mat and use a wooden or rubber mallet to crush them into pieces no larger than ¼ inch. (Use a double bag for any pieces that might cut through.)

BUST MY BOURBON BALLS ICE CREAM

You will need 8 Bourbon Balls/160 grams/about 1 cup (page 182). When ready to churn the ice cream, cut the bourbon balls in half or quarter them. During churning, when the ice cream has reached the consistency of soft serve and begins to ball up around the dasher, remove the dasher and use a large spoon or spatula to fold in the bourbon balls.

CHERRY VANILLA ICE CREAM

Brandied cherries are a delicious counterpoint in both color and flavor to the ivory creaminess of vanilla ice cream. The brandy keeps them from freezing rock hard. Increase the sugar in the ice cream base to a total of 133 grams/⅔ cup to balance the slight tartness of the cherries. You will need 1½ cups/242 grams lightly packed Brandied Cherries (page 206). When ready to churn the ice cream, cut the cherries in half. During churning, when the ice cream has reached the consistency of soft serve and begins to ball up around the dasher, remove the dasher and use a large spoon or spatula to fold in the cherries.

GRAPE-NUTS ICE CREAM

My friend Nancy Weber, who grew up in New England, sings the praises of this addition to vanilla ice cream. She calls it "brown bread," because Grape-Nuts cereal is made with caramelized dried crumbs, traditionally from Irish wheat and barley black bread. These crunchy morsels contribute a malty, salty-sweet crunch to the ice cream.

You will need about 116 grams/1 cup of Grape-Nuts cereal. Add the Grape-Nuts during churning, after the ice cream has reached soft serve consistency.

SOUR CREAM ICE CREAM

Makes: About 1 quart/1 liter

Sour cream gives this ice cream a creamy texture that is slightly denser than its vanilla ice cream counterpart. It also contributes a mildly tangy flavor. I like to add only a small touch of vanilla so as not to override the flavor of the sour cream.

ICE CREAM BASE

7 (to 11) large egg yolks (see page xxxii)	130 grams	½ cup (118 ml)
heavy cream	464 grams	2 cups (473 ml), *divided*
sugar	150 grams	¾ cup
glucose or reduced corn syrup (see page xxi)	42 grams	2 tablespoons (30 ml)
fine sea salt	.	a pinch
sour cream	242 grams	1 cup
pure vanilla extract	.	¾ teaspoon (3.7 ml)

❖ Have ready a fine-mesh strainer suspended over a medium bowl.

1) In a medium saucepan, with a silicone spatula, stir together the egg yolks, 232 grams/1 cup/237 ml of the cream, and the sugar. Stir in the glucose and salt until well blended.

2) Heat the mixture on medium-low, stirring constantly, until slightly thicker than heavy cream. When a finger is run across the back of the spatula, it will leave a well-defined track. An instant-read thermometer should read 170° to 180°F/77° to 82°C.

3) Immediately pour the mixture into the strainer, scraping up the thickened mixture that has settled on the bottom of the pan. Press it through the strainer and scrape any mixture clinging to the underside into the bowl. Set the strainer over a second bowl and stir the remaining cream (232 grams/1 cup/237 ml) into the hot cream mixture.

4) Cool the custard in an ice water bath or refrigerator until cool or just barely warm. Whisk in the sour cream and vanilla. Press it through the strainer into the bowl and scrape in the mixture from the underside of the strainer. Cover and refrigerate for a minimum of 8 hours or until no warmer than 43°F/6°C. (Alternatively, cool in an ice water bath.) Set a covered storage container in the freezer.

5) Churn the sour cream custard in a prechilled ice cream maker. Transfer the ice cream to the chilled container. Press a piece of plastic wrap on the surface of the ice cream, cover the container, and allow the ice cream to firm in the freezer for at least 4 hours before serving.

STORE Covered storage container: frozen, 3 days

CORDON ROSE CHEESECAKE ICE CREAM

Makes: About 1 quart/1 liter

Anyone who loves this cheesecake from *The Cake Bible* will be as overjoyed as I am that after 30 years I have successfully turned it into an ice cream. The cake batter is so delicious I could never resist saving out a little to eat plain. Years ago I tried to turn it into an ice cream but it was terribly icy. But with my new understanding of the ingredients and methods for making ice cream, I decided to revisit it.

This ice cream tastes just like the cheesecake, and has an extraordinarily dense, silky, and creamy consistency. It can be enhanced further with Sour Cherry Topping (page 208), fresh macerated strawberries, or Apricot Purée (page 97), either laced through it or drizzled on top.

ICE CREAM BASE

cream cheese, preferably Philadelphia brand	200 grams	¾ cup
cornstarch	9 grams	1 tablespoon
heavy cream	261 grams	1 cup plus 2 tablespoons (267 ml), *divided*
sugar	150 grams	¾ cup
glucose or reduced corn syrup (see page xxi)	53 grams	2½ tablespoons (37.5 ml)
fine sea salt	.	a pinch
4 (to 6) large egg yolks (see page xxxii)	74 grams	¼ cup plus 2 teaspoons (69 ml)
sour cream	363 grams	1½ cups
pure vanilla extract	.	1 teaspoon (5 ml)
lemon oil, preferably Boyajian (see Scoops)	.	⅛ teaspoon

Continued

✣ Cut the cream cheese into pieces (about 1 inch), and allow it to soften at room temperature (65° to 75°F/18° to 24°C) while mixing the rest of the base.

✣ Have ready a fine-mesh strainer suspended over a medium bowl.

✣ Prepare an ice water bath (see page xvii).

1) In a custard cup or small bowl, stir together the cornstarch and 29 grams/ 2 tablespoons/30 ml of the cream until smooth. (Add the cream slowly as you mix it in.) Cover with plastic wrap.

2) In a medium saucepan, with a silicone spatula, stir together the remaining cream (232 grams/1 cup/237 ml), the sugar, glucose, and salt until well blended.

3) In a medium bowl, place the egg yolks and whisk them lightly. Set it near the cooktop.

4) Over medium heat, bring the cream and sugar mixture to a boil, stirring constantly. Lower the heat and cook at a slow boil, stirring, for 2 to 3 minutes to evaporate some of the water in the mixture. Remove the pan from the heat. Allow the mixture to cool for a few minutes (to about 180°F/82°C).

5) Stir the cornstarch mixture to make sure it is smooth and then whisk it into the hot mixture. Return the pan to the heat and bring the mixture to a slow boil. Cook for 1 minute, whisking gently. It will thicken slightly.

6) Remove the cornstarch mixture from the heat and gradually whisk about ½ cup/118 ml of the mixture into the egg yolks to temper them. Then use a whisk to stir the egg yolk mixture back into the pot. Check the temperature. If an instant-read thermometer reads at least 170°F/77°C, there is no need to heat it further. If it is lower, heat the mixture on low, stirring constantly, until thickened a little further. When a finger is run across the back of the spatula, it will leave a well-defined track. An instant-read thermometer should read 170° to 180°F/77° to 82°C.

7) Immediately remove the pan from the heat and pour the mixture into the strainer, scraping up the thickened mixture that has settled on the bottom of the pan. Press it through the strainer into the bowl and scrape any mixture clinging to the underside into the bowl. Remove the residue and set the strainer over the medium bowl used for the egg yolks, for the second straining.

8) Set the bowl containing the custard mixture in the ice water bath and allow it to cool until no longer warm to the touch, stirring occasionally. Whisk in the cream cheese, sour cream, vanilla, and lemon oil. It will be mostly smooth, but the cream cheese will be slightly lumpy.

9) Scrape the mixture into a food processor and process until as smooth as possible, then press it through the strainer again.

10) Cover and refrigerate for a minimum of 8 hours or until no warmer than 43°F/6°C. (Alternatively, continue cooling it in the ice water bath.) Set a covered storage container in the freezer.

11) Churn the cheesecake custard in a prechilled ice cream maker. Transfer the ice cream to the chilled container. Press a piece of plastic wrap on the surface of the ice cream, cover the container, and allow the ice cream to firm in the freezer for at least 4 hours before serving.

STORE Covered storage container: frozen, 3 days

SCOOPS

❊ Lemon oil is made from the oil residing in the zest of lemons. It is different from lemon extract and has a much more pure and powerful flavor. Alternatively, use about 6 grams/1 tablespoon of grated lemon zest (from 1 or 2 lemons, scrubbed with liquid detergent first, then rinsed and dried). Add it to the base in Step 9 after processing but before chilling it. It will infuse into the base and be strained out after chilling.

CARAMEL ICE CREAM

Makes: About 5 cups/1.2 liters

Caramel is one of my favorite ice creams. Caramelized sugar adds depth of flavor and also an extra creamy texture. It is so rich that for this recipe I lowered the proportion of cream to milk.

ICE CREAM BASE

heavy cream	464 grams	2 cups (473 ml), *divided*
sugar	200 grams	1 cup
water	45 grams	3 tablespoons (45 ml)
cream of tartar	.	⅛ plus ¹⁄₁₆ teaspoon
glucose or reduced corn syrup (see page xxi)	63 grams	3 tablespoons (45 ml)
milk	242 grams	1 cup (237 ml)
fine sea salt	.	a big pinch
6 (to 9) large egg yolks (see page xxxii)	112 grams	¼ cup plus 3 tablespoons (104 ml)
pure vanilla extract	.	1 teaspoon (5 ml)

❖ Have ready a fine-mesh strainer suspended over a medium bowl.

1) Into a 1 cup/237 ml glass measure with a spout, weigh or measure 116 grams/½ cup/118 ml of the cream. Heat it in a microwave until hot and then cover it.

2) In a medium heavy saucepan, preferably nonstick, with a silicone spatula, stir together the sugar, water, and cream of tartar until all the sugar is moistened. Heat, stirring constantly, until the sugar has dissolved and the syrup is bubbling.

3) Stop stirring completely and allow the syrup to boil undisturbed until it turns a deep amber. (An instant-read thermometer should read 375° to 380°F/ 190° to 193°C.) Remove it immediately from the heat, or even slightly before it reaches temperature, as the temperature will continue to rise, and just as soon as it reaches the correct temperature, pour in the hot cream. The mixture will bubble up furiously.

4) Use a clean silicone spatula to stir the mixture gently, scraping the thicker part that has settled on the bottom of the pan. If necessary, return it to very low heat, continuing to stir gently for 1 minute, until the mixture is uniform in color and the caramel has dissolved completely. Remove the pan from the heat.

5) Stir in the glucose, and then the milk and salt.

6) In a small bowl, place the egg yolks and whisk them lightly. Set it near the cooktop.

7) Whisk about ½ cup/118 ml of the hot mixture into the egg yolks to temper them. Then stir the egg yolk mixture back into the pot. Check the temperature. If it is under 170°F/77°C, heat it briefly on low heat, stirring constantly, until a finger run across the back of the spatula leaves a well-defined track. An instant-read thermometer should read 170° to 180°F/ 77° to 82°C.

8) Immediately pour the mixture into the strainer, scraping up the thickened mixture that has settled on the bottom of the pan. Press it through the strainer and scrape any mixture clinging to the underside into the bowl.

9) Stir in the remaining cream (348 grams/1½ cups/355 ml) and the vanilla.

10) Cover and refrigerate for a minimum of 8 hours or until no warmer than 43°F/6°C. (Alternatively, cool in an ice water bath.) Set a covered storage container in the freezer.

STORE
Covered storage container: frozen, 3 days

11) Churn the caramel custard in a prechilled ice cream maker. Press a piece of plastic wrap on the surface of the ice cream, cover the container, and allow the ice cream to firm in the freezer for at least 4 hours before serving.

VARIATION

SALTED CARAMEL ICE CREAM
This is one of the most popular flavors because the sharp brightness of salt is a perfect counterpoint to the sweetness of the caramel. Use a total of ¾ teaspoon/4 grams fine sea salt. Alternatively, you can use Maldon salt, firmly packed, or fleur de sel, but it is not necessary to use a flaky salt because any salt you add will dissolve into the ice cream base.

DULCE DE LECHE ICE CREAM

Makes: About 5 cups/1.2 liters

Häagen-Dazs Dulce de Leche has long been my favorite commercial ice cream, so I was delighted to discover that it is even more delicious when homemade! I have tried innumerable methods of making dulce de leche, and the absolute best and smoothest texture is achieved by using the same method as for canning preserves. You can make several jars at the same time. They make great gifts and will keep refrigerated for several weeks.

Dulce de leche is made from sweetened milk that is cooked until the sugar in the milk and the added sugar caramelize. It is paler in color than caramel, and has a more mellow flavor. It stays soft on freezing, so you can enjoy finding little pockets of the dulce in the ice cream.

DULCE DE LECHE

Makes: 350 grams/about 1 generous cup/276 ml

1 can sweetened condensed milk	396 grams	1 cup plus 3 tablespoons (281 ml)

1) Place a small rack or metal trivet in a canning pot or deep pot. Fill the pot about two-thirds full with hot water and bring it to a boil.

2) Scrape the condensed milk into the canning jar. Cover with the lid and the screw cap. Set it on the rack. Add boiling water to cover the jar by at least 2 inches. Cover the pot and simmer for about 3 hours, or until the condensed milk is dark tan, checking the level of the water every 30 minutes and adding more boiling water if needed. (Note: If you can set your burner so that the water is just below a simmer, it will take about 6½ hours but will result in the silkiest, smoothest possible dulce.)

3) Transfer the jar to a wire rack and allow it to cool completely before opening. Once opened, it will keep refrigerated for up to 2 weeks. Bring it

Continued

SPECIAL EQUIPMENT

One 2 cup/473 ml canning jar

A disposable pastry bag or quart-size reclosable freezer bag

A 9 by 5 inch loaf pan, preferably Pyrex

to room temperature before using to soften it for piping. If it is not perfectly smooth, a vigorous stirring with a spoon works well.

ICE CREAM BASE

Dulce de Leche	350 grams	1 cup plus 2½ tablespoons (276 ml), *divided*
6 (to 9) large egg yolks (see page xxxii)	112 grams	¼ cup plus 3 tablespoons (104 ml)
milk	121 grams	½ cup (118 ml)
glucose or reduced corn syrup (see page xxi)	63 grams	3 tablespoons (45 ml)
fine sea salt	.	a pinch
heavy cream	522 grams	2¼ cups (532 ml)
pure vanilla extract	.	1 teaspoon (5 ml)

✿ Have ready a fine-mesh strainer suspended over a medium bowl.

1) In a medium saucepan, with a silicone spatula, stir together 200 grams/ about ⅔ cup/158 ml of the dulce de leche, the egg yolks, milk, glucose, and salt until well blended.

2) Heat the mixture on medium-low, stirring constantly, until slightly thicker than heavy cream. When a finger is run across the back of the spatula, it will leave a well-defined track. An instant-read thermometer should read 170° to 180°F/77° to 82°C.

3) Immediately pour the mixture into the strainer, scraping up the thickened mixture that has settled on the bottom of the pan. Press it through the strainer and scrape any mixture clinging to the underside into the bowl.

4) Stir in the cream and vanilla. Cover and refrigerate for a minimum of 8 hours or until no warmer than 43°F/6°C. (Alternatively, cool in an ice water bath.) Set the loaf pan in the freezer.

5) Churn the dulce de leche custard in a prechilled ice cream maker.

Continued

6) While the ice cream is churning, scrape the remaining 150 grams/½ cup/ 118 ml of the dulce de leche into the pastry bag. Cut off a small semicircle from the point of the bag and close it with a binder clamp until ready to pipe the dulce. (Alternatively, you can use a spoon to apply the dulce, but it's easier and faster with a pastry bag.)

7) Pipe about one-third of the dulce in zigzags onto the bottom of the pan. Spread about one-third of the ice cream on top. Quickly pipe more zigzags on top, using about half of the remaining dulce. Repeat with another one-third of the ice cream and then the remaining dulce. Top with the remaining ice cream.

8) Press a piece of plastic wrap on the surface of the ice cream, cover the pan, and allow the ice cream to firm in the freezer for at least 4 hours before serving.

STORE Covered storage container: frozen, 3 days

SCOOPS

✳ Canning jars are not recommended for reuse for canning because the bottoms can fracture off into the water bath.

✳ The darker the dulce, the thicker it will be, but it always stays soft enough even when frozen.

✳ Pyrex retains the cold best. If using a metal pan, set it in an ice water bath while filling it with the ice cream and dulce.

HONEY ICE CREAM

Makes: About 1 quart/1 liter

Honey comes in many flavors and intensities, resulting in subtle to pronounced flavor. Choose your favorite and experiment. Honey replaces the glucose to give this mellifluous ice cream its smooth and creamy texture. A higher than usual proportion of milk to cream works well for this super creamy and dense ice cream.

ICE CREAM BASE

full-flavored honey	222 grams	²⁄₃ cup (158 ml)
8 (to 12) large egg yolks (see page xxxii)	149 grams	½ cup plus 4 teaspoons (138 ml)
milk	363 grams	1½ cups (355 ml)
sugar	67 grams	⅓ cup
fine sea salt	.	a pinch
heavy cream	348 grams	1½ cups (355 ml)

❖ Have ready a fine-mesh strainer suspended over a medium bowl containing the honey.

1) In a medium saucepan, with a silicone spatula, stir together the egg yolks, milk, sugar, and salt until well blended.

2) Heat the mixture on medium-low, stirring constantly, until slightly thicker than heavy cream. When a finger is run across the back of the spatula, it will leave a well-defined track. An instant-read thermometer should read 170° to 180°F/77° to 82°C.

3) Immediately pour the mixture into the strainer, scraping up the thickened mixture that has settled on the bottom of the pan. Press it through the strainer and scrape any mixture clinging to the underside into the bowl.

4) Stir in the honey until well blended, then stir in the cream. Cover and refrigerate for a minimum of 8 hours or until no warmer than 43°F/6°C.

Continued

(Alternatively, cool in an ice water bath.) Set a covered storage container in the freezer.

5) Churn the honey custard in a prechilled ice cream maker. Transfer the ice cream to the chilled container. Press a piece of plastic wrap on the surface of the ice cream, cover the container, and allow the ice cream to firm in the freezer for at least 4 hours before serving.

STORE Covered storage container: frozen, 3 days

SCOOPS

✳ Chestnut honey, especially the Agrimontana brand from Italy, is one of my favorites. Its intense flavor perfectly balances its sweetness. If using a milder honey, it is advisable to use only 50 grams/¼ cup of sugar.

DARK BROWN SUGAR ICE CREAM WITH BLACK PEPPER

Makes: 1 generous quart/1 generous liter

The butterscotch and molasses overtones of this ice cream meld beautifully with a grinding of black pepper, which adds a spark of smokiness and a hint of heat. This is a great blending of sugar and spice. Muscovado sugar has depth, complexity, and a spiciness of its own. India Tree Muscovado comes from the volcanic island of Mauritius, off the coast of India, and really smokes in this ice cream.

ICE CREAM BASE

dark brown sugar, preferably India Tree Muscovado	168 grams	¾ cup, firmly packed
heavy cream	464 grams	2 cups (473 ml)
7 (to 11) large egg yolks (see page xxxii)	130 grams	½ cup (118 ml)
glucose or reduced corn syrup (see page xxi)	42 grams	2 tablespoons (30 ml)
fine sea salt	.	a pinch
milk	160 grams	⅔ cup (158 ml)
pure vanilla extract	.	½ tablespoon (7.5 ml)
freshly ground black pepper	.	to taste

✣ Have ready a fine-mesh strainer suspended over a medium bowl.

1) In a medium saucepan, place the sugar. With a silicone spatula, stir in the cream and then the egg yolks. Stir in the glucose and salt until well blended.

2) Heat the mixture on medium-low, stirring constantly with a silicone spatula, until it thickly coats the spatula but is still liquid enough to pour. When a finger is run across the back of the spatula, it will leave a well-defined track. An instant-read thermometer should read 170° to 180°F/77° to 82°C.

Continued

3) Immediately remove the pan from the heat and pour the mixture into the strainer, scraping up the thickened mixture that has settled on the bottom of the pan. Press it through the strainer and scrape any mixture clinging to the underside into the bowl.

4) Stir in the milk and vanilla.

5) Cover and refrigerate for a minimum of 8 hours or until no warmer than 43°F/6°C. (Alternatively, cool in an ice water bath.) Set a covered storage container in the freezer.

6) Churn the dark brown sugar custard in a prechilled ice cream maker. Transfer the ice cream to the chilled container. Press a piece of plastic wrap on the surface of the ice cream, cover the container, and allow the ice cream to firm in the freezer for at least 4 hours before serving.

Pass the pepper mill!

STORE Covered storage container: frozen, 3 days

SCOOPS

✳ The cream is heated with the sugar and egg custard and then the milk is added at the end because the acidity in the brown sugar can cause the proteins in the milk to coagulate.

VARIATION

SAGE ICE CREAM

Sage is an unexpectedly welcome addition and makes this ice cream a perfect accompaniment to pumpkin pie. The sage stays in the background, imperceptible at first taste, but then appears briefly and compellingly, making you want to take another and yet another taste to find it again.

Add about 15 leaves/10 grams of fresh sage to the hot custard before stirring in the milk and vanilla. Cover and refrigerate, allowing the sage leaves to steep for 1 hour before removing them. Omit the black pepper.

EGGNOG ICE CREAM

Makes: About 1 quart/1 liter

Growing up, I hated eggnog, but of course it wasn't frozen, nor did it have rum. My grandmother would make it for me as a meal-in-one breakfast drink, and when she walked out of the room I would quickly pour it down the side of the building from our sixth floor apartment overlooking Central Park West. No one ever questioned the strange stripe on the side of the building. Interesting how a dash of rum and the cold texture of the ice cream cuts through the thick richness of eggnog. Eggnog ice cream has now become a holiday dessert tradition.

ICE CREAM BASE

6 (to 9 large) egg yolks (see page xxxii)	112 grams	1/4 cup plus 3 tablespoons (104 ml)
milk	121 grams	1/2 cup (118 ml)
heavy cream	406 grams	1 3/4 cups (414 ml), *divided*
sugar	133 grams	2/3 cup
glucose or reduced corn syrup (see page xxi)	42 grams	2 tablespoons (30 ml)
fine sea salt	.	a pinch
pure vanilla extract	.	1/2 tablespoon (7.5 ml)
nutmeg, freshly grated	.	3/8 teaspoon
dark rum (optional)	28 grams	2 tablespoons (30 ml)

✲ Have ready a fine-mesh strainer suspended over a medium bowl.

1) In a medium saucepan, with a silicone spatula, stir together the egg yolks, milk, and 174 grams/3/4 cup/177 ml of the cream until well blended. Stir in the sugar, glucose, and salt until the sugar has dissolved.

2) Heat the mixture on medium-low, stirring constantly, until slightly thicker than heavy cream. When a finger is run across the back of the spatula, it will leave a well-defined track. An instant-read thermometer should read 170° to 180°F/77° to 82°C.

3) Immediately pour the mixture into the strainer, scraping up the thickened mixture that has settled on the bottom of the pan. Press it through the strainer and scrape any mixture clinging to the underside into the bowl.

4) Stir in the remaining cream (232 grams/1 cup/237 ml), the vanilla, nutmeg, and rum, if desired. Cover and refrigerate for a minimum of 8 hours or until no warmer than 43°F/6°C. (Alternatively, cool in an ice water bath.) Set a covered storage container in the freezer.

5) Churn the eggnog custard in a prechilled ice cream maker. Transfer the ice cream to the chilled container. Press a piece of plastic wrap on the surface of the ice cream, cover the container, and allow the ice cream to firm in the freezer for at least 4 hours before serving.

STORE Covered storage container: frozen, 3 days

ESPRESSO ICE CREAM

Makes: About 1 quart/1 liter

The best coffee ice cream is made with freshly roasted and ground coffee beans. Espresso is more concentrated than regular brewed coffee, which is ideal to get the flavor without too many water-forming ice crystals. Homemade chocolate chips (page 175) are a great addition.

ICE CREAM BASE

8 (to 12) large egg yolks (see page xxxii)	149 grams	½ cup plus 4 teaspoons (138 ml)
heavy cream	464 grams	2 cups (473 ml), *divided*
sugar	180 grams	1 cup minus 5 teaspoons
glucose or reduced corn syrup (see page xxi)	42 grams	2 tablespoons (30 ml)
fine sea salt	.	a pinch
brewed espresso	237 grams	1 cup (237 ml)
coffee extract	.	2 teaspoons (10 ml)
Kahlúa (optional)	67 grams	¼ cup (59 ml)

❖ Have ready a fine-mesh strainer suspended over a medium bowl.

1) In a medium saucepan, with a silicone spatula, stir together the egg yolks and 232 grams/1 cup/237 ml of the cream until well blended. Stir in the sugar, glucose, and salt until the sugar has dissolved.

2) Heat the mixture on medium-low, stirring constantly, until slightly thicker than heavy cream. When a finger is run across the back of the spatula, it will leave a well-defined track. An instant-read thermometer should read 170° to 180°F/77° to 82°C.

3) Immediately pour the mixture into the strainer, scraping up the thickened mixture that has settled on the bottom of the pan. Press it through the strainer and scrape any mixture clinging to the underside into the bowl.

4) Stir in the espresso, coffee extract, and remaining cream (232 grams/ 1 cup/237 ml). Cover and refrigerate for a minimum of 8 hours or until no warmer than 43°F/6°C. (Alternatively, cool in an ice water bath.) Set a covered storage container in the freezer.

5) Whisk the Kahlúa into the espresso custard, if desired, and churn it in a prechilled ice cream maker. Transfer the ice cream to the chilled container. Press a piece of plastic wrap on the surface of the ice cream, cover the container, and allow the ice cream to firm in the freezer for at least 4 hours before serving.

STORE Covered storage container: frozen, 3 days

BACK ROAD WILD MINT CHIP ICE CREAM

Makes: About 1 quart/1 liter

Bright green specks of extra fresh mint leaf, added to the ice cream base before churning, greatly enhance the deep minty flavor. Chocolate curls provide the ideal texture to complement rather than override the mint flavor. A scattering of fresh blueberries on top can make both an attractive and synergistic addition.

ICE CREAM BASE

fresh mint leaves, preferably peppermint (see Scoops)	53 grams (about 150 grams on the stem)	2 cups, lightly packed
milk	136 grams	½ cup plus 1 tablespoon (133 ml)
heavy cream	392 grams	1½ cups plus 3 tablespoons (400 ml), *divided*
sugar	133 grams	⅔ cup
fine sea salt	.	a pinch
6 (to 9) large egg yolks (see page xxxii)	112 grams	¼ cup plus 3 tablespoons (104 ml)
glucose or reduced corn syrup (see page xxi)	32 grams	1½ tablespoons (22.5 ml)
green liquid food color (optional)	.	2 to 4 drops
extra fresh mint leaves	13 grams (about 38 grams on the stem)	½ cup, lightly packed
dark chocolate, curls or thickly grated (see page 175)	64 grams	¾ cup

Continued

* Have ready a fine-mesh strainer suspended over a medium bowl.

* Rinse the mint leaves and strip them from the stems. Discard the stems.

1) In a medium saucepan, heat the milk, 196 grams/¾ cup plus 1½ tablespoons/200 ml of the cream, the sugar, and salt, stirring with a silicone spatula, until very warm (130° to 140°F/54° to 60°C). Stir in the mint. Cover and remove from the heat. Allow the mixture to steep for 1 hour. Strain and squeeze the leaves to release all the liquid. Discard the leaves.

2) With a silicone spatula, stir the egg yolks into the mint mixture until incorporated. Then stir in the glucose until well blended.

3) Heat the mixture on medium-low, stirring constantly, until about the thickness of light cream. When a finger is run across the back of the spatula, it will leave a faint track. An instant-read thermometer should read 170° to 180°F/77° to 82°C.

4) Immediately pour the mixture into the strainer, scraping up the thickened mixture that has settled on the bottom of the pan. Press it through the strainer and scrape any mixture clinging to the underside into the bowl.

5) Stir in the remaining cream (196 grams/¾ cup plus 1½ tablespoons/ 200 ml) and food color, if desired, to achieve a pale green color. Cover and refrigerate for a minimum of 8 hours or until no warmer than 43°F/6°C. (Alternatively, cool in an ice water bath.) Set a covered storage container in the freezer.

6) Shortly before churning the mint custard, use sharp scissors to snip the extra mint leaves into fine pieces. Add the mint to the custard mixture and scrape it into a prechilled ice cream maker. After the ice cream has reached soft serve consistency and begins to ball up around the dasher, add the chocolate curls and continue spinning for just a few seconds, just until they are mixed in. (If using grated chocolate, mix it in gently with a spatula.)

7) Transfer the ice cream to the chilled container. Press a piece of plastic wrap on the surface of the ice cream, cover the container, and allow the ice cream to firm in the freezer for at least 4 hours before serving.

STORE Covered storage container: frozen, 3 days

SCOOPS

* There are many varieties of mint. Peppermint has the strongest flavor. If using spearmint, or a less flavorful variety, you may want to supplement the mint flavor with mint extract to taste.

* Mint has an enzyme that inhibits the egg yolk custard from thickening as much as usual, and also causes slight curdling of some of the egg yolk. Any curds will be removed by straining the custard.

GREEN TEA ICE CREAM

Makes: About 1 quart/1 liter

I fell in love with matcha (the powdered green tea of the Japanese tea ceremony) on my first trip to Japan, and when I returned home I began using it in cakes, meringue, and whipped cream. A few years later, on a visit to Vancouver, Canada, I delighted in it as a cold drink. So, of course, it had to become an ice cream as well. Matcha is the finest possible powder, which makes it difficult to measure and impossible to integrate fully into the custard base without the use of a blender.

ICE CREAM BASE

matcha green tea powder	11 grams	2 tablespoons, packed
7 (to 11) large egg yolks (see page xxxii)	130 grams	½ cup (118 ml)
milk	181 grams	¾ cup (177 ml)
heavy cream	522 grams	2¼ cups (532 ml), *divided*
sugar	133 grams	⅔ cup
glucose or reduced corn syrup (see page xxi)	42 grams	2 tablespoons (30 ml)
fine sea salt	.	a pinch

✤ Have ready a fine-mesh strainer suspended over a medium bowl containing the matcha.

1) In a medium saucepan, with a silicone spatula, stir together the egg yolks, milk, and 290 grams/1¼ cups/296 ml of the cream, until well blended. Stir in the sugar, glucose, and salt until the sugar has dissolved.

2) Heat the mixture on medium-low, stirring constantly with a silicone spatula, until slightly thicker than heavy cream. When a finger is run across the back of the spatula, it will leave a well-defined track. An instant-read thermometer should read 170° to 180°F/77° to 82°C.

Continued

3) Immediately pour the mixture into the strainer, scraping up the thickened mixture that has settled on the bottom of the pan. Press it through the strainer and scrape any mixture clinging to the underside into the bowl.

4) Stir in the matcha and then stir in the remaining cream (232 grams/ 1 cup/237 ml). Transfer the mixture to a blender and whirl it on low speed to break up the particles of green tea, or use an immersion blender. Cover and refrigerate for a minimum of 8 hours or until no warmer than 43°F/6°C. (Alternatively, cool in an ice water bath.) Set a covered storage container in the freezer.

5) Churn the green tea custard in a prechilled ice cream maker. Transfer the ice cream to the chilled container. Press a piece of plastic wrap on the surface of the ice cream, cover the container, and allow the ice cream to firm in the freezer for at least 4 hours before serving.

STORE Covered storage container: frozen, 3 days

ROYAL VELVET LAVENDER ICE CREAM

Makes: About 1 quart/1 liter

I was intrigued by a version of this ice cream many years ago on a trip to Florence, Italy. I'm not a fan of herbs in sweets, but the exquisitely floral flavor of lavender is an exception.

This ice cream is smooth, dense, and creamy, and perfumed with lavender. The day that I tested this ice cream I also happened to make a rhubarb compote (see page 205). When I tasted the two together, I was amazed to discover that the assertive rhubarb hits first, but with each bite the more subtle, aromatic lavender rose like a high note above it. I also love the colors of lavender and deep rose together. Since the color of the lavender disappears in the ice cream, I decided it deserved to have its color restored with a few drops of food coloring. Alternatively, garnish with a sprig of lavender.

ICE CREAM BASE

fresh lavender buds (see Scoops)	9 grams	3 tablespoons
sugar	113 grams	½ cup plus 1 tablespoon
cornstarch	12 grams	4 teaspoons
heavy cream	522 grams	2¼ cups (532 ml), *divided*
milk	181 grams	¾ cup (177 ml)
glucose or reduced corn syrup (see page xxi)	42 grams	2 tablespoons (30 ml)
fine sea salt	.	a pinch
7 (to 11) large egg yolks (see page xxxii)	130 grams	½ cup (118 ml)
lavender or purple liquid food color (optional)	.	a few drops

- Have ready a fine-mesh strainer suspended over a medium bowl.
- Prepare an ice water bath (see page xvii).

Continued

1) In a small food processor, process the lavender with the sugar until the lavender is in very fine particles.

2) In a custard cup or small bowl, stir together the cornstarch and 58 grams/¼ cup/59 ml of the cream until smooth, adding the cream slowly as you mix it in. Cover with plastic wrap.

3) In a medium saucepan, with a silicone spatula, stir together the remaining cream (464 grams/2 cups/473 ml), the milk, 50 grams/¼ cup of the lavender sugar, the glucose, and salt until well blended.

4) Scrape the remaining lavender sugar into the bowl beneath the strainer. (The moisture from the lavender buds will make the sugar stick to the sides of the processor.)

5) In a medium bowl, place the egg yolks and whisk them lightly. Set it near the cooktop.

6) Over medium heat, bring the cream mixture to a boil, stirring constantly. Lower the heat and cook at a slow boil, stirring, for 2 to 3 minutes to evaporate some of the water in the mixture. Remove the pan from the heat. Allow the mixture to cool for a few minutes, to about 180°F/82°C.

7) Stir the cornstarch mixture to make sure it is smooth and then whisk it into the hot cream mixture. Return the pan to the heat and bring the mixture to a slow boil. Cook for 1 minute, whisking gently. It will thicken slightly.

8) Remove the cornstarch mixture from the heat and gradually whisk about ½ cup/118 ml of the mixture into the egg yolks to temper them. Then use a whisk to stir the egg yolk mixture back into the pot. Check the temperature. If an instant-read thermometer reads 170°F/77°C, there is no need to heat it further. If it is lower, heat the mixture on low, stirring constantly, until thickened a little further. When a finger is run across the back of the spatula, it will leave a well-defined track. An instant-read thermometer should read 170° to 180°F/77° to 82°C.

9) Immediately remove the pan from the heat and pour the mixture into the strainer, scraping up the thickened mixture that has settled on the bottom of the pan. Press it through the strainer into the bowl and scrape any mixture clinging to the underside into the bowl. Stir to mix in the remaining lavender sugar and add the food color, if desired.

10) Set the bowl containing the custard mixture in the ice water bath and allow it to cool until no longer warm to the touch, stirring occasionally. Cover and refrigerate for a minimum of 8 hours or until no warmer than 43°F/6°C. Set a covered storage container in the freezer.

11) Churn the lavender custard in a prechilled ice cream maker. Transfer the ice cream to the chilled container. Press a piece of plastic wrap on the surface of the ice cream, cover the container, and allow the ice cream to firm in the freezer for at least 4 hours before serving.

12) If you make the rhubarb compote on page 205, gently spoon some rhubarb into the bowl and top it with a large scoop of the ice cream.

SCOOPS

❋ I like to let the fresh lavender buds sit in the sugar for 1 hour at room temperature or up to 24 hours in the refrigerator, covered, so that some of the moisture in the buds is absorbed into the sugar, which prevents it from sticking to the food processor.

❋ Fresh lavender buds can be frozen in an airtight container for a year. They can also be dried and stored in an airtight container in a cool spot for up to 2 years.

❋ If using dried lavender, make sure it is food-grade (avoid the potpourri variety because it has likely been sprayed with pesticides). Some dried lavenders are unpleasantly pungent. Kalustyan's carries a good variety of edible dried lavender. You can also dry your own by hanging the lavender branches upside down in a cool, dry place for several weeks. Use 1½ tablespoons/3 grams in place of the fresh lavender buds.

❋ Monica Hamway, of Orchard View Lavender Farm in Port Murray, New Jersey, offered some valuable information about lavender. She told me that there are 450 varieties of lavender, and while French lavender varieties are most suited for potpourri, English lavenders are most suited for cooking. She also told me that the flavorful lavender oil is more prevalent in the buds than after they flower.

❋ Woody and I harvested four English varieties at Monica's orchard in June of 2017 and 2018: Royal Velvet, Hidcote, Munstead, and Folgate. We found that all four varieties had the unmistakable scent of lavender, but some had a spicier aroma. When combined with the ingredients for this ice cream, however, we could not distinguish the difference.

RED WINE ICE CREAM

Makes: About 1 quart/1 liter

I first discovered this exceptional idea on a wine trip to Germany many years ago. How enchanting to be able to turn your favorite red wine into an exquisite pale pink ice cream! Choose a red wine that is intense in flavor to stand up to the softening effect of the creamy custard. A scoop would be a lovely complement to fresh strawberries or a fruit pie.

ICE CREAM BASE

nonfat dry milk (see Scoops)	18 grams	2 tablespoons plus 2 teaspoons
heavy cream	522 grams	2¼ cups (532 ml), *divided*
sugar	100 grams	½ cup
glucose or reduced corn syrup (see page xxi)	42 grams	2 tablespoons (30 ml)
fine sea salt	.	a pinch
6 (to 9) large egg yolks (see page xxxii)	112 grams	¼ cup plus 3 tablespoons (104 ml)
red wine, such as Côte-Rôtie, Croze-Hermitage, zinfandel, or cabernet	173 grams	¾ cup (177 ml)

❖ Have ready a fine-mesh strainer suspended over a medium bowl.

1) In a small saucepan, with a silicone spatula, stir together the dry milk, 232 grams/1 cup/237 ml of the heavy cream, the sugar, glucose, and salt. Bring it to a slow boil and cook, stirring, for 2 minutes. Allow it to cool slightly.

2) In a medium saucepan, place the egg yolks. Whisk a little of the cream mixture into the yolks and then gradually whisk in the remainder.

3) Heat the mixture on medium-low, stirring constantly with a silicone spatula, until slightly thicker than heavy cream. When a finger is run across the back of the spatula, it will leave a well-defined track. An instant-read thermometer should read 170° to 180°F/77° to 82°C.

4) Immediately pour the mixture into the strainer, scraping up the thickened mixture that has settled on the bottom of the pan. Press it through the strainer and scrape any mixture clinging to the underside into the bowl.

5) Stir in the remaining cream (290 grams/1¼ cups/296 ml). Cover and refrigerate for a minimum of 8 hours or until no warmer than 43°F/6°C. (Alternatively, cool in an ice water bath.) Set a covered storage container in the freezer.

6) Stir in the wine and churn the red wine custard in a prechilled ice cream maker. The alcohol in the red wine makes this ice cream base very soft at this stage, so if your ice cream machine has a removable container, cover it and set it in the freezer for about an hour or until it firms up well enough to transfer to the chilled storage container. Press a piece of plastic wrap on the surface of the ice cream, cover the container, and allow the ice cream to firm in the freezer for at least 4 hours before serving.

STORE Covered storage container: frozen, 3 days

SCOOPS

✻ Adding dry milk helps keep the ice cream from becoming icy from the addition of wine, which has a high water content compared to milk. I don't reduce the wine because it would dull the flavor.

OLIVE OIL ICE CREAM

Makes: About 1 quart/1 liter

I first tasted this exceptional ice cream two decades ago at the Monkey Bar in New York City. It was the silkiest ice cream I had ever experienced. I had no idea it contained olive oil until Chef Andrew Chase gave me his recipe. It called for a large amount of glucose powder, which is not readily available to home cooks, but now that liquid glucose is more readily available, I finally decided to adapt the recipe. The flavor of the olive oil is very melodious and subtle and stays in the background but, of course, it depends on your choice of olive oil. I especially like Greek olive oils with a slightly grassy aroma and not too much peppery flavor. If desired, serve the ice cream with a garnish of sliced fresh kumquats.

ICE CREAM BASE

milk	322 grams	1⅓ cups (315 ml)
heavy cream	310 grams	1⅓ cups (315 ml), *divided*
nonfat dry milk	13 grams	2 tablespoons
sugar	133 grams	⅔ cup
glucose or reduced corn syrup (see page xxi)	42 grams	2 tablespoons (30 ml)
fine sea salt	.	a pinch
4 (to 6) large egg yolks (see page xxxii)	74 grams	¼ cup plus 2 teaspoons (69 ml)
extra virgin olive oil	71 grams	⅓ cup (79 ml)

✢ Have ready a fine-mesh strainer suspended over a medium bowl.

✢ Prepare an ice water bath (see page xvii).

1) In a small saucepan, with a silicone spatula, stir together the milk, 155 grams/ ⅔ cup/158 ml of the cream, and the dry milk until well blended. Stir in the sugar, glucose, and salt until the sugar has dissolved. Bring the milk mixture to a slow boil, stirring constantly. Lower the heat and cook at a slow boil, stirring,

Continued

for 2 to 3 minutes to evaporate some of the water in the mixture. Allow it to cool slightly.

2) In a medium saucepan, place the egg yolks. Whisk a little of the milk mixture into the yolks and then gradually whisk in the remainder.

3) Heat the mixture on medium-low, stirring constantly with a silicone spatula until slightly thicker than heavy cream. When a finger is run across the back of the spatula, it will leave a well-defined track. An instant-read thermometer should read 170° to 180°F/77° to 82°C.

4) Immediately pour the mixture into the strainer, scraping up the thickened mixture that has settled on the bottom of the pan. Press it through the strainer and scrape any mixture clinging to the underside into the bowl.

5) Stir in the remaining cream (155 grams/²⁄₃ cup/158 ml).

6) Set the bowl in the ice water bath and allow it to cool until no longer warm to the touch, stirring occasionally. Stir in the olive oil. Cover and refrigerate for a minimum of 8 hours or until no warmer than 43°F/6°C. (Alternatively, continue cooling it in the ice water bath.) Set a covered storage container in the freezer.

7) Churn the olive oil custard in a prechilled ice cream maker. Transfer the ice cream to the chilled container. Press a piece of plastic wrap on the surface of the ice cream, cover the container, and allow the ice cream to firm in the freezer for at least 4 hours before serving.

STORE Covered storage container: frozen, 3 days

TURKISH STRETCHY ICE CREAM

Makes: About 3 cups/0.7 liters

The uniqueness of this extraordinary Turkish ice cream is its texture—sticky, chewy, and incredibly stretchy. After my grandson, Owen Daw, enjoyed a trip to Turkey, he described ice cream vendors teasing customers by leaving the long ice cream paddle in place after handing them the ice cream topped cone, and then magically lifting away the ice cream right out of the cone.

It took a bit of research to unveil the romantic mystery of the ice cream. My pastry chef friend from Turkey, Yusuf Yaran, explained that the key ingredient is a powder called salep, which comes from the root of an orchid. He wrote that there are tons of orchids in the city of Kahramanmaraş, Turkey, but it is a long process and only a few grams come from each flower's root. You can order it on the internet. Aside from procuring the salep, this recipe couldn't be easier.

The flavor is up to you—a few drops of rosewater or a little vanilla extract or raspberry essence are all lovely additions. A topping of chopped pistachios is also traditional.

ICE CREAM BASE

salep powder	4 grams	1¼ teaspoons
sugar	156 grams	¾ cup plus ½ tablespoon
milk	726 grams	3 cups (710 ml)
heavy cream	43 grams	3 tablespoons (45 ml)
flavoring (see headnote)	.	to taste

✲ Prepare an ice water bath (see page xvii).

1) In a small bowl, whisk together the salep powder and sugar.

2) In a medium saucepan, on medium-low heat, stirring constantly with a silicone spatula, bring the milk and cream to a boil.

Continued

3) Gradually stir the salep and sugar mixture into the milk. Boil for about 8 minutes, stirring constantly.

4) Pour the mixture into a bowl and set it in the ice water bath until no longer warm.

5) Stir in your choice of flavoring. Cover and refrigerate for a minimum of 8 hours or until no warmer than 43°F/6°C. (Alternatively, cool in the ice water bath.) Set a covered storage container in the freezer.

6) Churn the Turkish ice cream base in a prechilled ice cream maker. Transfer the ice cream to the chilled container. Press a piece of plastic wrap on the surface of the ice cream, cover the container, and allow the ice cream to firm in the freezer for at least 4 hours before serving.

STORE Covered storage container: frozen, 3 days

SCOOPS

✣ Some recipes for Turkish ice cream include a small amount of mastic—a resinous gum derived from the mastic tree on the island of Chios in Greece. It is available as "pearls" or small pieces called "tears." Mastic adds an extra chewy quality to the ice cream. If you want to try it, you will need to pound a small piece using a heavy-duty reclosable plastic bag and rolling pin, or a mortar and pestle, to pulverize it into a powder. Add about ½ teaspoon/2 grams to the milk mixture before boiling it.

SUVIR SARAN'S CARDAMOM "RICE CREAM" WITH SAFFRON SAUCE

Makes: 4 to 6 servings

This is not technically an ice cream because it isn't served frozen, but it is as satisfying as one, and doesn't require an ice cream maker. My friend, Chef Suvir Saran, makes a fabulous version of firni, the beloved Indian rice pudding. It is flavored with cardamom and topped with a gilding of saffron cream sauce. It is refreshingly light yet creamy and delicious. I am most grateful to him for sharing this recipe.

Plan Ahead The rice needs to be soaked in Step 2 for a minimum of 8 and up to 12 hours.

basmati rice	35 grams	¼ cup
water	118 grams	½ cup (118 ml)
half-and-half	968 grams	1 quart (about 1 liter)
6 cardamom pods	.	½ teaspoon (seeds from about 6 cardamom pods)
sugar	100 grams	½ cup
saffron threads	.	¼ teaspoon
heavy cream	29 grams	2 tablespoons (30 ml)

✽ Have ready six ramekins or custard cups (6 ounce/177 ml capacity).

1) In a spice grinder, process the rice until finely ground.

2) In a large saucepan, scrape in the rice and add the water. Cover the pan and allow the rice to soak for at least 8 and up to 12 hours.

3) Drain away most of the water and add the half-and-half. Bring it to a boil, stirring constantly with a whisk.

4) Lower the heat to a slow boil and reduce the mixture to about three-quarters of the original volume, continuing to stir constantly for about 20 minutes. The mixture should be the consistency of a thin pudding, and just begin to mound slightly when dropped from the whisk before disappearing into the surface.

5) Scrape the rice cream into a pitcher with a spout.

6) Remove the seeds from the cardamom pods and discard the pods. In a mortar and pestle, grind the seeds into a powder. (Alternatively, grind the cardamom seeds, with the sugar, in a spice grinder or food processor.)

7) Whisk the cardamom and sugar into the rice cream. Pour it into the ramekins and allow it to cool for about 20 minutes. Cover the ramekins tightly and refrigerate for at least 4 and up to 48 hours. It will thicken on chilling.

8) In a small skillet, on low heat, warm the saffron for about 3 minutes or until it begins to smell aromatic and darkens slightly. Scrape it into a mortar or a small custard cup and with a pestle or the back of a spoon, crush it into a fine powder. Scrape it into a small glass measure with a spout and stir in the heavy cream.

9) Shortly before serving, pour the saffron cream onto the puddings.

STORE Airtight (without the saffron cream): refrigerated, 2 days. The saffron cream can be made ahead. Store in a separate airtight container, refrigerated, for up to 2 days.

SCOOPS

✻ If you don't happen to have half-and-half on hand, you can substitute 363 grams/ 1½ cups/355 ml whole milk plus 116 grams/ ½ cup/118 ml heavy cream.

BERRY, FRUIT, AND VEGETABLE ICE CREAMS

This chapter includes berries, stone fruit, citrus fruit, dried fruit, and vegetables such as rhubarb and pumpkin. Those that are seasonal are organized in that order, but many are available year-round, and some are best when used frozen, such as strawberries, or even canned, such as mango.

Berries, fruits, and vegetables are the most challenging to turn into creamy ice cream because of their high water content, but the flavors and textures they contribute make it well worth the effort.

Berry and citrus fruit ice creams lend themselves beautifully to making Creamsicle-style swirl ice creams. The ideal balance is one part vanilla ice cream to one-quarter fruit ice cream. Simply soften the two ice creams and swirl the fruit ice cream into the vanilla ice cream. Serve immediately or refreeze for a firmer consistency.

SPECIAL NOTES ON BERRY, PEACH, AND CHERRY ICE CREAMS

Berries, such as strawberries, and especially thorn berries such as blackberries, black raspberries, and raspberries, make some of the most intense, creamy, and flavorful ice creams. But berries are tricky because they contain as much as 80% to 89% water. Water will turn to ice when frozen and can ruin the texture of the ice cream. Another major challenge is that the berries' ripeness, sugar content, water content, and flavor vary significantly depending on the season, where they are harvested, and how they are stored.

My goal has been to make the most of the berries' flavor, and sometimes to enhance their flavor so that the results always fall between an acceptable margin of predictable deliciousness. I have found that concentrating the juices of the berries (but not the pulp) maintains the fresh flavor of the berry and helps eliminate iciness. Frozen berries, when thawed, release a significant amount of their juices. These juices can be boiled down and concentrated, while the pulp remains uncooked and retains its full flavor. I usually prefer commercially picked and frozen strawberries, raspberries, and blackberries because they are picked at the perfect ripeness and their flavor and sugar level are fairly consistent. If using fresh berries, be sure to freeze them for a minimum of 24 hours before thawing to help release their juices. Frozen berries will keep at 0°F/−18°C for as long as 2 years.

The next challenge is separating and removing the hard and undesirable seeds from the pulp. Using a food processor risks bruising the seeds and releasing a bitter flavor. If you plan to make berry purée, a Squeezo Tomato Strainer with berry screen or a food mill with fine berry screen (3/64 inch holes) will pay for itself as it releases the most pulp and in the shortest time. The berries can be pressed through a fine-mesh strainer with the back of a large spoon, but it will take at least four times as long.

The exact yield of berry juice and purée varies depending on the berry, how long it has been frozen, and your equipment (measuring cups and puréeing device), but not to worry; using the specified weight or volume of berries should give you at least the 341 grams/ 1¼ cups/296 ml of sweetened purée needed for each recipe, and even if slightly less, these purées are so vibrant that the ice cream will still be delicious. In all likelihood you will have extra to use as sauce for pancakes or berries, or to drizzle on top of the ice cream. Alternatively, because each purée will be sweetened to the correct level, after collecting enough of the leftover purées in the freezer, you can combine them and add them proportionately to the custard base to make a mixed berry ice cream (I like to call it "many berry" ice cream).

When it comes to strawberries, I like to leave the tiny seeds in the purée because they are soft and also are such an intrinsic part of eating a strawberry. There is, therefore, no waste, and if there is less juice released there will be more pulp. I therefore have standardized the sweetness by basing the amount of sugar on the initial weight of the berry at about 9%. This can't be done with thorn berries because the amount of seeds removed varies, so it has to be determined by the finished weight or volume of the purée rather than the initial weight of the berries.

Even after concentrating a berry's juices, there is still enough water in the purée to produce a slightly icy texture. This is effectively eliminated by adding a cornstarch slurry, made with water or dairy (cream and milk) from the base, to the custard base. Using this technique requires heating the rest of the dairy to thicken the cornstarch. This means that there isn't any cold dairy or liquid to add at the end to cool down the custard base quickly, so an ice water bath is required. This method also requires tempering the egg yolks when adding the hot dairy to them instead of simply adding them to the unheated mixture initially, as I do for other ice creams. These extra steps make the process more laborious than my other ice creams. But it is worth it for the exceptionally smooth, creamy, and flavorful results.

A berry such as raspberry has such an intense flavor it is unmistakable and requires no further enhancement, but strawberries (and also fruits such as peaches and pears) benefit immensely from just a few drops of a fruit essence. Mandy Aftel, a gifted perfumer, carries exquisite essences on her site (see Ingredients, page xxxiii).

Some fruits, such as peaches and sweet Bing cherries, have a high water content, so they would freeze like rocks in the ice cream. Peaches also lose their flavor when eaten frozen. They are often better served *with* the ice cream, rather than *in* the ice cream. To maintain the best flavor of a ripe, juicy peach, I prefer to slice it and macerate it briefly with sugar, and then serve it with the ice cream. I do, however, offer a special technique for concentrating the peach juices and puréeing the pulp (see Peach Perfect Ice Cream, page 68), to make exceptional peach ice cream. Cherries can be brandied and are wonderful when added to the ice cream after the ice cream reaches the consistency of soft serve (see page 7).

Bottled pomegranate juice happens to be delicious when concentrated. It makes an excellent ice cream, and a stunning translucent garnet syrup to swirl through or lace on top of the ice cream. However, concentrating does not work for all fruit—for example, concentrated mango purée has a decidedly cooked flavor.

STRAWBERRY ICE CREAM

Makes: 1 generous quart/1 generous liter

Strawberry ice cream was my dad's favorite. My version is dense and creamy, with a slight pleasant crunch of strawberry seeds and a true strawberry flavor. Rather than having large icy pieces of strawberry in the ice cream, I process the berries until only small bits remain and then top the ice cream with fresh strawberries, cut in half or quarters and macerated in sugar.

Plan Ahead The strawberries will take anywhere from several hours to as long as 2 days to thaw.

SWEETENED STRAWBERRY PURÉE

Makes: About 530 grams/about 2 cups plus 2 tablespoons/500 ml (Amount needed to add to the custard base: 341 grams/about 1¼ cups/296 ml)

frozen strawberries	567 grams (20 ounces)	about 4 cups
lemon juice, freshly squeezed and strained	10 grams	2 teaspoons (10 ml)
sugar	50 grams	¼ cup

1) In a colander suspended over a deep bowl, thaw the strawberries completely. This will take several hours or as long as 2 days in the refrigerator. Press and stir the berries to force out the juice until you have about 88 grams/7 tablespoons/100 ml of juice.

2) Transfer the juice to a small saucepan and boil until dark, thickened, and reduced to about one-quarter of its original weight or volume (about 4 teaspoons/20 ml). (Alternatively, you can do this in the microwave, in a 4 cup/1 liter glass measure with a spout, lightly coated with nonstick cooking spray, swirling or stirring every 20 to 30 seconds. I prefer this method for purity of flavor.) Allow it to cool until no longer hot.

Continued

3) In a food processor, purée the strawberries until only little bits remain. Scrape the purée into the cooled juice. Add the lemon juice and sugar and stir until the sugar has dissolved.

The sweetened strawberry purée keeps in an airtight container for 10 days refrigerated or 6 months frozen.

ICE CREAM BASE

Sweetened Strawberry Purée	341 grams	1¼ to 1¾ cups (296 to 414 ml)
pure vanilla extract	.	½ teaspoon (2.5 ml)
cornstarch	9 grams	1 tablespoon
milk	106 grams	¼ cup plus 3 tablespoons (104 ml), *divided*
heavy cream	290 grams	1¼ cups (296 ml)
sugar	175 grams	¾ cup plus 2 tablespoons
glucose or reduced corn syrup (see page xxi)	42 grams	2 tablespoons (30 ml)
salt	.	a pinch
6 (to 9) large egg yolks (see page xxxii)	112 grams	¼ cup plus 3 tablespoons (104 ml)
strawberry essence, preferably Aftelier (optional)	.	about 6 drops, to taste

✲ Have ready a fine-mesh strainer suspended over a medium bowl.

✲ Prepare an ice water bath (see page xvii).

1) Into a medium bowl, weigh or measure the strawberry purée. Stir in the vanilla. Cover and refrigerate it.

2) In a custard cup or small bowl, stir together the cornstarch and 30 grams/ 2 tablespoons/30 ml of the milk until smooth, adding the milk slowly as you mix it in. Cover with plastic wrap.

3) In a medium saucepan, with a silicone spatula, stir together the remaining milk (76 grams/5 tablespoons/74 ml), the cream, sugar, glucose, and salt until well blended.

4) In a small bowl, place the egg yolks and whisk them lightly. Set it near the cooktop.

5) Over medium heat, bring the milk mixture to a slow boil, stirring constantly. Lower the heat and cook at a slow boil, stirring, for 2 to 3 minutes to evaporate some of the water in the mixture. Remove the pan from the heat. Allow the mixture to cool for a few minutes, to about 180°F/82°C.

6) Stir the cornstarch mixture to make sure it is smooth and then whisk it into the hot milk mixture. Return the pan to the heat and bring the mixture to a slow boil. Cook for 1 minute, whisking gently. It will thicken slightly.

7) Remove the cornstarch mixture from the heat and gradually whisk about ½ cup/118 ml of the mixture into the egg yolks to temper them. Then use a whisk to stir the egg yolk mixture back into the pot. Check the temperature. If an instant-read thermometer reads 170°F/77°C, there is no need to heat it further. If it is lower, heat the mixture on low, stirring constantly, until thickened a little further. When a finger is run across the back of the spatula, it will leave a well-defined track. An instant-read thermometer should read 170° to 180°F/77° to 82°C.

8) Immediately remove the pan from the heat and pour the mixture into the strainer, scraping up the thickened mixture that has settled on the bottom of the pan. Press it through the strainer into the bowl and scrape any mixture clinging to the underside into the bowl.

9) Set the bowl in the ice water bath and allow it to cool until no longer warm to the touch, stirring occasionally. Stir in the strawberry purée mixture and the strawberry essence, if desired. Cover and refrigerate for a minimum of 8 hours or until no warmer than 43°F/6°C. (Alternatively, continue cooling it in the ice water bath.) Set a covered storage container in the freezer.

10) Churn the strawberry custard in a prechilled ice cream maker. Transfer the ice cream to the chilled container. Press a piece of plastic wrap on the surface of the ice cream, cover the container, and allow the ice cream to firm in the freezer for at least 4 hours before serving.

STORE Covered storage container: frozen, 3 days

SCOOPS

✻ When reducing the strawberry juice, it is important to stir it every 20 to 30 seconds to prevent spattering.

THORN BERRY ICE CREAMS

Makes: About 5 cups/1.2 liters

This family of berries makes some of the most flavorful, lilting, creamy, and colorful of all ice creams. They have the biggest overrun (increase in volume when churned—about 38%) of all my ice creams and are very scoopable even when frozen at −7°F/−22°C. All this makes the somewhat labor intensive process of removing the seeds and reducing the juices well worth the effort.

I love all thorn berry ice creams, but I favor the flavor of black raspberry most of all. It also has the largest overrun (as much as 50%). I call it my silver lining recipe, because for years I have picked black raspberries every July from the back road, and in 2017, I cracked a tooth on one of the hard, angular seeds. Rather than continuing to risk eating the berries straight off the bush, I was inspired to turn them into ice cream. Black raspberries can be found fresh at farmers' markets and also frozen online. And we have now planted our own garden of black raspberry bushes!

Blackberries are the least sweet of the three berries listed here, black raspberries a little sweeter, and raspberries sweeter still. I add sugar to equal about half the volume of the blackberry purée and a little less for the other berries, but it is easiest to determine the exact amount by the percentage listed in the chart. Also, since the sweetness varies slightly from batch to batch, I recommend you taste the completed berry custard before churning, and add a little more sugar if needed to taste. It should be slightly sweeter than desired because it will seem a little less sweet once frozen.

Plan Ahead The berries will take anywhere from several hours to as long as 24 hours to thaw.

Continued

Blackberry, black raspberry, and raspberry ice creams

SWEETENED BERRY PURÉE

Makes: About 400 grams/about 1½ cups/348 ml (Amount needed to add to the custard base: 341 grams/about 1¼ cups/296 ml)

frozen blackberries, raspberries, or black raspberries	680 grams (24 ounces; to yield a minimum of 244 grams of unsweetened purée)	about 6 cups (to yield a minimum of 1 cup plus 2 tablespoons/266 ml unsweetened purée)
percentage of sugar (for minimum yield of 244 grams/ 1 cup/237 ml purée)	**weight of sugar**	**approximate volume of sugar**
1) blackberries: 41%	1) 100 grams	1) 8 tablespoons
2) black raspberries: 38.5%	2) 94 grams	2) 7½ tablespoons
3) raspberries: 35%	3) 88 grams	3) 7 tablespoons
lemon juice, freshly squeezed and strained	16 grams	1 tablespoon (15 ml)

1) In a colander suspended over a deep bowl, thaw the berries completely. This will take several hours or as long as 24 hours in the refrigerator. Press the berries to force out as much of the juice as possible. There should be over ¾ cup/177 ml of juice, but don't worry if you have less because that means you will have more of the pulp. If desired, weigh the juice to make reducing it easier.

2) Transfer the juice to a small saucepan and boil, stirring often, until dark and thickened and concentrated to about one-quarter to one-third of its original weight or volume (4 to 5 tablespoons/60 to 75 ml). Watch carefully toward the end as it reduces very quickly and could scorch. Pour it into a glass measure with a spout that has been lightly coated with nonstick cooking spray. (Alternatively, you can do this in the microwave, in a 4 cup/1 liter glass measure with a spout, lightly coated with nonstick cooking spray, swirling or stirring every 20 to 30 seconds. I prefer this method for purity of flavor, but it takes 15 to 20 minutes—about twice as long as on the cooktop—monitoring constantly.)

3) Press the berries through a food mill with a fine berry screen (³⁄₆₄ inch holes) or a fine-mesh strainer, using the back of a spoon. You should have more than ¾ cup/177 ml (about 200 grams). (This will take about 20 minutes if using a strainer.) Stir in the reduced berry syrup. You should now have at least 244 grams/1 cup/237 ml of purée.

4) Add sugar according to the chart on the previous page, either by percentage or volume/weight.

5) Add the lemon juice and stir until the sugar has fully dissolved.

The sweetened berry purée keeps in an airtight container for 10 days refrigerated or 6 months frozen.

ICE CREAM BASE

Sweetened Berry Purée	341 grams	1¼ cups (296 ml)
pure vanilla extract	.	½ teaspoon (2.5 ml)
cornstarch	9 grams	1 tablespoon
milk	106 grams	¼ cup plus 3 tablespoons (104 ml), *divided*
heavy cream	290 grams	1¼ cups (296 ml)
sugar	150 grams	¾ cup
glucose or reduced corn syrup (see page xxi)	32 grams	1½ tablespoons (22.5 ml)
salt	.	a pinch
6 (to 9) large egg yolks (see page xxxii)	112 grams	¼ cup plus 3 tablespoons (104 ml)

✲ Have ready a fine-mesh strainer suspended over a medium bowl.

✲ Prepare an ice water bath (see page xvii).

1) Into a medium bowl, weigh or measure the berry purée. Stir in the vanilla. Cover and refrigerate it.

2) In a custard cup or small bowl, stir together the cornstarch and 45 grams/ 3 tablespoons/45 ml of the milk until smooth, adding the milk slowly as you mix it in. Cover with plastic wrap.

3) In a medium saucepan, with a silicone spatula, stir together the remaining milk (61 grams/¼ cup/59 ml), the cream, sugar, glucose, and salt until well blended.

Continued

❋ Perfect Purée of Napa Valley sells an excellent raspberry purée that can be substituted in equal weight or volume for the unsweetened purée.

❋ When reducing the berry juice, it is important to stir it every 20 to 30 seconds to prevent spattering.

❋ When making the raspberry ice cream, be sure to try it with Cranberry Topping (page 204)— the synergy is staggeringly good, but chocolate fudge is also an amazing combination.

4) In a small bowl, place the egg yolks and whisk them lightly. Set it near the cooktop.

5) Over medium heat, bring the milk mixture to a boil, stirring constantly. Lower the heat and cook at a slow boil, stirring, for 2 to 3 minutes to evaporate some of the water in the mixture. Remove the pan from the heat. Allow the mixture to cool for a few minutes, to about 180°F/82°C.

6) Stir the cornstarch mixture to make sure it is smooth and then whisk it into the hot milk mixture. Return the pan to the heat and bring the mixture to a slow boil. Cook for 1 minute, whisking gently. It will thicken slightly.

7) Remove the cornstarch mixture from the heat and gradually whisk about ½ cup/118 ml of the mixture into the egg yolks. Then whisk the egg yolk mixture back into the pot. Check the temperature. If an instant-read thermometer reads 170°F/77°C, there is no need to heat it further. If it is lower, heat the mixture on low, stirring constantly with a silicone spatula, until thickened a little further. When a finger is run across the back of the spatula, it will leave a well-defined track. An instant-read thermometer should read 170° to 180°F/77° to 82°C.

8) Immediately remove the pan from the heat and pour the mixture into the strainer, scraping up the thickened mixture that has settled on the bottom of the pan. Press it through the strainer into the bowl and scrape any mixture clinging to the underside into the bowl.

9) Set the bowl containing the custard mixture in the ice water bath and allow it to cool until no longer warm to the touch, stirring occasionally. Stir in the berry purée mixture. Cover and refrigerate for a minimum of 8 hours or until no warmer than 43°F/6°C. (Alternatively, continue cooling it in the ice water bath.) Set a covered storage container in the freezer.

10) Churn the berry custard in a prechilled ice cream maker. Transfer the ice cream to the chilled container. Press a piece of plastic wrap on the surface of the ice cream, cover the container, and allow the ice cream to firm in the freezer for at least 4 hours before serving.

STORE Covered storage container: frozen, 3 days

BLUEBERRY ICE CREAM

Makes: About 5 cups/1.2 liters

I fell in love with the gorgeous purple color of this ice cream in Erin McDowell's wonderful book *The Fearless Baker*. Despite being a major proponent of custard-style ice creams, I realized that the subtle flavor of blueberry would benefit from this eggless Philadelphia-style ice cream base, and the berries' high fiber would keep the ice cream from being icy. I used my usual 3 to 1 cream to milk ratio, decreased the amount of dairy in proportion to the blueberries to make it as creamy as possible, and boiled away some of the liquid in the blueberries. This gives it the creamiest texture, and it is scoopable right from the freezer!

Erin's inspiration to pulverize the entire vanilla bean gives it an amazing flavor that brings out the special qualities of the blueberry. The vanilla bean's seeds also add a delightful little crunch. Wait to make this ice cream when blueberries are in season for the best flavor and color, and freeze some of the berries for sweet summer memories in winter. Also be sure to freeze some red rhubarb, which has an earlier season. Adding Rhubarb Compote (page 205) is a sensational way to enhance the blueberry flavor without overwhelming it; swirl it into the base as described on page 64.

SWEETENED BLUEBERRY PURÉE

Makes: About 556 grams/1⅔ cups/394 ml

blueberries	568 grams	about 4 cups
sugar	250 grams	1¼ cups
1 vanilla bean, split in half lengthwise	.	.

✣ If you are measuring by weight, weigh the pan and tare out the weight before adding the ingredients. This way you can use the weight as a guide when reducing the mixture in Step 2.

Continued

1) In a medium saucepan, with a silicone spatula, stir together the blueberries, sugar, and vanilla bean.

2) Over medium-high heat, stirring constantly, cook the mixture until the sugar has dissolved and the juices are bubbling. Then lower the heat to medium and continue cooking at a rapid boil, stirring often, until the berries are very soft and the mixture is very thick, about 10 minutes. As it begins to thicken, turn down the heat to medium-low. As long as the juices are bubbling very thickly it will be fine. But the more water that evaporates, the creamier the ice cream will be. Reduce to about 556 grams/$1\frac{2}{3}$ cups/394 ml.

3) Scrape the mixture, including the vanilla bean, into a large mixing bowl or blender container.

ICE CREAM BASE

heavy cream	464 grams	2 cups (473 ml)
milk	161 grams	$\frac{2}{3}$ cup (158 ml)
Sweetened Blueberry Purée	about 556 grams	about $1\frac{2}{3}$ cups (394 ml)
lemon juice, freshly squeezed and strained	10 grams	2 teaspoons (10 ml)

✲ Have ready a fine-mesh strainer suspended over a large bowl.

1) Add the cream and milk to the blueberry mixture. Use an immersion blender to purée it until very smooth. (Alternatively, use a countertop blender, but be sure to scrape out as much as possible from the sides and lid—it helps to set a piece of plastic wrap on top before closing the lid.)

2) Pour the purée into the strainer and press it through the strainer into the bowl. Scrape any mixture clinging to the underside into the bowl. Stir in the lemon juice.

3) Cover and refrigerate for a minimum of 8 hours or until no warmer than 43°F/6°C. (Alternatively, cool it in the ice water bath.) Set a covered storage container in the freezer.

4) Churn the blueberry purée in a prechilled ice cream maker. Transfer the ice cream to the chilled container. Press a piece of plastic wrap on the surface of the ice cream, cover the container, and allow the ice cream to firm in the freezer for at least 4 hours before serving.

SCOOPS

✲ Commercially frozen blueberries (or your own frozen ones) can replace the fresh. While still delicious, however, the commercially frozen berries are not as vibrant.

STORE

Covered storage container: frozen, 3 days

Blueberry Ice Cream and Thai Corn Ice Cream, page 72

RHUBARB ICE CREAM

Makes: About 5 cups/1.2 liters

This dense and creamy ice cream has the true flavor of rhubarb, and here's why: Rhubarb purée makes a subtle, slightly tangy ice cream base but could never be identified as rhubarb on its own. Instead, swirling part of the rhubarb purée into the spun ice cream not only gives the pale pink base little splotches of beautiful color, it also gives it the incomparable rhubarb flavor. Cooking the rhubarb with the sugar until most of the watery juices are concentrated both adds intensity of flavor and keeps the ice cream from becoming icy.

ICE CREAM BASE

unsalted butter	64 grams	4½ tablespoons (½ stick plus ½ tablespoon)
rhubarb, preferably red (see Scoops)	850 grams	about 2 pounds
sugar	275 grams	1¼ cups plus 2 tablespoons, *divided*
fine sea salt	.	a pinch
6 (to 9) large egg yolks (see page xxxii)	112 grams	¼ cup plus 3 tablespoons (104 ml)
glucose or reduced corn syrup (see page xxi)	28 grams	4 teaspoons (20 ml)
milk	136 grams	½ cup plus 1 tablespoon (133 ml)
heavy cream	387 grams	1⅔ cups (394 ml), *divided*

✣ About 1 hour ahead, cut the butter into four pieces and set it on the counter at room temperature (65° to 75°F/18° to 24°C).

MAKE THE RHUBARB PURÉE

1) Trim off and discard the leaves and the wider part of the base of the rhubarb and cut the stalks into ½ inch pieces. Stalks that are wider than ¾ inch should be sliced in half. Weigh out 681 grams/1½ pounds (about 6 cups).

2) Set the rhubarb pieces in a large skillet. Sprinkle with 150 grams/¾ cup of the sugar and the salt and allow the rhubarb to sit for about 15 minutes, or until the sugar is moistened and mostly dissolved.

SCOOPS

❋ Red rhubarb and green rhubarb can be used interchangeably, but the red offers a more beautiful color.

❋ It is easiest to slice rhubarb by stacking two stalks, rib sides down.

❋ Rhubarb freezes well for many months. To keep its color and texture, it is best to sprinkle the sliced rhubarb with about 25 grams/ 2 tablespoons of sugar for 454 grams/1 pound of rhubarb (5% by weight). Allow it to thaw until the rhubarb pieces can be separated easily before cooking. Remember to remove the extra sugar from the recipe!

3) Cover and simmer the rhubarb on low heat for about 10 minutes (6 minutes if using frozen rhubarb), or until the rhubarb softens completely. Raise the heat to medium and continue cooking, uncovered, for about 10 minutes more, stirring constantly, to concentrate the juices and reduce the purée to 390 grams/about 1 cup plus 2 tablespoons/267 ml. (When most of the juices have evaporated, turn down the heat to low.)

4) Scrape the mixture into two bowls, dividing it into 260 grams/¾ cup/177 ml for the ice cream base and 130 grams/¼ cup plus 2 tablespoons/89 ml for the swirl. Cover the rhubarb for the swirl and refrigerate it.

MAKE THE RHUBARB ICE CREAM

❋ Have ready a fine-mesh strainer suspended over a medium bowl.

5) In a medium saucepan, with a silicone spatula, stir together the egg yolks, butter, and glucose until well blended. Stir in the rhubarb purée for the base, the milk, and 155 grams/⅔ cup/158 ml of the cream.

6) Heat the mixture on medium-low, stirring constantly, until it just about begins to bubble. (The acidity of the rhubarb prevents the mixture from curdling.) An instant-read thermometer should read 170° to 180°F/ 77° to 82°C.

7) Immediately pour the mixture into the strainer, scraping up the thickened mixture that has settled on the bottom of the pan. Press it through the strainer and scrape any mixture clinging to the underside into the bowl.

8) Whisk in the remaining sugar (125 grams/½ cup plus 2 tablespoons), and then the remaining cream (232 grams/1 cup/237 ml). Cover and refrigerate for a minimum of 8 hours or until no warmer than 43°F/6°C. (Alternatively, cool in an ice water bath.) Set a covered storage container in the freezer.

9) Churn the rhubarb custard in a prechilled ice cream maker. Transfer the ice cream to the chilled container in 3 or 4 layers, alternating with little dollops of the purée and using a small metal spatula or spoon to swirl the purée slightly in between each layer. Press a piece of plastic wrap on the surface of the ice cream, cover the container, and allow the ice cream to firm in the freezer for at least 4 hours before serving.

STORE Covered storage container: frozen, 3 days

PEACH PERFECT ICE CREAM

Makes: About 5 cups/1.2 liters

Fresh peaches are a glorious fruit, but they tend to freeze rock hard in ice cream. One way around this is to macerate peach slices in sugar (and maybe a little peach brandy) and then top them with vanilla ice cream. But for true peach ice cream I use a special puréeing technique that concentrates and caramelizes the peach juices but leaves the peach pulp uncooked. I love the combination of peaches and ginger, as long as the ginger stays in the background, where it serves to elevate the peach flavor. This ice cream is just what I wanted it to be, and is indeed excellent with sliced fresh peaches. But a few drops of peach essence from Aftelier by Mandy Aftel adds immeasurably to the true peach flavor of the ice cream.

FRESH PEACH PURÉE AND SYRUP

Makes: 284 grams/1 cup plus 2 tablespoons/266 ml of purée; 400 grams/1½ cups/355 ml of syrup

4 to 5 ripe peaches (1½ pounds/680 grams)	567 grams	3 cups peeled, pitted, and cubed (see Scoops)
sugar, preferably turbinado	162 grams	¾ cup plus 1 tablespoon
fine sea salt	.	a pinch
lemon juice, freshly squeezed and strained	8 grams	½ tablespoon (7.5 ml)

✲ Have ready a fine-mesh strainer suspended over a 2 cup/473 ml glass measure with a spout.

1) In a medium bowl, place the peach cubes, sugar, salt, and lemon juice. Toss to mix well. Allow the peaches to sit for a minimum of 30 minutes, up to 1 hour. Transfer the peach cubes and the syrup to a colander suspended over a bowl to capture the syrup. The peaches will have released their juices to yield about 400 grams/1½ cups/355 ml of syrup.

2) Into a medium saucepan, pour the syrup and cover it.

3) In a food processor, purée the peaches. Press the purée through the strainer to remove any little fibers. You should have about 284 grams/1 cup plus 2 tablespoons/266 ml of purée. Cover the purée and refrigerate it.

The peach purée and syrup keep in airtight containers for 2 days refrigerated or 6 months frozen.

ICE CREAM BASE

fresh ginger, peeled and coarsely grated	10 grams	2 teaspoons
cornstarch	12 grams	4 teaspoons
milk	121 grams	½ cup (118 ml), *divided*
6 (to 9) large egg yolks (see page xxxii)	112 grams	¼ cup plus 3 tablespoons (104 ml)
heavy cream	348 grams	1½ cups (355 ml)
Fresh Peach Syrup	400 grams	1½ cups (355 ml)
glucose or reduced corn syrup (see page xxi)	42 grams	2 tablespoons (30 ml)
Fresh Peach Purée	284 grams	1 cup plus 2 tablespoons (266 ml)
peach essence, preferably Aftelier (optional)	.	3 or 4 drops, to taste

❖ Have ready a fine-mesh strainer suspended over a medium bowl.

❖ Prepare an ice water bath (see page xvii).

❖ Set the prepared ginger near the cooktop.

1) In a custard cup or small bowl, stir together the cornstarch and 30 grams/ 2 tablespoons/30 ml of the milk until smooth, adding the milk slowly as you mix it in. Cover with plastic wrap.

2) In a small bowl, place the egg yolks and whisk them lightly. Set it near the cooktop.

3) In a 2 cup/473 ml or larger glass measure with a spout, combine the remaining milk (91 grams/6 tablespoons/89 ml) and the cream and heat in

Continued

the microwave, stirring every 20 to 30 seconds with a silicone spatula, until it is hot. (Alternatively, heat the mixture in a saucepan on medium-low, stirring constantly.) Set aside.

4) To the saucepan containing the peach syrup, add the glucose. Over medium heat, bring the mixture to a boil, stirring constantly with a silicone spatula. Lower the heat and continue boiling until it reduces and caramelizes to a deep golden amber. An instant-read thermometer should read 225°F/107°C (or about 275°F/135°C if you used fine granulated sugar).

5) Remove the pan from the heat and immediately, but gradually, add the hot milk mixture. Stir until uniform in color. Stir in the ginger.

6) Stir the cornstarch mixture to make sure it is smooth and then whisk it into the hot peach mixture. Return the pan to the heat and bring the mixture to a slow boil. Cook for 1 minute, whisking gently. It will thicken slightly.

7) Remove the cornstarch mixture from the heat and gradually whisk about ½ cup/118 ml of the mixture into the egg yolks to temper them. Then use a whisk to stir the egg yolk mixture back into the pot. Check the temperature. If an instant-read thermometer reads 170°F/77°C, there is no need to heat it further. If it is lower, heat the mixture on low, stirring constantly with a silicone spatula, until thickened a little further. When a finger is run across the back of the spatula, it will leave a well-defined track. An instant-read thermometer should read 170° to 180°F/77° to 82°C.

8) Immediately remove the pan from the heat and pour the mixture into the strainer, scraping up the thickened mixture that has settled on the bottom of the pan. Press it through the strainer and scrape any mixture clinging to the underside into the bowl. Discard the ginger and residue.

9) Set the bowl in the ice water bath and allow it to cool until no longer warm to the touch, stirring occasionally. Stir in the cold peach purée. If desired, add the peach essence by the droplet. It is very powerful, so add just a drop at a time. Cover and refrigerate for a minimum of 8 hours or until no warmer than 43°F/6°C. (Alternatively, cool in an ice water bath.) Set a covered storage container in the freezer.

10) Churn the peach custard in a prechilled ice cream maker. Transfer the ice cream to the chilled container. Press a piece of plastic wrap on the surface of the ice cream, cover the container, and allow the ice cream to firm in the freezer for at least 4 hours before serving.

STORE Covered storage container: frozen, 3 days

SCOOPS

✳ Peaches peel easily when ripe. Bring a large pot of water to a boil. Remove it from the heat and add the peaches. Let the peaches sit for 1 minute and then remove one and run it under cold water. If the peel does not slip off easily, return it to the pot for another minute. Empty the peaches into a colander and run cold water over them. Peel the peaches. Cut them in half and remove the pits. Then cut them into cubes.

✳ Frozen peaches can be substituted in equal weight for fresh. If measuring by volume, allow them to soften enough to cut them into cubes. In either case, place them in a bowl and sprinkle with the sugar, salt, and lemon juice. Cover and allow them to thaw, preferably overnight in the refrigerator.

THAI CORN ICE CREAM

Makes: About 1 quart/1 liter

I could move to Thailand for its lovely people and large variety of tropical fruit, but I don't have to move there for their amazing and mysteriously delicious corn ice cream. I can make it right in my own home in the U.S.

It is best to make this recipe at the height of the summer corn season, when the corn is at its sweetest and most flavorful. The cob contains even more flavor than the kernels, so I steep both in the milk before making the custard. When I ate this in Thailand, each serving came with a baby corn cob as decor. But I like to add a scattering of blueberries, which share the same season and give a fresh burst of texture and flavor that does not override the corn.

ICE CREAM BASE

heavy cream	464 grams	2 cups (473 ml)
milk	181 grams	3/4 cup (177 ml)
nonfat dry milk	13 grams	2 tablespoons
1 large ear of corn, kernels removed and cob cut into about 8 pieces	180 grams (kernels)	1 cup plus 2 tablespoons (kernels)
sugar	100 grams	1/2 cup
glucose or reduced corn syrup (see page xxi)	42 grams	2 tablespoons (30 ml)
fine sea salt	.	a pinch
7 (to 11) large egg yolks (see page xxxii)	130 grams	1/2 cup (118 ml)
pure vanilla extract	.	1 teaspoon (5 ml)

✲ Have ready a fine-mesh strainer suspended over a medium bowl.

✲ Prepare an ice water bath (see page xvii).

1) In a small saucepan, with a silicone spatula, stir together the cream, milk, and dry milk. Bring it to a slow boil, stirring constantly. Lower the heat and cook at a slow boil, stirring, for 2 to 3 minutes to evaporate some of the water in the mixture.

2) Add the corn kernels and cob pieces and return the mixture to a boil. Remove it from the heat, cover it, and allow it to steep for 1 hour.

3) Remove and discard the cob pieces. With an immersion blender or countertop blender, purée the mixture until the corn kernels are in very small pieces.

4) With a silicone spatula, stir in the sugar, glucose, salt, and then the egg yolks until well combined (or add them to the blender and blend).

5) Transfer the mixture to a saucepan and heat on medium-low, stirring constantly, until slightly thicker than heavy cream. When a finger is run across the back of the spatula, it will leave a well-defined track. An instant-read thermometer should read 170° to 180°F/77° to 82°C.

6) Immediately pour the mixture into the strainer, scraping up the thickened mixture that has settled on the bottom of the pan. Press the custard through the strainer and scrape any mixture clinging to the underside into the bowl. Discard the corn residue in the strainer.

7) Set the bowl in the ice water bath and allow it to cool until no longer warm to the touch, stirring occasionally. Stir in the vanilla. Cover and refrigerate for a minimum of 8 hours or until no warmer than 43°F/6°C. (Alternatively, continue cooling it in the ice water bath.) Set a covered storage container in the freezer.

8) Churn the corn custard in a prechilled ice cream maker. Transfer the ice cream to the chilled container. Press a piece of plastic wrap on the surface of the ice cream, cover the container, and allow the ice cream to firm in the freezer for at least 4 hours before serving.

STORE
Covered storage container: frozen, 3 days

SCOOPS

❊ Raw corn is about 72.7% water. After steeping in the hot milk mixture, it releases about 27% of its water into the custard, which is why dry milk is added to help absorb it and prevent iciness in the churned ice cream.

VARIATION

ROASTED CORN ICE CREAM

Roasting the corn brings out a slightly smoky, caramelized flavor. Husk the corn and remove the silk. Brush with about a teaspoon of melted butter, wrap in foil, and set it on a baking sheet. Roast in a preheated 450°F/230°C oven for 20 minutes.

PINEAPPLE ICE CREAM

Makes: About 5 cups/1.2 liters

This creamy tropical ice cream has a pleasing, slightly crunchy texture from the fibers of the pineapple. It is a labor of love that entails steeping fresh pineapple in a hot sugar syrup and then concentrating some of the syrup for amazing flavor. To take it really over the top, you can then make a beautifully clear, tangy pineapple caramel sauce from the poaching syrup.

Plan Ahead Prepare the Pineapple Purée a minimum of 8 hours and up to 3 days before churning the ice cream.

FRESH PINEAPPLE PURÉE AND SYRUP

Makes: About 550 grams/2 cups/473 ml of purée; about 828 grams/3 cups/710 ml of syrup

sugar	133 grams	⅔ cup
water	280 grams	1 cup plus 3 tablespoons (281 ml)
a pineapple, peeled, cored, eyes removed, and cut into chunks	770 grams	3 cups

1) In a small saucepan, with a silicone spatula, stir together the sugar and water and bring it to a boil, stirring constantly. Add the pineapple chunks and swirl them into the pan without stirring. Return it to a boil.

2) Cover and cool at room temperature for 8 to 12 hours.

3) Transfer the pineapple chunks and the syrup to a colander suspended over a bowl to capture the syrup. There will be about 828 grams/3 cups/710 ml of syrup, and about 550 grams/3 cups of pineapple chunks.

4) Into a medium saucepan, weigh or measure 414 grams/1½ cups/355 ml of the syrup for the base. Cover and refrigerate it. In another medium saucepan, reserve the remaining syrup, tightly covered and refrigerated, for the Clear Pineapple Caramel Sauce.

Continued

5) In a food processor, purée the pineapple. If you start with 550 grams of pineapple cubes you will end up with about 550 grams/2 cups/473 ml of purée.

6) Into a 2 cup/473 ml glass measure with a spout, weigh or measure 386 grams/1½ cups/355 ml of the purée. Cover and refrigerate it. Freeze any remainder for future use.

The pineapple purée keeps in an airtight container for 5 days refrigerated or 6 months frozen.

ICE CREAM BASE

cornstarch	9 grams	1 tablespoon
milk	121 grams	½ cup (118 ml), *divided*
6 (to 9) large egg yolks (see page xxxii)	112 grams	¼ cup plus 3 tablespoons (104 ml)
heavy cream	348 grams	1½ cups (355 ml)
fine sea salt	.	a pinch
Fresh Pineapple Syrup	414 grams	1½ cups (355 ml)
Fresh Pineapple Purée	386 grams	1½ cups (355 ml)
pure vanilla extract	.	½ teaspoon (2.5 ml)
dark rum (optional)	26 grams	2 tablespoons (30 ml)

❖ Have ready a fine-mesh strainer suspended over a medium bowl.

❖ Prepare an ice water bath (see page xvii).

1) In a custard cup or small bowl, stir together the cornstarch and 21 grams/2 tablespoons/30 ml of the milk until smooth, adding the milk slowly as you mix it in. Cover with plastic wrap.

2) In a small bowl, place the egg yolks and whisk them lightly. Set it near the cooktop.

3) In a medium saucepan, with a silicone spatula, stir together the remaining milk (100 grams/6 tablespoons/89 ml), the cream, and salt. Heat it until it is hot and set it aside.

4) Set the medium saucepan containing the pineapple syrup over medium heat and bring the syrup to a boil, stirring constantly with a silicone spatula. Lower the heat and continue boiling, stirring often, until the syrup reduces and caramelizes to a deep golden amber. An instant-read thermometer should read 290°F/143°C.

5) Remove the pan from the heat and immediately but gradually add the hot milk mixture. Stir until uniform in color.

6) Stir the cornstarch mixture to make sure it is smooth and then whisk it into the hot mixture. Return the pan to the heat and bring the mixture to a slow boil. Cook for 1 minute, whisking gently. It will thicken slightly.

7) Remove the cornstarch mixture from the heat and gradually whisk about ½ cup/118 ml of the mixture into the egg yolks to temper them. Then use a whisk to stir the egg yolk mixture back into the pot. Check the temperature. If an instant-read thermometer reads 170°F/77°C, there is no need to heat it further. If it is lower, heat the mixture on low, stirring constantly, until thickened a little further. When a finger is run across the back of the spatula, it will leave a well-defined track. An instant-read thermometer should read 170° to 180°F/77° to 82°C.

8) Immediately remove the pan from the heat and pour the mixture into the strainer, scraping up the thickened mixture that has settled on the bottom of the pan. Press it through the strainer and scrape any mixture clinging to the underside into the bowl.

STORE

Covered storage container: frozen, 3 days

9) Set the bowl in the ice water bath and allow it to cool until no longer warm to the touch, stirring occasionally. Stir in the cold pineapple purée and vanilla. Cover and refrigerate for a minimum of 8 hours or until no warmer than 43°F/6°C. (Alternatively, cool in an ice water bath.) Set a covered storage container in the freezer.

10) Churn the pineapple custard in a prechilled ice cream maker. If adding the rum, add it when the ice cream has reached the consistency of soft serve and begins to ball up around the dasher. Transfer the ice cream to the chilled container. Press a piece of plastic wrap on the surface of the ice cream, cover the container, and allow the ice cream to firm in the freezer for at least 4 hours before serving.

Continued

SCOOPS

✻ 1 pineapple, peeled, cored, and eyes removed, will yield about 770 grams/ 3 cups cubed. After soaking, the cubes will release about 270 grams of juice and weigh about 550 grams.

✻ When cooking the pineapple syrup in Step 4 on page 77, the acidity of the pineapple causes the sugar to become invert sugar, so I use it in place of glucose in this ice cream recipe.

CLEAR PINEAPPLE CARAMEL SAUCE

Makes: About 231 grams/½ cup plus 2 tablespoons/148 ml

water	79 grams	⅓ cup (79 ml)
reserved pineapple syrup	about 414 grams	about 1½ cups (355 ml)

✻ Have ready a 1 cup/237 ml glass measure with a spout, lightly coated with nonstick cooking spray.

1) In a small saucepan on the cooktop or in a glass measure in the microwave, heat the water until hot.

2) Set the medium saucepan containing the reserved syrup over medium heat and bring to a boil. Lower the heat and continue boiling, stirring often with a silicone spatula, until it reduces and caramelizes to a deep golden amber. An instant-read thermometer should read 290°F/143°C.

3) Remove the pan from the heat and immediately stir in the hot water, until evenly incorporated. Return the pan to the cooktop and continue boiling until the syrup deepens in color. An instant-read thermometer should read 230° to 240°F/110° to 115°C.

4) Immediately pour the pineapple caramel into the prepared measuring cup. It will be pretty thin but thickens considerably when cooled, and still more when it encounters the ice cream. Cover it, and allow it to cool until warm or room temperature. If desired, transfer it to a squeeze bottle for easy drizzling onto the ice cream.

The sauce keeps in an airtight container for 1 week at room temperature or 1 month refrigerated.

MANGO ICE CREAM

Makes: 1 generous quart/1 generous liter

The tropical, bright, and luscious flavor of mango makes for a terrific ice cream. Canned mango pulp from India has far more flavor than the fresh mangoes available in the U.S. It is well worth seeking out the best mango pulp, such as the Ratna brand, which is made from the Alphonso mango, often referred to in India as the "king of mangoes." The pulp is very smooth and contains sugar, but because of the mango's high water content I use a cornstarch slurry to ensure that there is not even the slightest iciness. This ice cream deserves the best of everything.

ICE CREAM BASE

Alphonso mango pulp, preferably Ratna brand (see Scoops)	333 grams	1¼ cups (296 ml)
cornstarch	9 grams	1 tablespoon
milk	121 grams	½ cup (118 ml), *divided*
heavy cream	348 grams	1½ cups (355 ml)
sugar	150 grams	¾ cup
glucose or reduced corn syrup (see page xxi)	63 grams	3 tablespoons (45 ml)
fine sea salt	.	a pinch
6 (to 9) large egg yolks (see page xxxii)	112 grams	¼ cup plus 3 tablespoons (104 ml)
pure vanilla extract	.	½ teaspoon (2.5 ml)
freshly ground cardamom to taste (optional)		

✲ Have ready a fine-mesh strainer suspended over a medium bowl.

✲ Prepare an ice water bath (see page xvii).

1) Into a small bowl, weigh or measure the mango pulp. Cover and refrigerate it.

Continued

2) In a custard cup or small bowl, stir together the cornstarch and 21 grams/ 2 tablespoons/30 ml of the milk until smooth, adding the milk slowly as you mix it in. Cover with plastic wrap.

3) In a medium saucepan, with a silicone spatula, stir together the remaining milk (100 grams/6 tablespoons/89 ml), the cream, sugar, glucose, and salt until well blended.

4) In a small bowl, place the egg yolks and whisk them lightly. Set it near the cooktop.

5) Over medium heat, bring the milk mixture to a boil, stirring constantly. Lower the heat and cook at a slow boil for 2 to 3 minutes to evaporate some of the water in the mixture. Remove the pan from the heat. Allow the mixture to cool for a few minutes (to about 180°F/82°C).

6) Stir the cornstarch mixture to make sure it is smooth and then whisk it into the hot mixture. Return the pan to the heat and bring the mixture to a slow boil. Cook for 1 minute, whisking gently. It will thicken slightly.

7) Remove the cornstarch mixture from the heat and gradually whisk about ½ cup/118 ml of the mixture into the egg yolks to temper them. Then use a whisk to stir the egg yolk mixture back into the pot. Check the temperature. If an instant-read thermometer reads 170°F/77°C, there is no need to heat it further. If it is lower, heat the mixture on low, stirring constantly, until thickened a little further. When a finger is run across the back of the spatula, it will leave a well-defined track. An instant-read thermometer should read 170° to 180°F/77° to 82°C.

8) Immediately remove the pan from the heat and pour the mixture into the strainer, scraping up the thickened mixture that has settled on the bottom of the pan. Press it through the strainer into the bowl and scrape any mixture clinging to the underside into the bowl.

9) Set the bowl in the ice water bath and allow it to cool until no longer warm to the touch, stirring occasionally. Stir in the mango pulp and vanilla. Cover and refrigerate for a minimum of 8 hours or until no warmer than 43°F/6°C. (Alternatively, continue cooling it in the ice water bath.) Set a covered storage container in the freezer.

SCOOPS

❊ Many canned brands of mango pulp taste more like peach than mango. The Ratna brand is renowned for its bright orange flesh and intense mango flavor.

Continued

10) Churn the mango custard in a prechilled ice cream maker. Transfer the ice cream to the chilled container. Press a piece of plastic wrap on the surface of the ice cream, cover the container, and allow the ice cream to firm in the freezer for at least 4 hours before serving.

If desired, sprinkle each serving with a little ground cardamom.

VARIATION

MANGO GINGER ICE CREAM

My talented colleague and longtime friend Nathan Fong recommended this terrific flavor combination. Chop about 55 grams/¼ cup crystallized ginger into small pieces and add it during churning when the ice cream has reached the consistency of soft serve.

SUBLIME BANANA ICE CREAM

Makes: About 3½ cups/0.8 liter

I didn't appreciate the presence of banana in ice cream until I fell in love with this recipe from Dana Cree's ice cream book *Hello, My Name Is Ice Cream.* The technique of infusing the banana into the base gives the most blissful flavor to this dense and creamy ice cream. Dana generously gave me permission to offer it in this book. It's well worth taking the time to allow the bananas to get really ripe and also to infuse them in the dairy for a full 24 hours.

Plan Ahead The banana flavor will be best the longer the milk mixture infuses, up to 24 hours.

ICE CREAM BASE

3 large or 4 medium very ripe bananas (see Scoops), about 510 grams before peeling	about 400 grams peeled	
milk	403 grams	1⅔ cups (394 ml)
heavy cream	309 grams	1⅓ cups (315 ml)
sugar	150 grams	¾ cup
glucose or reduced corn syrup (see page xxi)	53 grams	2½ tablespoons (37.5 ml)
cornstarch	12 grams	4 teaspoons
milk	30 grams	2 tablespoons (30 ml)
5 (to 8) large egg yolks (see page xxxii)	93 grams	¼ cup plus 2 tablespoons (89 ml)
pure vanilla extract	.	1 teaspoon (5 ml)
fine sea salt	.	a big pinch

Continued

1) Into a 2 quart/2 liter bowl, peel and place the bananas.

2) In a medium saucepan, with a silicone spatula, stir together the 403 grams/1⅔ cups/394 ml of milk, the cream, sugar, and glucose until well blended. Over medium-high heat, stirring constantly, bring the mixture to a full boil. Pour it over the bananas and allow them to infuse for about 1 hour. Then cover them and refrigerate for at least 1 hour and up to 24 hours. (The longer they infuse, the more intense the banana flavor.)

✢ Have ready a fine-mesh strainer suspended over a medium saucepan.

✢ Prepare an ice water bath (see page xvii).

3) Stir the milk mixture to wash any butterfat from the dairy that clings to the bananas back into the mixture. Empty the mixture into the strainer. Discard the bananas, then rinse and dry the strainer. Set the strainer back over the bowl.

4) In a custard cup or small bowl, stir together the cornstarch and the 30 grams/2 tablespoons/30 ml of milk until smooth, adding the milk slowly as you mix it in. Cover with plastic wrap.

5) In a small bowl, place the egg yolks and whisk them lightly. Set it near the cooktop.

6) Over medium heat, bring the milk mixture to a boil, stirring constantly. Lower the heat and cook at a slow boil for 2 to 3 minutes to evaporate some of the water in the mixture. Remove the pan from the heat. Allow the mixture to cool for a few minutes, to about 180°F/82°C.

7) Stir the cornstarch mixture to make sure that it is smooth and then whisk it into the hot mixture. Return the pan to the heat and bring the mixture to a slow boil. Cook for 1 minute, whisking gently. It will thicken slightly.

8) Remove the cornstarch mixture from the heat and gradually whisk about ½ cup/118 ml of the mixture into the egg yolks to temper them. Then use a whisk to stir the egg yolk mixture back into the pot. Check the temperature. If an instant-read thermometer reads 170°F/77°C, there is no need to heat it further. If it is lower, heat the mixture on low, stirring constantly, until thickened a little further. When a finger is run across the back of the spatula,

Continued

it will leave a well-defined track. An instant-read thermometer should read 170° to 180°F/77° to 82°C.

9) Immediately pour the mixture into the strainer, scraping up the thickened mixture that has settled on the bottom of the pan. Press it through the strainer and scrape any mixture clinging to the underside into the bowl.

10) Set the bowl in the ice water bath and allow it to cool until no longer warm to the touch, stirring occasionally. Stir in the vanilla and salt. Cover and refrigerate for a minimum of 8 hours or until no warmer than 43°F/6°C. (Alternatively, continue cooling it in the ice water bath.) Set a covered storage container in the freezer.

11) Churn the banana custard in a prechilled ice cream maker. Transfer the ice cream to the chilled container. Press a piece of plastic wrap on the surface of the ice cream, cover the container, and allow the ice cream to firm in the freezer for at least 4 hours before serving.

STORE Covered storage container: frozen, 3 days

SCOOPS

❋ For the best flavor, use bananas that have ripened to mostly black.

CONCORD GRAPE ICE CREAM

Makes: About 1 quart/1 liter

Late August is Concord grape picking time down the back roads near my home in western New Jersey. They make wonderful pies, preserves, ice cream, and sorbet. Letting the purée steep overnight with the skins gives the ice cream an enticing hue; concentrating and reducing the grape purée evaporates enough of its water to produce an exceptionally creamy consistency.

Plan Ahead For the deepest color, let the grape purée and the skins steep for up to 24 hours.

ICE CREAM BASE

Concord grapes	907 grams (2 pounds)	about 5½ cups
glucose or reduced corn syrup (see page xxi)	42 grams	2 tablespoons (30 ml)
sugar	238 grams	1 cup plus 3 tablespoons
fine sea salt	.	a pinch
heavy cream	290 grams	1¼ cups (296 ml), *divided*
6 (to 9) large egg yolks (see page xxxii)	112 grams	¼ cup plus 3 tablespoons (104 ml)
lemon juice, freshly squeezed and strained	10 grams	2 teaspoons (10 ml)

MAKE THE CONCORD GRAPE PURÉE

✣ Have ready a fine-mesh strainer suspended over a medium saucepan.

1) Rinse the grapes well and drain away any water. Place the grapes in a bowl and remove the skins by pressing the grapes between thumb and forefinger (see Scoops), but leave the skins in the bowl with the grapes. Allow them to sit at cool room temperature, covered, for 8 to 12 hours, or refrigerate for up to 24 hours. (If you are using a food mill fitted with a fine disc to purée the

Continued

grapes, there is no need to remove the skins, as they will be left behind along with the seeds, nor to allow the grapes to sit overnight; proceed to Step 3).

2) Remove and reserve the skins in a small bowl.

3) In a food processor, pulsing briefly, break up the pulp. (The seeds are very hard, so they will not be cracked open.) Press the grape pulp through the strainer and scrape any mixture clinging to the underside into the pan. (This will take about 30 minutes.) Squeeze the liquid from the peels into the pan. (Alternatively, pass the grapes, skins and all, through a food mill fitted with a fine disc.) You should have about 500 grams/about 2 cups/473 ml. Discard the skins and the seeds.

4) Over medium-low heat, stirring constantly with a silicone spatula, cook at a slow boil until the purée reduces to about 300 grams/1 cup/237 ml. Watch carefully as it will bubble up. It should be very thick. Remove it from the heat.

MAKE THE CONCORD GRAPE ICE CREAM

✼ Have ready a fine-mesh strainer suspended over a medium bowl.

5) Into the hot grape purée, stir the glucose, sugar, salt, and 58 grams/¼ cup/ 59 ml of the cream. If it is still hot (above 100°F/38°C), allow it to cool until warm.

6) In a small bowl, whisk together the egg yolks. Stir them into the grape mixture.

7) Heat the mixture on medium-low, stirring constantly, until it thickens slightly more. An instant-read thermometer should read 170° to 180°F/77° to 82°C.

8) Immediately pour the mixture into the strainer, scraping up any remaining mixture that has settled on the bottom of the pan. Press as much as possible of this thick mixture through the strainer and scrape any mixture clinging to the underside into the bowl.

9) Stir in the remaining cream (232 grams/1 cup/237 ml) and the lemon juice. Cover and refrigerate for a minimum of 8 hours or until no warmer than 43°F/6°C. (Alternatively, cool in an ice water bath.) Set a covered storage container in the freezer.

STORE

Covered storage container: frozen, 3 days

10) Churn the Concord grape custard in a prechilled ice cream maker. Transfer the ice cream to the chilled container. Press a piece of plastic wrap on the surface of the ice cream, cover the container, and allow the ice cream to firm in the freezer for at least 4 hours before serving.

SCOOPS

❉ It is recommended that you wear disposable gloves when skinning the grapes by hand to prevent irritation from the acidity.

❉ Depending on the ripeness or even the year, some grapes may release more liquid. I still reduce the purée to the same volume and weight.

❉ Concord grapes freeze very well for over a year due to their thick skins. Freezing also helps release the pulp and juices from the skins.

❉ Concord grape jam or jelly adds a delicious and bright purple swirl. Different brands will vary in consistency, so if it seems a bit thin, it may work best to boil it for a few minutes before straining it. Any leftover add-ins can be passed in a pitcher or small bowl to use as a topping. Spoon up to ½ cup of the jam into a small bowl and stir it lightly until smooth. Scrape it into a disposable piping bag. Cut off a small semicircle from the point of the bag and close it with a binder clamp until ready to pipe the jam. (Alternatively you can use a spoon to apply it, but it's easier and faster with a piping bag.)

❉ Use a 9 by 5 inch loaf pan, preferably Pyrex, as your storage container. Pipe zigzags of about one-third of the grape jam onto the bottom of the pan. Spread about one-third of the ice cream on top. Quickly pipe zigzags of about half of the remaining jam on top. Repeat with another one-third of the ice cream and then the remaining jam. Top with the remaining ice cream.

PEAR ICE CREAM

Makes: About 5 cups/1.2 liters

Joël Robuchon was a culinary genius, so when years ago I discovered his pear and star anise clafoutis (a crustless custard tart) in his book *Simply French*, I knew it would be really special. It was, in fact, even more wonderful than I had imagined, so it stayed in my memory and reappeared when I was thinking about potential ice cream flavors. I dedicate this recipe to Chef Robuchon's memory.

FRESH PEAR PURÉE AND SYRUP

Makes: 400 grams/1½ cups/355 ml of purée; 60 grams/¾ cup/177 ml of syrup

3 large or 2 medium firm ripe Bartlett pears (1½ pounds/680 grams), peeled, cored, and cubed (see Scoops)	567 grams cubes	3 cups cubes
sugar	100 grams	½ cup
fine sea salt	.	a pinch
lemon juice, freshly squeezed and strained	8 grams	½ tablespoon (7.5 ml)

✻ Have ready a medium or fine-mesh strainer suspended over a 2 cup/473 ml glass measure with a spout.

1) In a medium bowl, place the pear cubes, sugar, salt, and lemon juice. Toss to mix well. Allow it to sit for a minimum of 30 minutes. Transfer the pear cubes and the syrup to a colander suspended over a bowl to capture the syrup. The pears will have released their juices to yield about 60 grams/¾ cup/177 ml of syrup.

2) Into a medium saucepan, pour the syrup and cover it.

3) In a food processor, purée the pears. Press it through the strainer to remove any little fibers. You should have about 400 grams/1½ cups/355 ml of purée. Cover the purée and refrigerate it.

The pear purée keeps in an airtight container for 2 days refrigerated or 6 months frozen.

ICE CREAM BASE

6 whole star anise, including any seeds (see Scoops)	about 6 grams	.
sugar	25 grams	2 tablespoons
cornstarch	12 grams	4 teaspoons
milk	121 grams	½ cup (118 ml), *divided*
6 (to 9) large egg yolks (see page xxxii)	112 grams	¼ cup plus 3 tablespoons (104 ml)
crème fraîche or heavy cream	348 grams	1½ cups (355 ml)
1 vanilla bean, cut in half lengthwise	.	OR 2 teaspoons (10 ml) pure vanilla extract
Fresh Pear Syrup	60 grams	¾ cup (177 ml)
glucose or reduced corn syrup (see page xxi)	84 grams	¼ cup (59 ml)
Fresh Pear Purée	400 grams	1½ cups (355 ml)
Aftelier pear essence (optional)	.	3 to 4 drops, to taste
Poire Williams (pear eau-de-vie, optional)	28 grams	2 tablespoons (30 ml)

✲ Have ready a fine-mesh strainer suspended over a medium bowl.

✲ Prepare an ice water bath (see page xvii).

1) In a small coffee mill or a mortar and pestle, grind the star anise (including any seeds) together with the sugar to a fine powder. Cover and set it aside.

2) In a custard cup or small bowl, stir together the cornstarch and 21 grams/2 tablespoons/30 ml of the milk until smooth, adding the milk slowly as you mix it in. Cover with plastic wrap.

3) In a small bowl, place the egg yolks, and whisk them lightly. Set it near the cooktop.

4) In a 2 cup/473 ml or larger glass measure with a spout, whisk together the remaining milk (100 grams/6 tablespoons/89 ml) and the crème fraîche. With a small knife, scrape the vanilla bean seeds into the milk mixture.

Continued

(Store the vanilla bean pod for another use.) Heat in the microwave until hot, stirring every 20 to 30 seconds. (Or combine the mixture in a medium saucepan and heat on the cooktop, stirring with a silicone spatula.) Cover and set it aside.

5) In the medium saucepan containing the pear syrup, add the glucose. Over medium heat, bring the syrup and glucose to a boil, stirring constantly with a silicone spatula. Lower the heat and continue boiling until it reduces and just begins to caramelize to a light golden amber. An instant-read thermometer should read 244°F/118°C.

6) Remove the pan from the heat and immediately but gradually add the hot milk mixture. Stir until uniform in color.

7) Stir the cornstarch mixture to make sure it is smooth and then whisk it into the hot milk mixture. Return the pan to the heat and bring the mixture to a slow boil. Cook for 1 minute, whisking gently. It will thicken slightly.

8) Remove the cornstarch mixture from the heat and gradually whisk about ½ cup/118 ml of the mixture into the egg yolks to temper them. Then use a whisk to stir the egg yolk mixture back into the pot. Check the temperature. If an instant-read thermometer reads 170°F/77°C, there is no need to heat it further. If it is lower, heat the mixture on low, stirring constantly until thickened a little further. When a finger is run across the back of the spatula, it will leave a well-defined track. An instant-read thermometer should read 170° to 180°F/77° to 82°C.

9) Immediately remove the pan from the heat and pour the mixture into the strainer, scraping up the thickened mixture that has settled on the bottom of the pan. Press it through the strainer into the bowl and scrape any mixture clinging to the underside into the bowl.

10) Set the bowl in the ice water bath and allow it to cool until no longer warm to the touch, stirring occasionally. Stir in the pear purée, the vanilla extract (if not using the vanilla bean seeds), and the star anise mixture. If desired, add the pear essence by the droplet. It is very powerful, so add just a drop at a time. Cover and refrigerate for a minimum of 8 hours or until no warmer than 43°F/6°C. (Alternatively, cool in an ice water bath.) Set a covered storage container in the freezer.

11) Churn the pear custard in a prechilled ice cream maker. If adding the eau-de-vie, add it during churning when the ice cream has reached the consistency of soft serve and begins to ball up around the dasher. Transfer the ice cream to the chilled container. Press a piece of plastic wrap on the surface of the ice cream, cover the container, and allow the ice cream to firm in the freezer for at least 4 hours before serving.

STORE Covered storage container: frozen, 3 days

SCOOPS

✻ Bartlett pears from California are available beginning in June, but the most flavorful Bartlett pears come from Washington State in the fall.

✻ Star anise has the best flavor when no older than 3 months.

PUMPKIN ICE CREAM

Makes: About 1 quart/1 liter

I tasted pumpkin ice cream for the first time at an ice cream stand in Belvidere, New Jersey, near where we live. It was love at first lick! So I created this version based on my pumpkin pie, in which I cook the pumpkin purée with the brown sugar and spices and then process it to make it silky smooth and creamy when frozen.

Pumpkin is a tricky ingredient because without sugar the flavor is not pleasant. It needs just the right balance of sugar and spice without overriding the pumpkin flavor. This ice cream is dense, earthy, and just a little spicy.

ICE CREAM BASE

canned pure unsweetened pumpkin, preferably Libby's	243 grams	1 cup
light brown sugar, preferably Muscovado, or dark brown sugar	163 grams	¾ cup, firmly packed, *divided*
ground ginger	.	1½ teaspoons
ground cinnamon	.	1½ teaspoons
fine sea salt	.	a big pinch
heavy cream	348 grams	1½ cups (355 ml), *divided*
milk	121 grams	½ cup (118 ml)
7 (to 11) large egg yolks (see page xxxii)	130 grams	½ cup (118 ml)
glucose or reduced corn syrup (see page xxi)	84 grams	¼ cup (59 ml)

1) In a small heavy saucepan, stir together the pumpkin, 109 grams/½ cup of the brown sugar, the spices, and salt. On low heat, bring the mixture to a sputtering simmer, stirring constantly. Reduce the heat to low and cook, stirring constantly, for 3 minutes, until smooth and glossy.

2) Scrape the pumpkin mixture into a food processor and process for 1 minute. With the motor on, add 116 grams/½ cup/118 ml of the cream and the milk,

Continued

processing until incorporated. Scrape the mixture into a medium bowl and set a fine-mesh strainer on top.

3) In a medium saucepan, with a silicone spatula, stir together the egg yolks and the remaining cream (232 grams/1 cup/237 ml) until well blended. Stir in the remaining brown sugar (54 grams/¼ cup) and the glucose until the sugar has dissolved.

4) Heat the mixture on medium-low, stirring constantly, until slightly thicker than heavy cream. When a finger is run across the back of the spatula, it will leave a well-defined track. An instant-read thermometer should read 170° to 180°F/77° to 82°C.

5) Immediately pour the mixture into the strainer, scraping up the thickened mixture that has settled on the bottom of the pan. Press it through the strainer and scrape any mixture clinging to the underside into the bowl.

6) Stir the pumpkin mixture into the custard mixture until evenly blended. Cover and refrigerate for a minimum of 8 hours or until no warmer than 43°F/6°C. (Alternatively, cool in an ice water bath.) Set a covered storage container in the freezer.

7) Churn the pumpkin custard in a prechilled ice cream maker. Transfer the ice cream to the chilled container. Press a piece of plastic wrap on the surface of the ice cream, cover the container, and allow the ice cream to firm for about 2 hours in the freezer before serving. This ice cream is very dense, so if frozen for a longer time, it is best to allow it to soften before eating.

STORE Covered storage container: frozen, 3 days

SCOOPS

✻ I tried a version adding 100 grams/ 1 cup of buttered pecans, but although delicious it seriously diminished the pumpkin flavor. I also tried a bit of bourbon, which did the same thing. Best not to gild the lily here, with the possible exception of hot fudge (page 198)— a surprising made-in-heaven marriage. The pineapple caramel on page 78 is also a synergistic pairing!

ALL SEASON APRICOT ICE CREAM

Makes: About 1 quart/1 liter

Fresh apricots have a relatively short season, but dried apricots offer an even more intense flavor. Not only is this dense and creamy ice cream beautiful to behold, with little pockets of glistening orange apricot purée running through the golden apricot custard base, it is absolutely addictive to eat. Pushing the purée through a sieve is admittedly a slow process; a food mill with a fine berry screen (³⁄₆₄ inch holes) will speed things up.

SPECIAL EQUIPMENT

One 9 by 5 inch loaf pan, preferably Pyrex

APRICOT PURÉE

Makes: 505 grams/about 2 cups minus 2 tablespoons/443 ml

dried apricots, preferably Mediterranean or Californian	340 grams	2 cups, packed
water	355 grams	1½ cups (355 ml)
lemon juice, freshly squeezed and strained	23 grams	1½ tablespoons (22.5 ml)
sugar (see Step 5)	about 100 grams	about ½ cup
glucose for the swirl filling (see Step 7)	about 56 grams	about 2 tablespoons plus 2 teaspoons (40 ml)

❖ Have ready a fine-mesh strainer suspended over a medium bowl.

1) In a small saucepan, place the apricots and water. Cover the pan and let it sit for 2 hours.

2) On very low heat, simmer the mixture, covered, for 20 minutes or until the apricots are very soft.

3) Into the bowl of a food processor, scrape the apricots and any liquid remaining in the pan. Process until uniform in consistency, scraping down the sides of the bowl as needed.

Continued

4) Press the mixture through the strainer until you have a minimum of 1½ cups/355 ml. Stir in the lemon juice.

5) Transfer the purée to a 4 cup/1 liter glass measure with a spout. Measure the volume and add one-third as much sugar (or weigh it and add one-quarter as much sugar). Stir until the sugar has dissolved.

6) Into a medium bowl, weigh or measure out 362 grams/1⅓ cups/315 ml of purée for the ice cream base.

7) In another bowl, weigh or measure out the remainder for the swirl. You should have about 136 grams/½ cup/118 ml of purée. Add the glucose. The amount of glucose should be one-third the volume of the purée; if you have less purée, adjust accordingly, using less glucose. Cover and refrigerate.

The apricot purée keeps in an airtight container for 5 days refrigerated or 6 months frozen.

ICE CREAM BASE

Apricot Purée	362 grams	1⅓ cups (315 ml)
heavy cream	232 grams	1 cup (237 ml)
pure vanilla extract	.	⅓ teaspoon (1.6 ml)
5 (to 8) large egg yolks (see page xxxii)	93 grams	¼ cup plus 2 tablespoons (89 ml)
milk	81 grams	⅓ cup (79 ml)
sugar	125 grams	½ cup plus 2 tablespoons
glucose or reduced corn syrup (see page xxi)	14 grams	2 teaspoons (10 ml)
fine sea salt	.	a pinch

✽ Have ready a fine-mesh strainer suspended over a medium bowl.

1) In the medium bowl containing the apricot purée, whisk in the cream and vanilla. Cover and refrigerate.

2) In a medium saucepan, with a silicone spatula, stir together the egg yolks and milk until well blended. Stir in the sugar, glucose, and salt until the sugar has dissolved.

Continued

3) Heat the mixture on medium-low, stirring constantly, until slightly thicker than heavy cream. When a finger is run across the back of the spatula, it will leave a well-defined track. An instant-read thermometer should read 170° to 180°F/77° to 82°C.

4) Immediately pour the mixture into the strainer, scraping up the thickened mixture that has settled on the bottom of the pan. Press it through the strainer and scrape any mixture clinging to the underside into the bowl.

5) Stir the apricot mixture into the custard mixture. Cover and refrigerate for a minimum of 8 hours or until no warmer than 43°F/6°C. (Alternatively, cool in an ice water bath.) Set the loaf pan in the freezer.

6) Churn the apricot custard in a prechilled ice cream maker. When it is fully churned, set the ice cream machine bowl or canister in the freezer to firm up for about 30 minutes. Into the loaf pan, spread layers of the ice cream alternating with layers of the purée. Press a piece of plastic wrap on the surface of the ice cream and return it to the freezer. You can leave it in the pan, covered with a second sheet of plastic wrap or, when it's firm enough, scoop it into a chilled covered storage container. Allow it to firm in the freezer for about 2 hours before serving.

STORE Covered storage container: frozen, 3 days

SCOOPS

❄ Mediterranean apricots have the most zing.

CHRISTMAS ICE CREAM

Makes: About 5 cups/1.2 liters

I have never been a fan of mincemeat pie, finding it overly intense and sweet; however, tempered by vanilla ice cream, it is nothing short of glorious. The intense holiday sweet spices blend beautifully with the cold creaminess of the ice cream, and the cognac and rum absorbed by the fruit makes the ice cream extra smooth. For a special treat, make your own mincemeat or rum-soaked glacéed fruit (see below); both are best stored for a minimum of three weeks ahead. Alternatively, you can use your favorite commercial brand.

I adapted this recipe from a large-scale one given to me by chef Anna Higham from Scotland. I met Anna in the fall of 2016 when she was doing a stage (apprenticeship) with executive pastry chef Miro Uskokovic at Gramercy Tavern in New York City. She made a mincemeat pie for their annual Thanksgiving in-house pie contest. Although traditional mincemeat contains beef suet, Anna's recipe does not, and with all the other delicious components I don't miss it.

Plan Ahead Make the mincemeat a minimum of 3 weeks and up to 1 year ahead. The glacéed fruit alternative needs a minimum of 1 week to absorb the rum.

MINCEMEAT ICE CREAM

1 recipe Vanilla Ice Cream (page 3)	.	1 quart/1 liter
Mincemeat (page 102) or Glacéed Fruit (page 104)	.	1 cup

1) Once the ice cream is churned, transfer it to a chilled covered storage container. Press a piece of plastic wrap on the surface of the ice cream, cover the container, and allow the ice cream to firm slightly in the freezer for 30 minutes to an hour.

2) Fold in the mincemeat. Replace the plastic wrap, cover, and return it to the freezer for at least 4 hours before serving.

STORE Covered storage container: frozen, 3 days

Continued

MINCEMEAT

Makes: 300 grams/1 cup

½ cinnamon stick, broken into pieces	.	.
1 whole clove	.	.
½ star anise, optional	.	.
1 small apple, peeled, cored, and finely diced	87 grams	⅔ cup
golden raisins, cut in half	44 grams	⅓ cup
dried cherries, cut in quarters	20 grams	1½ tablespoons
currants	20 grams	2 tablespoons
candied orange rind, finely diced	30 grams	¼ cup, firmly packed
dark brown sugar	30 grams	2 tablespoons, firmly packed
lemon zest, finely grated	2 grams	1 teaspoon
lemon juice, freshly squeezed and strained	10 grams	2 teaspoons (10 ml)
orange zest, finely grated	3 grams	½ tablespoon
orange juice, freshly squeezed and strained	15 grams	1 tablespoon (15 ml)
nutmeg, grated	1.2 grams	½ tablespoon
fine sea salt	1.5 grams	¼ teaspoon
cognac	21 grams	1½ tablespoons (22.5 ml)
rum	21 grams	1½ tablespoons (22.5 ml)

MAKE THE MINCEMEAT

1) In a small piece of cheesecloth or large tea caddy, place the cinnamon stick pieces, whole clove, and star anise. If using cheesecloth, tie it together to make a little bundle.

2) In a small saucepan, stir together all the remaining ingredients except the cognac and rum. Add the spice bundle.

3) Over medium heat, bring the mixture to a boil, stirring constantly with a silicone spatula.

Continued

4) Lower the heat and simmer, stirring constantly, for 5 minutes, or until the apple exudes its juice and most of the liquid gets absorbed by the dried fruit.

5) Remove the pan from the heat and allow it to cool until warm or room temperature. Remove and discard the spice bundle, and stir in the cognac and rum.

6) Transfer the mincemeat to a 2 cup/473 ml canning jar or other jar with a tight fitting lid.

7) Refrigerate for a minimum of 3 weeks to allow it to mellow.

The mincemeat can be stored, refrigerated, for about a year. If planning to store for more than 3 weeks, add enough cognac and rum to cover the fruit.

GLACÉED FRUIT ALTERNATIVE

Glacéed fruit used for fruitcake can be substituted for the mincemeat. For 1 cup, use 52 grams/¼ cup plus 2 tablespoons of glacéed mixed fruit, preferably lemon and orange peel, 50 grams/¼ cup plus 2 tablespoons of golden raisins, 37 grams/¼ cup of glacéed red cherries (cut into quarters), and 28 grams/2 tablespoons/30 ml of dark rum.

Add all the ingredients to a 1 cup/237 ml canning jar. Screw the cap on tightly and lay it on its side. Allow it to sit for a week at room temperature, turning it one-quarter turn every day or so until almost all the rum has been absorbed into the fruit.

The glacéed fruit will keep at room temperature indefinitely. Add rum if it appears to be dry.

RUM RAISIN ICE CREAM

Makes: About 1 quart/1 liter

I love the flavor of raisins plumped with dark rum. In a blind taste test, several of my tasters preferred the flavor of golden raisins to dark raisins, but you can substitute an equal weight and volume of dark if desired.

Plan Ahead The raisins need 2 days to absorb the rum fully.

RUM SOAKED RAISINS

Makes: 163 grams/1 cup

golden raisins	108 grams	¾ cup
dark rum	55 grams	¼ cup (59 ml)

1) Set the raisins in a 2 cup/473 ml canning jar or jar with a tight fitting lid. Add the rum.

2) Let the raisins soak in the rum at room temperature for a minimum of 48 hours to absorb all the rum. Invert the jar a few times to help distribute the rum. (If the raisins are not soaked long enough, any rum that doesn't get absorbed will soften the churned ice cream if it is added.)

ICE CREAM BASE

6 (to 9) large egg yolks (see page xxxii)	112 grams	¼ cup plus 3 tablespoons (104 ml)
milk	160 grams	⅔ cup (158 ml)
heavy cream	464 grams	2 cups (473 ml), *divided*
sugar	120 grams	½ cup plus 1½ tablespoons
glucose or reduced corn syrup (see page xxi)	42 grams	2 tablespoons (30 ml)
fine sea salt	.	a pinch
Rum Soaked Raisins	163 grams	1 cup

Continued

✽ Have ready a fine-mesh strainer suspended over a medium bowl.

1) In a medium saucepan, with a silicone spatula, stir together the egg yolks, milk, and 174 grams/¾ cup/177 ml of the cream until well blended. Stir in the sugar, glucose, and salt until the sugar has dissolved.

2) Heat the mixture on medium-low, stirring, until slightly thicker than heavy cream. When a finger is run across the back of the spatula, it will leave a well-defined track. An instant-read thermometer should read 170° to 180°F/77° to 82°C.

3) Immediately pour the mixture into the strainer, scraping up the thickened mixture that has settled on the bottom of the pan. Press it through the strainer and scrape any mixture clinging to the underside into the bowl.

4) Stir in the remaining cream (290 grams/1¼ cups/296 ml). Cover and refrigerate for a minimum of 8 hours or until no warmer than 43°F/6°C. (Alternatively, cool in an ice water bath.) Set a covered storage container in the freezer.

5) Churn the custard in a prechilled ice cream maker. Transfer the ice cream to the chilled container. Press a piece of plastic wrap on the surface of the ice cream, cover the container, and allow the ice cream to firm in the freezer for 30 minutes to an hour.

6) Stir in the rum soaked raisins. Replace the plastic wrap, cover, and return it to the freezer for at least 4 hours before serving.

STORE Covered storage container: frozen, 3 days

SCOOPS

✽ The texture of this ice cream is very slightly icy but not noticeably thanks to the presence of the raisins.

PRUNES AND ARMAGNAC ICE CREAM

Makes: About 1 quart/1 liter

This recipe, which I adore, was introduced to me by my friend and esteemed colleague Paula Wolfert. The region of Gascony, in France, is known for its prunes and Armagnac, and together they give ice cream a velvety texture and luscious flavor. I like to make a big batch of the prunes in Armagnac to have at the ready. It will keep, refrigerated, for years, and the longer it sits, the more mellow the Armagnac becomes.

Plan Ahead Macerate the prunes a minimum of 24 hours ahead of making the ice cream base.

PRUNES IN ARMAGNAC

Makes: 275 grams/1¼ cups

pitted prunes	165 grams	¾ cup, tightly packed
Armagnac	179 grams	¾ cup (177 ml)

1) Use scissors to cut the prunes into small pieces. Set the prunes in a 2 cup/473 ml canning jar or jar with a tight fitting lid. Add the Armagnac and, if necessary, add a little extra to cover the prunes. (If the time frame in Step 2 does not allow, add only 119 grams/½ cup/118 ml, because that is the amount absorbed by a freshly opened container of prunes. Once the container is opened, the prunes tend to dry quickly.)

2) Let the prunes soak in the Armagnac at room temperature for a minimum of 24 hours. If soaking for longer than 2 days, it is best to refrigerate them.

3) Empty the prunes and Armagnac into a fine-mesh strainer suspended over a medium bowl. Press lightly to release any excess liquid. There should be about 60 grams/¼ cup/59 ml of Armagnac, which can be poured into a pitcher to serve as topping. (This step can be done while the ice cream is churning.)

Continued

The prunes in Armagnac keep in the canning jar for 2 years, refrigerated.

ICE CREAM BASE

6 (to 9) large egg yolks (see page xxxii)	112 grams	¼ cup plus 3 tablespoons (104 ml)
milk	121 grams	½ cup (118 ml)
heavy cream	406 grams	1¾ cups (414 ml), *divided*
sugar	100 grams	½ cup
glucose or reduced corn syrup (see page xxi)	42 grams	2 tablespoons (30 ml)
fine sea salt	.	a big pinch
Prunes in Armagnac, strained	275 grams	1¼ cups

✳ Have ready a fine-mesh strainer suspended over a medium bowl.

1) In a medium saucepan, with a silicone spatula, stir together the egg yolks, milk, and 174 grams/¾ cup/177 ml of the cream until well blended. Stir in the sugar, glucose, and salt until the sugar has dissolved.

2) Heat the mixture on medium-low, stirring constantly, until slightly thicker than heavy cream. When a finger is run across the back of the spatula, it will leave a well-defined track. An instant-read thermometer should read 170° to 180°F/77° to 82°C.

3) Immediately pour the mixture into the strainer, scraping up the thickened mixture that has settled on the bottom of the pan. Press it through the strainer and scrape any mixture clinging to the underside into the bowl.

4) Stir in the remaining cream (232 grams/1 cup/237 ml). Cover and refrigerate for a minimum of 8 hours or until no warmer than 43°F/6°C. (Alternatively, cool in an ice water bath.) Set a covered storage container in the freezer.

5) Churn the custard in a prechilled ice cream maker. Transfer the ice cream to the chilled container. Press a piece of plastic wrap on the surface of the ice cream, cover the container, and allow the ice cream to firm in the freezer for 30 minutes to an hour.

STORE
Covered storage container: frozen, 3 days

6) Fold in the Armagnac soaked prunes. Replace the plastic wrap, cover, and return it to the freezer for at least 4 hours before serving.

POMEGRANATE PRIDE ICE CREAM

Makes: About 1 quart/1 liter

This luscious, tangy ice cream is so unique and delicious it deserves its name. Evaporating the water in bottled pomegranate juice is the secret to making the ice cream silky smooth, with no ice crystals and no need for a stabilizer to keep it that way! It maintains its creamy, scoopable texture perfectly in the freezer for at least a week—I've never managed to keep it longer. Pama pomegranate liqueur, or additional reduced pomegranate syrup (see Scoops), is a glorious topping.

ICE CREAM BASE

bottled pomegranate juice, preferably POM	573 grams	2¼ cups (532 ml)
unsalted butter	56 grams	4 tablespoons (½ stick)
sugar	262 grams	1¼ cups plus 1 tablespoon
fine sea salt	1.5 grams	¼ teaspoon
heavy cream	522 grams	2¼ cups (532 ml), *divided*
6 (to 9) large egg yolks (see page xxxii)	112 grams	¼ cup plus 3 tablespoons (104 ml)
lemon juice, freshly squeezed and strained	8 grams	½ tablespoon (7.5 ml)
red liquid food color (optional)	.	about 6 drops
pomegranate arils (optional)	30 grams	3 tablespoons
Pama pomegranate liqueur (optional)	120 grams	½ cup (118 ml)

✤ Have ready a fine-mesh strainer suspended over a medium bowl.

1) In a medium saucepan, preferably nonstick, boil the pomegranate juice over medium heat, stirring often with a silicone spatula, until it is reduced

Continued

to about one-quarter its original weight or volume (143 grams/½ cup plus 1 tablespoon/133 ml).

2) Cut the butter into four pieces and stir it in until melted. Stir in the sugar and salt, and then 174 grams/¾ cup/177 ml of the cream. Allow the mixture to cool until just barely warm or room temperature. Then stir in the egg yolks.

3) Heat the mixture on medium-low, stirring constantly, until slightly thicker than heavy cream. When a finger is run across the back of the spatula, it will leave a well-defined track. An instant-read thermometer should read 170° to 180°F/77° to 82°C.

4) Immediately pour the mixture into the strainer, scraping up the thickened mixture that has settled on the bottom of the pan. Press it through the strainer and scrape any mixture clinging to the underside into the bowl.

5) Stir in the remaining cream (348 grams/1½ cups/355 ml) and then the lemon juice and food color, if desired, to achieve a pale pink color. Cover and refrigerate for a minimum of 8 hours or until no warmer than 43°F/6°C. (Alternatively, cool in an ice water bath.) Set a covered storage container in the freezer.

6) Churn the pomegranate custard in a prechilled ice cream maker. Transfer the ice cream to the chilled container. Press a piece of plastic wrap on the surface of the ice cream, cover the container, and allow the ice cream to firm in the freezer for at least 4 hours before serving.

7) Top with a sprinkling of pomegranate arils and/or a drizzle of pomegranate liqueur, if desired.

STORE Covered storage container: frozen, 3 days

SCOOPS

❖ You can make a second batch of the reduced pomegranate syrup (using the same amount of pomegranate juice, sugar, and lemon juice) to use as a topping or to swirl through the ice cream after churning; the syrup doesn't freeze hard and adds a delicious tang. After reducing the pomegranate juice, remove it from the heat and stir in the sugar until dissolved. Return it to the heat and bring it to a boil, stirring constantly, to ensure that the sugar has dissolved completely. Let cool and then stir in the lemon juice. It will keep for several months, refrigerated, but after about three weeks there will be slight crystallization of the sugar. It can be restored by bringing it to a boil in a microwave, but be sure to cover it to prevent evaporation. Then stir it to ensure that all the sugar crystals have dissolved.

To swirl the pomegranate syrup into the ice cream, use a 9 by 5 inch loaf pan, preferably Pyrex, to store the ice cream. (Set it in the freezer for a minimum of 30 minutes before adding the ice cream.) Scrape the pomegranate syrup into a disposable piping bag. Cut off a small semicircle from the point of the bag and close it with a binder clamp until ready to pipe the pomegranate syrup. (Alternatively, you can use a spoon to apply it, but it's easier and faster with a piping bag.)

Pipe zigzags of about one-third of the pomegranate syrup onto the bottom of the pan. Spread about one-third of the ice cream on top. Quickly pipe zigzags of about half of the remaining pomegranate syrup on top. Repeat with another third of the ice cream and then the remaining pomegranate syrup. Top with the remaining ice cream. Press a piece of plastic wrap on the surface of the ice cream, cover the pan, and allow the ice cream to firm in the freezer for at least 4 hours before serving.

GINGER ICE CREAM

Makes: 1 generous quart/1 generous liter

I love the contrast of cold, creamy ice cream with the fiery bite of ginger in the background, gently softened with aromatic vanilla.

ICE CREAM BASE

sugar	138 grams	½ cup plus 3 tablespoons, *divided*
Tahitian vanilla bean (see Scoops), cut in half lengthwise	.	1½ inch piece
fresh ginger, peeled and chopped into small pieces (see Scoops)	50 grams	½ cup, loosely packed
water	118 grams	½ cup (118 ml)
8 (to 12) large egg yolks (see page xxxii)	149 grams	½ cup plus 4 teaspoons (138 ml)
milk	181 grams	¾ cup (177 ml)
glucose or reduced corn syrup (see page xxi)	63 grams	3 tablespoons (45 ml)
fine sea salt	.	a pinch
heavy cream	522 grams	2¼ cups (532 ml)

❃ Have ready a fine-mesh strainer suspended over a medium bowl.

1) In a small saucepan, place 100 grams/½ cup of the sugar and the vanilla bean. Use your fingers to rub the seeds from the center of the vanilla bean into the sugar. Leave the pod in the saucepan.

2) Add the ginger and water to the sugar mixture and stir with a silicone spatula until the sugar has dissolved.

3) Heat over medium-high heat, stirring constantly, until the mixture comes to a boil. Stop stirring, reduce the heat to low, and simmer for 5 minutes without stirring. Remove the ginger syrup from the heat. Cover and allow it to cool for about 30 minutes, or until room temperature.

4) In a medium saucepan, with a silicone spatula, stir together the egg yolks and milk until well blended. Stir in the remaining sugar (38 grams/3 tablespoons), the glucose, and salt until the sugar has dissolved.

5) Heat the mixture on medium-low, stirring constantly, until slightly thicker than heavy cream. When a finger is run across the back of the spatula, it will leave a well-defined track. An instant-read thermometer should read 170° to 180°F/77° to 82°C.

6) Immediately pour the mixture into the strainer, scraping up the thickened mixture that has settled on the bottom of the pan. Press it through the strainer and scrape any mixture clinging to the underside into the bowl.

7) Stir in the cream and vanilla extract if not using the vanilla bean (see Scoops).

8) Pour the ginger syrup into a small food processor and add enough of the custard base to be able to process the ginger into fine particles. Cover and refrigerate for a minimum of 8 hours or until no warmer than 43°F/6°C. (Alternatively, cool in an ice water bath.) Set a covered storage container in the freezer.

9) Strain the ginger custard into a prechilled ice cream maker and discard the ginger. Churn the ginger custard. Transfer the ice cream to the chilled container. Press a piece of plastic wrap on the surface of the ice cream, cover the container, and allow the ice cream to firm in the freezer for at least 4 hours before serving.

STORE Covered storage container: frozen, 3 days

SCOOPS

✻ If using a Tahitian vanilla bean and the seeds are pulpy, you will need to process the seeds with the sugar. If using a Madagascar vanilla bean, use a 3 inch piece. Alternatively, use ½ tablespoon/7.5 ml of pure vanilla extract.

✻ If you don't have a small food processor for Step 8, instead of finely chopping the ginger, grate the ginger on a fine grater with small round holes (not the shredder with oval openings). You will need about 3 tablespoons/50 grams.

LEMON GINGER ICE CREAM

Makes: About 1 quart/1 liter

I love, love, love this refreshingly flavorful ice cream. It was inspired by a talented colleague from New Zealand, Annabel Langbein, and adapted from her book *The Free Range Cook: Simple Pleasures*. Not only is it the easiest ice cream to make, it doesn't even use an ice cream machine (no churning necessary). It is billowy and creamy and never icy, even after 3 to 4 weeks in the freezer. A silky Italian meringue made with sugar syrup is the miracle ingredient!

ICE CREAM BASE

2 large egg whites	60 grams	¼ cup (59 ml)
cream of tartar	.	¼ teaspoon
crystallized ginger	54 grams	¼ cup
superfine sugar (see Scoops)	150 grams	¾ cup
lemon zest, finely chopped (see Scoops)	.	¾ teaspoon
lemon juice, freshly squeezed and strained (2 lemons)	95 grams	6 tablespoons (89 ml)
heavy cream	116 grams	½ cup (118 ml)
plain Greek yogurt, full fat	54 grams	¼ cup (59 ml)

❖ Thirty minutes to 1 hour ahead, weigh or measure the egg whites and cream of tartar into a stand mixer bowl. Cover the bowl.

1) In a food processor, process the ginger with the sugar until the ginger is in very small pieces. Alternatively, chop it with a knife and mix it with the sugar.

2) In a medium saucepan (preferably with a spout), with a silicone spatula, stir together the ginger sugar, lemon zest, and lemon juice. Continue stirring, on medium heat, until it comes to a boil, then lower the heat and simmer for 5 minutes. An instant-read thermometer should read 228°F/109°C.

Continued

3) While the syrup is simmering, attach the whisk beater to the stand mixer. Beat the egg whites and cream of tartar until stiff peaks form when the beater is raised.

4) On low speed, add the hot syrup to the egg whites, avoiding the whisk. Turn the mixer to high and beat until very thick, 7 to 10 minutes. At first it will be very soupy; it will take several minutes before it begins to thicken. Scrape the meringue into a large bowl. Without rinsing the stand mixer bowl, add the cream and whip it to soft peaks. (Alternatively, whip the cream in a small bowl with a handheld mixer; see Scoops.)

5) Detach the whisk beater and use it to fold the yogurt into the whipped cream. Scrape this mixture into the meringue and continue folding with the whisk until evenly incorporated, then use a large silicone spatula to reach to the bottom of the bowl.

6) Transfer the mixture to a covered storage container. Press a piece of plastic wrap on the surface of the ice cream, cover the container, and allow the ice cream to firm in the freezer for at least 6 hours before serving (or 3 hours if you like it semifreddo, or the consistency of soft serve).

STORE Covered storage container: frozen, 1 week

SCOOPS

✳ If processing the sugar with the crystallized ginger, you can use fine granulated sugar.

✳ Be sure to scrub the lemon with a little liquid dishwashing detergent, rinse well, and dry before zesting. If desired, a little extra lemon zest can be grated directly onto the ice cream shortly before serving.

✳ If whipping the cream with a handheld mixer, pour the cream into a chilled metal bowl and refrigerate it, covered, for at least 15 minutes. Chill the handheld mixer's beaters alongside the bowl.

TRUE LEMON ICE CREAM

Makes: About 1 quart/1 liter

Of all desserts, lemon curd has the purest, most intense, and full-flavored lemon flavor I know, so I use it as a base for lemon ice cream. All that's added is heavy cream, a little milk, and a little extra sugar to produce an exceptionally smooth, creamy, and refreshing ice cream. The same basic technique works for other citrus fruits, too, but because their acidity varies, I concentrate the juice and adjust the amount of sugar accordingly (see Orange Ice Cream, page 121, and Grapefruit Ice Cream, page 126). Limes and Seville oranges, however, are very high in acid, so the juice can be substituted for lemon juice (see Variations, page 120).

ICE CREAM BASE

unsalted butter	64 grams	4½ tablespoons (½ stick plus ½ tablespoon)
lemon zest, finely grated (2 lemons), see Scoops	6 grams	1 tablespoon
6 (to 9) large egg yolks (see page xxxii)	112 grams	¼ cup plus 3 tablespoons (104 ml)
sugar	200 grams	1 cup, *divided*
glucose or reduced corn syrup (see page xxi)	28 grams	4 teaspoons (20 ml)
lemon juice, freshly squeezed and strained (3 lemons)	126 grams	½ cup (118 ml)
fine sea salt	.	a pinch
heavy cream	387 grams	1⅔ cups (394 ml)
milk	136 grams	½ cup plus 1 tablespoon (133 ml)

❖ About 1 hour ahead, cut the butter into four pieces and set it on the counter at room temperature (65° to 75°F/18° to 24°C).

❖ Have ready a fine-mesh strainer suspended over a medium bowl containing the lemon zest.

Continued

1) In a medium saucepan, with a silicone spatula, stir together the egg yolks, butter, 100 grams/½ cup of the sugar, and the glucose until well blended. Stir in the lemon juice and salt.

2) Heat the mixture on medium-low, stirring constantly, until slightly thicker than heavy cream. It should thickly coat the spatula and will pool slightly when a little is dropped back on its surface.

3) Immediately pour the mixture into the strainer, scraping up the thickened mixture that has settled on the bottom of the pan. Press it through the strainer and scrape any mixture clinging to the underside into the bowl.

4) Whisk the remaining sugar (100 grams/½ cup) into the hot lemon curd, and then the cream and milk. Cover and refrigerate for a minimum of 8 hours or until no warmer than 43°F/6°C. (Alternatively, cool in an ice water bath.) Set a covered storage container in the freezer.

5) Churn the lemon custard in a prechilled ice cream maker. Transfer the ice cream to the chilled container. Press a piece of plastic wrap on the surface of the ice cream, cover the container, and allow the ice cream to firm in the freezer for at least 4 hours before serving.

STORE Covered storage container: frozen, 3 days

SCOOPS

✽ Be sure to scrub the lemon with a little liquid dishwashing detergent, rinse well, and dry before zesting.

✽ Fresh blueberries or raspberries scattered on top make a harmonious combination of flavors and textures.

VARIATIONS

LIME ICE CREAM

Substitute an equal weight or volume of freshly squeezed and strained lime juice for the lemon juice. Substitute 8 grams/4 teaspoons of finely grated lime zest for the lemon zest. Use only 175 grams/¾ cup plus 2 tablespoons of sugar: Add 100 grams/½ cup to the egg mixture and the remaining 75 grams/¼ cup plus 2 tablespoons to the hot lime curd.

SEVILLE ORANGE ICE CREAM

Replace the lemon juice with an equal weight or volume of freshly squeezed and strained Seville orange juice. Replace the lemon zest with 8 grams/4 teaspoons of finely grated navel orange zest (the zest from Seville oranges is unpleasantly bitter, except when used in marmalade).

ORANGE ICE CREAM

Makes: About 1 quart/1 liter

Orange juice makes a wonderful orange curd provided it is concentrated to increase acidity and flavor. You can concentrate it completely in a saucepan, preferably nonstick, but for the purest flavor, the final reduction in the microwave is best.

ICE CREAM BASE

unsalted butter	64 grams	4½ tablespoons (½ stick plus ½ tablespoon)
orange peel (2 to 3 navel oranges, see Scoops)	12 grams	.
orange juice, freshly squeezed and strained (6 oranges)	644 grams	2⅔ cups (630 ml)
5 (to 8) large egg yolks (see page xxxii)	93 grams	¼ cup plus 2 tablespoons (89 ml)
sugar	171 grams	⅔ cup plus 3 tablespoons, *divided*
glucose or reduced corn syrup (see page xxi)	28 grams	4 teaspoons (20 ml)
fine sea salt	.	a pinch
heavy cream	387 grams	1⅔ cups (394 ml)
milk	136 grams	½ cup plus 1 tablespoon (133 ml)
milk for rinsing the peel	60 grams	¼ cup (59 ml)

✽ About 1 hour ahead, cut the butter into four pieces and set it on the counter at room temperature (65° to 75°F/18° to 24°C).

✽ Have ready a fine-mesh strainer suspended over a medium bowl containing the orange peel.

1) In a medium saucepan over medium-high heat, boil the orange juice, stirring constantly, until reduced to ¾ to 1 cup/177 to 237 ml. Pour it into a 4 cup/1 liter glass measure with a spout that has been lightly coated with nonstick cooking spray, and microwave, stirring every 20 to 30 seconds, for about 10 minutes, until reduced to no less than 150 grams/9 tablespoons/133 ml and no more

Continued

Orange Ice Cream, Blood Orange
Ice Cream (page 124), and
Grapefruit Ice Cream (page 126)

than 176 grams/²⁄₃ cup/158 ml (about one-quarter of its original weight or volume). Set it aside to cool until no longer hot to the touch.

2) In a medium saucepan, with a silicone spatula, stir together the egg yolks, butter, 133 grams/²⁄₃ cup of the sugar, and the glucose until well blended. Stir in the orange juice and salt. It will be very thick.

3) Heat the mixture on medium-low, stirring constantly, until slightly thicker than heavy cream. It should thickly coat the spatula and will pool slightly when a little is dropped back on its surface.

4) Immediately pour the mixture into the strainer, scraping up the thickened mixture that has settled on the bottom of the pan. Press it through the strainer and scrape any mixture clinging to the underside into the bowl.

5) Whisk the remaining sugar (38 grams/3 tablespoons) into the hot orange curd, and then the cream and milk. Cover and refrigerate for a minimum of 8 hours or until no warmer than 43°F/6°C. Set a covered storage container in the freezer.

6) Strain the mixture into a bowl. Transfer the peel to another bowl and add the 60 grams/¼ cup/59 ml of milk for rinsing the peel. Stir the peel and milk together to remove the custard mixture that clings to the peel. Remove and discard the peel, and add the milk to the rest of the custard mixture.

7) Churn the orange custard in a prechilled ice cream maker. Transfer the ice cream to the chilled container. Press a piece of plastic wrap on the surface of the ice cream, cover the container, and allow the ice cream to firm in the freezer for at least 4 hours before serving.

STORE
Covered storage container: frozen, 3 days

SCOOPS

❄ Be sure to scrub the orange with a little liquid detergent, rinse well, and dry before removing the peel. When removing the peel, avoid the bitter white pith beneath or scrape it off if necessary.

❄ When reducing the orange juice, it is important to stir it every 20 to 30 seconds to prevent spattering.

VARIATIONS

TANGERINE ICE CREAM
Tangerines are slightly less tart than oranges but also a little more intense in flavor. Replace the orange juice with an equal weight or volume of tangerine juice. Use navel orange peel rather than tangerine peel, which is very bitter.

TANGELO ICE CREAM
Tangelos are a cross between oranges and grapefruits. Substitute an equal weight or volume of tangelo juice and peel, and add an extra 8 grams/2 teaspoons of sugar in Step 5.

BLOOD ORANGE ICE CREAM

Makes: About 1 quart/1 liter

Frozen blood orange concentrate makes the most amazing ice cream, with a lovely deeply orange flavor. It is well worth purchasing the concentrate either directly from Perfect Purée of Napa Valley or Kalustyan's. It keeps for well over a year in the freezer and also makes a great addition to margaritas. I adore this ice cream! You can also make your own blood orange concentrate from blood oranges when they are in season (see Note).

ICE CREAM BASE

unsalted butter	64 grams	4½ tablespoons (½ stick plus ½ tablespoon)
blood orange concentrate	150 grams	½ cup plus 1 tablespoon (133 ml)
orange zest, finely grated (1 navel orange)	6 grams	1 tablespoon
5 (to 8) large egg yolks (see page xxxii)	93 grams	¼ cup plus 2 tablespoons (89 ml)
sugar	238 grams	1 cup plus 3 tablespoons, *divided*
glucose or reduced corn syrup (see page xxi)	42 grams	2 tablespoons (30 ml)
fine sea salt	.	a pinch
heavy cream	387 grams	1⅔ cups (394 ml)
milk	121 grams	½ cup (118 ml)

❖ About 1 hour ahead, cut the butter into four pieces and set it on the counter at room temperature (65° to 75°F/18° to 24°C).

❖ In a 1 cup/237 ml glass measure with a spout, weigh the blood orange concentrate. (If measuring it by volume, allow it to defrost first.)

❖ Have ready a fine-mesh strainer suspended over a medium bowl containing the orange zest.

1) In a medium saucepan, with a silicone spatula, stir together the egg yolks, butter, 138 grams/½ cup plus 3 tablespoons of the sugar, and the glucose until well blended. Stir in the blood orange concentrate and salt. It will be very thick.

2) Heat the mixture on medium-low, stirring constantly, until thickened a little further. An instant-read thermometer should not exceed 196°F/91°C.

3) Immediately pour the mixture into the strainer, scraping up the thickened mixture that has settled on the bottom of the pan. Press it through the strainer and scrape any mixture clinging to the underside into the bowl.

4) Whisk the remaining sugar (100 grams/½ cup) into the hot blood orange curd, and then the cream and milk. Cover and refrigerate for a minimum of 8 hours or until no warmer than 43°F/6°C. (Alternatively, cool in an ice water bath.) Set a covered storage container in the freezer.

5) Churn the blood orange custard in a prechilled ice cream maker. Transfer the ice cream to the chilled container. Press a piece of plastic wrap on the surface of the ice cream, cover the container, and allow the ice cream to firm in the freezer for at least 4 hours before serving.

STORE Covered storage container: frozen, 3 days

NOTE To make blood orange concentrate, you will need 6 to 8 blood oranges. Be sure to scrub them with a little liquid dishwashing detergent, rinse well, and dry before zesting. Follow the quantities and instructions for the orange juice reduction in Step 1 of the Orange Ice Cream on page 121.

SCOOPS

✳ The finished temperature of the custard in Step 2 is higher than the usual 180°F/82°C of other ice creams because of the acidity of the blood orange juice.

GRAPEFRUIT ICE CREAM

Makes: About 1 quart/1 liter

Grapefruit adds a pleasantly bitter edge to the sweetness of ice cream. I use the same method for concentrating the juice as for the Orange Ice Cream on page 121, but it only needs to be reduced by half. For a lovely pale pink color, add a few drops of red food color. And for a luxurious accompaniment, serve with a garnish of Soft Candied Grapefruit Peel (page 185).

ICE CREAM BASE

unsalted butter	64 grams	4½ tablespoons (½ stick plus ½ tablespoon)
grapefruit zest, finely grated, preferably ruby red (2 grapefruits; see Scoops)	18 grams	3 tablespoons
grapefruit juice, freshly squeezed and strained (2 grapefruits)	252 grams	1 cup (237 ml)
6 (to 9) large egg yolks (see page xxxii)	112 grams	¼ cup plus 3 tablespoons (104 ml)
sugar	150 grams	¾ cup, *divided*
glucose or reduced corn syrup (see page xxi)	28 grams	4 teaspoons (20 ml)
fine sea salt	.	a pinch
heavy cream	387 grams	1⅔ cups (394 ml)
milk	136 grams	½ cup plus 1 tablespoon (133 ml)
red food color (optional)	.	about 6 drops

❈ About 1 hour ahead, cut the butter into four pieces and set it on the counter at room temperature (65° to 75°F/18° to 24°C).

❈ Have ready a fine-mesh strainer suspended over a medium bowl containing the grapefruit zest.

Continued

1) In a small saucepan, stirring often, boil the grapefruit juice until reduced to about half its original weight or volume, 126 grams/½ cup/118 ml. (Alternatively, you can do this in the microwave, in a 4 cup/1 liter glass measure with a spout, lightly coated with nonstick cooking spray, swirling or stirring every 20 to 30 seconds, for about 10 minutes.) Set it aside to cool until no longer hot to the touch.

2) In a medium saucepan, with a silicone spatula, stir together the egg yolks, butter, 100 grams/½ cup of the sugar, and the glucose until well blended. Stir in the grapefruit juice and salt. It will be very thick.

3) Heat the mixture on medium-low, stirring constantly, until slightly thicker than heavy cream. It should thickly coat the spatula and will pool slightly when a little is dropped back on its surface.

4) Immediately pour the mixture into the strainer, scraping up the thickened mixture that has settled on the bottom of the pan. Press it through the strainer and scrape any mixture clinging to the underside into the bowl.

5) Whisk the remaining sugar (50 grams/¼ cup) into the hot grapefruit curd, and then the cream, milk, and food color if desired. Cover and refrigerate for a minimum of 8 hours or until no warmer than 43°F/6°C. (Alternatively, cool in an ice water bath.) Set a covered storage container in the freezer.

6) Churn the grapefruit custard in a prechilled ice cream maker. Transfer the ice cream to the chilled container. Press a piece of plastic wrap on the surface of the ice cream, cover the container, and allow the ice cream to firm in the freezer for at least 4 hours before serving.

STORE Covered storage container: frozen, 3 days

SCOOPS

❋ Be sure to scrub the grapefruit with a little liquid detergent, rinse well, and dry before zesting.

❋ When reducing the grapefruit juice, it is important to stir it every 20 to 30 seconds to prevent spattering.

PASSION ICE CREAM

Makes: About 1 quart/1 liter

This fruit is called "passion" for a reason! It lends this creamy ice cream a perfect balance of lilting sweetness and acidity. Something magical happens when Tahitian vanilla bean is added to passion fruit—it enhances and rounds off the slightly metallic quality of the fruit. After I shared this ice cream with my dear friend and colleague Elizabeth Karmel, she bought the passion fruit concentrate and an ice cream maker so she could have it again and again!

ICE CREAM BASE

unsalted butter	64 grams	4½ tablespoons (½ stick plus ½ tablespoon)
passion fruit concentrate (see Scoops)	125 grams	7½ tablespoons (111 ml)
sugar	225 grams	1 cup plus 2 tablespoons, *divided*
¾ Tahitian vanilla bean, split lengthwise (see Scoops)	.	.
heavy cream	387 grams	1⅔ cups (394 ml)
milk	136 grams	½ cup plus 1 tablespoon (133 ml)
6 (to 9) large egg yolks (see page xxxii)	112 grams	¼ cup plus 3 tablespoons (104 ml)
glucose or reduced corn syrup (see page xxi)	28 grams	4 teaspoons (20 ml)
fine sea salt	.	a pinch

✣ About 1 hour ahead, cut the butter into four pieces and set it on the counter at room temperature (65° to 75°F/18° to 24°C).

✣ In a 1 cup/237 ml glass measure with a spout, weigh the passion fruit concentrate. (If measuring it by volume, allow it to defrost first.)

✣ Have ready a fine-mesh strainer suspended over a medium bowl.

Continued

1) In a medium saucepan, place 150 grams/¾ cup of the sugar and the vanilla bean. Use your fingers to rub the seeds from the center of the vanilla bean into the sugar. Remove the pod and set it in a medium bowl. Add the cream and milk. Cover and refrigerate.

2) Add the egg yolks and butter to the sugar mixture and, with a silicone spatula, stir them together. Stir in the glucose, passion fruit concentrate, and salt until well blended.

3) Heat the mixture on medium-low, stirring constantly, until slightly thicker than heavy cream. It should thickly coat the spatula and will pool slightly when a little is dropped back on its surface.

4) Immediately pour the mixture into the strainer, scraping up the thickened mixture that has settled on the bottom of the pan. Press it through the strainer and scrape any mixture clinging to the underside into the bowl.

5) Whisk the remaining sugar (75 grams/¼ cup plus 2 tablespoons) into the hot passion curd. Remove the vanilla bean pod and then whisk in the cream and milk mixture. Return the vanilla bean pod to the ice cream base. Cover and refrigerate for a minimum of 8 hours or until no warmer than 43°F/6°C. (Alternatively, cool in an ice water bath.) Set a covered storage container in the freezer.

6) Remove the vanilla bean pod and rinse and dry it for future use. Churn the passion fruit custard in a prechilled ice cream maker. Transfer the ice cream to the chilled container. Press a piece of plastic wrap on the surface of the ice cream, cover the container, and allow the ice cream to firm in the freezer for at least 4 hours before serving.

STORE Covered storage container: frozen, 3 days

SCOOPS

❊ I recommend Perfect Purée of Napa Valley passion fruit concentrate. If using fresh passion fruit, you will need about 7 ripe passion fruit (762 grams/1⅔ pounds flesh), strained and puréed to equal 164 grams/¾ cup/177 ml and a total of 200 grams/1 cup of sugar. Choose passion fruit that are very wrinkled to ensure ripeness.

❊ If using a Tahitian vanilla bean and the seeds are pulpy, you will need to process the seeds with the sugar.

❊ If Tahitian vanilla bean is unavailable, substitute 1½ Madagascar vanilla beans or 1 teaspoon/5 ml of pure vanilla extract.

CHOCOLATE AND NUT ICE CREAMS

This chapter is short and sweet but includes my best chocolate ice cream and a dreamy white chocolate ice cream in addition to ice creams featuring all my favorite nuts, from almond to hazelnut. It also has two ice creams that do not require an ice cream maker: the chocolate semifreddo and the nougat.

CHOCOLATE ICE CREAM

Makes: About 5 cups/1.2 liters

The secret to this chocolaty ice cream was given to me by Kelila Jaffe, professor in the food department at New York University. It is the subtle hint of malt—just enough to round out and enhance the chocolate. Either Butterscotch Toffee Sauce (page 203) or Caramel Sauce (page 194) would provide a fabulous accompaniment.

ICE CREAM BASE

dark chocolate, 60% to 62% cacao, finely chopped	44 grams (1.5 ounces)	about ¼ cup
sugar	94 grams	½ cup minus ½ tablespoon
malt powder, preferably Carnation	17 grams	2 tablespoons
unsweetened alkalized cocoa powder	28 grams	¼ cup plus 2 tablespoons (sifted before measuring)
fine sea salt	.	⅛ teaspoon plus 1/16 teaspoon
espresso powder, preferably Medaglia d'Oro	.	1/16 teaspoon
milk	121 grams	½ cup (118 ml)
heavy cream	580 grams	2½ cups (591 ml), *divided*
6 (to 9) large egg yolks (see page xxxii)	112 grams	¼ cup plus 3 tablespoons (104 ml)
glucose or reduced corn syrup (see page xxi)	63 grams	3 tablespoons (45 ml)
pure vanilla extract	.	1 teaspoon (5 ml)

✣ Have ready a fine-mesh strainer suspended over a medium bowl containing the finely chopped chocolate.

1) In a medium bowl, whisk together the sugar, malt powder, cocoa, salt, and espresso powder.

2) In a medium saucepan, with a silicone spatula, stir together the milk, 116 grams/½ cup/118 ml of the cream, and the egg yolks. Stir in the

Continued

glucose and the sugar mixture until the sugar has almost completely dissolved.

3) Heat the mixture on medium-low, stirring constantly, until slightly thicker than heavy cream. When a finger is run across the back of the spatula, it will leave a well-defined track. An instant-read thermometer should read 170° to 180°F/77° to 82°C.

4) Immediately pour the mixture into the strainer, scraping up the thickened mixture that has settled on the bottom of the pan. Press it through the strainer and scrape any mixture clinging to the underside into the bowl.

5) Stir until the chocolate has melted. Then stir in the remaining cream (464 grams/2 cups/473 ml) and the vanilla. Cover and refrigerate for a minimum of 8 hours or until no warmer than 43°F/6°C. (Alternatively, cool in an ice water bath.) Set a covered storage container in the freezer.

6) Churn the chocolate custard in a prechilled ice cream maker. Transfer the ice cream to the chilled container. Press a piece of plastic wrap on the surface of the ice cream, cover the container, and allow the ice cream to firm in the freezer for at least 4 hours before serving.

STORE Covered storage container: frozen, 3 days

LISA YOCKELSON'S WHITE CHOCOLATE SHEER BLISS ICE CREAM

Makes: About 1 quart/1 liter

I've added white chocolate to cake batters and buttercreams, enjoying the improved texture and intriguing flavor it yields, but I never before thought to add it to ice cream until my friend and cookbook author Lisa Yockelson shared this recipe. No one would ever guess that white chocolate is the secret ingredient that gives this dreamy vanilla-scented ice cream its luxuriously voluptuous texture. The cocoa butter and milk solids in the white chocolate are in good part responsible for the unique texture, but leave it to Lisa to create her own invert sugar instead of using glucose. She does this by making a simple sugar syrup. This ice cream deserves to be garnished with little flecks of gold leaf.

ICE CREAM BASE

fine quality white chocolate, preferably Valrhona	227 grams	8 ounces
water	118 grams	½ cup (118 ml)
sugar	125 grams	½ cup plus 2 tablespoons, *divided*
pure vanilla extract	15 grams	1 tablespoon (15 ml)
vanilla bean paste (optional, see Scoops)	.	½ teaspoon (2.5 ml)
7 (to 11) large egg yolks (see page xxxii)	130 grams	½ cup (118 ml)
heavy cream	522 grams	2¼ cups (532 ml), *divided*
fine sea salt	.	⅛ teaspoon

✲ Have ready a fine-mesh strainer suspended over a medium bowl.

Continued

1) Chop the white chocolate into medium-fine pieces and place in a medium glass bowl. Microwave, stirring every 15 seconds, until melted and smoothly combined. Alternatively, melt the chocolate in the top of a double boiler set over hot, not simmering, water. (Do not let the bottom of the container touch the water.) Stir often until the chocolate is completely melted. Set it aside in a warm place.

2) In a small saucepan, with a silicone spatula, stir together the water and 100 grams/½ cup of the sugar. Bring it to a boil over medium heat, stirring constantly. Stop stirring and allow it to boil for 3 minutes.

3) Remove the syrup from the heat and allow it to cool for 5 minutes. Stir in the vanilla extract and vanilla bean paste, if using. Cover tightly with plastic wrap.

4) In a small saucepan, with a silicone spatula, stir together the egg yolks, 464 grams/2 cups/473 ml of the cream, the remaining sugar (25 grams/ 2 tablespoons), and the salt until well blended.

5) Heat the mixture on medium-low, stirring constantly, until slightly thicker than heavy cream. When a finger is run across the back of the spatula, it will leave a well-defined track. An instant-read thermometer should read 170° to 180°F/77° to 82°C.

6) Immediately pour the mixture into the strainer, scraping up the thickened mixture that has settled on the bottom of the pan. Press it through the strainer and scrape any mixture clinging to the underside into the bowl.

7) Stir in the vanilla syrup and then the melted white chocolate until well blended. Stir in the remaining cream (58 grams/¼ cup/59 ml). Cover and refrigerate for a minimum of 8 hours or until no warmer than 43°F/6°C. (Alternatively, cool in an ice water bath.) Set a covered storage container in the freezer.

8) Churn the vanilla custard in a prechilled ice cream maker. Transfer the ice cream to the chilled container. Press a piece of plastic wrap on the surface of the ice cream, cover the container, and allow the ice cream to firm in the freezer for at least 4 hours before serving.

STORE Covered storage container: frozen, 3 days

SCOOPS

✳ If not using vanilla bean paste, add an additional ½ teaspoon/2.5 ml of pure vanilla extract.

CHOCOLATE SEMIFREDDO SEDUCTION

Makes: 1 cup/2 servings (it can be multiplied for more servings)

This could be the perfect Valentine's Day dessert. It takes 5 minutes to make and 30 minutes to chill, does not use an ice cream machine, and serves two.

It's hard to believe, but this rich chocolate cream is made with cocoa powder, not chocolate. I use cocoa because the cocoa butter in chocolate would become very hard when chilled, whereas a semifreddo, which means semi-frozen, should have a lighter, airier consistency, which the cocoa powder provides. The egg yolk adds shine and silkiness and enhances the flavor.

ICE CREAM BASE

sugar, preferably superfine	50 grams	¼ cup
unsweetened alkalized cocoa powder	28 grams	¼ cup plus 2 tablespoons (sifted before measuring)
salt	.	a tiny pinch
milk	60 grams	¼ cup (59 ml)
heavy cream	116 grams	½ cup (118 ml)
1 (to 2) large egg yolks (see page xxxii)	19 grams	1 tablespoon plus ½ teaspoon (17.5 ml)
pure vanilla extract	.	½ teaspoon (2.5 ml)

✣ Have ready a fine-mesh strainer suspended over a medium bowl.

1) In a small saucepan, whisk together the sugar, cocoa, and salt. Whisk in the milk until smooth. Then whisk in the cream.

2) Heat the mixture on low heat, stirring constantly with the whisk, until it begins to boil. Cook at a low boil for 1 minute, continuing to stir, until thickened.

Continued

3) Remove the pan from the heat and whisk in the egg yolk and vanilla. Scrape the chocolate custard into the strainer. Press it through the strainer and scrape any mixture clinging to the underside into the bowl.

4) Divide the chocolate custard into two pot de crème containers or 6 ounce custard cups. Cover tightly and freeze for at least 30 and up to 45 minutes before serving. It is at its best texture at this point, when only partially frozen. If you are making it ahead of time, refrigerate until 30 minutes before serving time, and then freeze it for 20 to 30 minutes.

STORE Covered storage container: refrigerated, 3 days

PEANUT BUTTER AND CHOCOLATE FUDGE ICE CREAM

Makes: About 1 quart/1 liter

Chocolate fudge is the secret ingredient that intensifies and rounds out the flavor of this incredibly creamy and delicious ice cream. It is also a great addition heated and drizzled on top.

ICE CREAM BASE

smooth peanut butter, preferably Jif	133 grams	½ cup
Hot Fudge Topping and Dipping Sauce, preferably homemade (page 198)	200 grams	⅔ cup plus 1 tablespoon (168 ml)
6 (to 9) large egg yolks (see page xxxii)	112 grams	¼ cup plus 3 tablespoons (104 ml)
milk	242 grams	1 cup (237 ml)
sugar	88 grams	½ cup minus 1 tablespoon
glucose or reduced corn syrup (see page xxi)	42 grams	2 tablespoons (30 ml)
fine sea salt	.	a pinch
heavy cream	290 grams	1¼ cups (296 ml)
pure vanilla extract	.	1 teaspoon (5 ml)

✲ About 30 minutes ahead, weigh or measure the peanut butter and Hot Fudge Topping and Dipping Sauce into a medium bowl and set aside at room temperature (65° to 75°F/18° to 24°C).

✲ Suspend a fine-mesh strainer over the bowl.

Continued

1) In a medium saucepan, with a silicone spatula, stir together the egg yolks and milk until well blended. Stir in the sugar, glucose, and salt until the sugar has dissolved.

2) Heat the mixture on medium-low, stirring constantly, until slightly thicker than heavy cream. When a finger is run across the back of the spatula, it will leave a well-defined track. An instant-read thermometer should read 170° to 180°F/77° to 82°C.

3) Immediately pour the mixture into the strainer, scraping up the thickened mixture that has settled on the bottom of the pan. Press it through the strainer and scrape any mixture clinging to the underside into the bowl.

4) Whisk the peanut butter–fudge custard until well blended. Then whisk in the cream and vanilla. Cover and refrigerate for a minimum of 8 hours or until no warmer than 43°F/6°C. (Alternatively, cool in an ice water bath.) Set a covered storage container in the freezer.

5) Churn the peanut butter and chocolate fudge custard in a prechilled ice cream maker. Transfer the ice cream to the chilled container. Press a piece of plastic wrap on the surface of the ice cream, cover the container, and allow the ice cream to firm in the freezer for at least 4 hours before serving.

STORE Covered storage container: frozen, 3 days

PURE PEANUT BUTTER ICE CREAM

Makes: About 5 cups/1.2 liters

Peanut butter not only offers a terrific flavor, it also gives this ice cream an exceptionally creamy texture. The optional black raspberry liqueur makes this the PB&J of ice creams. It has a subtle flavor but helps keep this dense ice cream softer. I love serving this ice cream with Concord grape pie, cherry pie, and chocolate tarts. And no one will complain if they find swirls of Concord grape jam; add it following the technique on page 172. It is fabulous topped with Hot Fudge (page 198) or extra Chambord.

ICE CREAM BASE

smooth peanut butter, preferably Jif	144 grams	½ cup plus 2 teaspoons
7 (to 11) large egg yolks (page xxxii)	130 grams	½ cup (118 ml)
milk	242 grams	1 cup (237 ml)
heavy cream	464 grams	2 cups (473 ml), *divided*
sugar	150 grams	¾ cup
glucose or reduced corn syrup (see page xxi)	42 grams	2 tablespoons (30 ml)
fine sea salt	.	a pinch
pure vanilla extract	.	1 teaspoon (5 ml)
Chambord (black raspberry liqueur), optional	49 grams	3 tablespoons (45 ml)

✲ About 30 minutes ahead, weigh or measure the peanut butter into a medium bowl on the counter at room temperature (65° to 75°F/18° to 24°C).

✲ Suspend a fine-mesh strainer over the bowl.

Continued

1) In a medium saucepan, with a silicone spatula, stir together the egg yolks, milk, and 116 grams/½ cup/118 ml of the cream until well blended. Stir in the sugar, glucose, and salt until the sugar has dissolved.

2) Heat the mixture on medium-low, stirring constantly, until slightly thicker than heavy cream. When a finger is run across the back of the spatula, it will leave a well-defined track. An instant-read thermometer should read 170° to 180°F/77° to 82°C.

3) Immediately pour the mixture into the strainer, scraping up the thickened mixture that has settled on the bottom of the pan. Press it through the strainer and scrape any mixture clinging to the underside into the strainer.

4) Whisk the peanut butter custard until well blended. Then whisk in the remaining cream (348 grams/1½ cups/355 ml) and the vanilla. Cover and refrigerate for a minimum of 8 hours or until no warmer than 43°F/6°C. (Alternatively, cool in an ice water bath.) Set a covered storage container in the freezer.

5) Churn the peanut butter custard in a prechilled ice cream maker. If adding the Chambord, add it during churning once the ice cream has reached the consistency of soft serve and begins to ball up around the dasher. Transfer the ice cream to the chilled container. Press a piece of plastic wrap on the surface of the ice cream, cover the container, and allow the ice cream to firm in the freezer for at least 4 hours before serving.

STORE Covered storage container: frozen, 3 days

SILKEN BLACK SESAME ICE CREAM

Makes: About 1 quart/1 liter

I've always enjoyed sesame paste, aka tahini, in savory dishes such as hummus or cold sesame noodles, but it wasn't until I tasted the Lebanese sesame halva marbled with dark chocolate at Kalustyan's, my favorite international food supply store in New York City, that it became a near addiction. So after completing the recipe testing for this book, my mind suddenly turned to "why not sesame ice cream?"

The fat content of tahini (which is 100% sesame paste) is only about 4% higher than peanut butter and much lower than praline paste. But it is much softer and silkier than either one. Be sure to soften the ice cream before serving; the nature of ground sesame seeds makes the ice cream very hard when frozen solid. Top it with a sprinkling of crumbled halva, preferably the marbled chocolate variety.

For a dramatic charcoal gray color and more intense flavor, I prefer black tahini. Beige tahini is more subtle but also delicious.

ICE CREAM BASE

tahini, preferably black (see Scoops)	155 grams	½ cup plus 2 tablespoons (150 ml)
7 (to 11) large egg yolks (see page xxxii)	130 grams	½ cup (118 ml)
milk	121 grams	½ cup (118 ml)
heavy cream	464 grams	2 cups (473 ml), *divided*
sugar	150 grams	¾ cup
glucose or reduced corn syrup (see page xxi)	42 grams	2 tablespoons (30 ml)
fine sea salt	.	a pinch

❖ About 30 minutes ahead, stir the tahini until the oil that has separated is completely incorporated. Then weigh or measure the tahini into a medium bowl

Continued

on the counter at room temperature (65° to 75°F/18° to 24°C). If the tahini has not been refrigerated, this can be done right before mixing the rest of the ingredients.

✻ Suspend a fine-mesh strainer over the bowl.

1) In a medium saucepan, with a silicone spatula, stir together the egg yolks, milk, and 116 grams/½ cup/118 ml of the cream until well blended. Stir in the sugar, glucose, and salt until the sugar has dissolved.

2) Heat the mixture on medium-low, stirring constantly, until slightly thicker than heavy cream. When a finger is run across the back of the spatula, it will leave a well-defined track. An instant-read thermometer should read 170° to 180°F/77° to 82°C.

3) Immediately pour the mixture into the strainer, scraping up the thickened mixture that has settled on the bottom of the pan. Press it through the strainer and scrape any mixture clinging to the underside into the strainer.

4) Whisk the tahini into the custard mixture until well blended. Then whisk in the remaining cream (348 grams/1½ cups/355 ml). Cover and refrigerate for a minimum of 8 hours or until no warmer than 43°F/6°C. (Alternatively, cool in an ice water bath.) Set a covered storage container in the freezer.

STORE

Covered storage container: frozen, 3 days

5) Churn the sesame custard in a prechilled ice cream maker. Transfer the ice cream to the chilled container. Press a piece of plastic wrap on the surface of the ice cream, cover the container, and allow the ice cream to firm in the freezer for at least 4 hours before serving.

SCOOPS

✻ Kevala organic black tahini, made in the United States, uses 100% unhulled, lightly roasted black sesame seeds. The Roland brand from Israel uses 100% hulled, lightly roasted black sesame seeds. Both are excellent choices. Soom tahini is made with 100% roasted tan sesame seeds.

✻ A sprinkling of lightly toasted sesame seeds adds a delightful crunch and indicates the flavor of the ice cream.

BROWN SUGAR BUTTER PECAN ICE CREAM

Makes: About 1 quart/1 liter

This fabulous ice cream is all the more so when made with light brown Muscovado sugar. The deliciously complex flavors of the sugar enhance, but do not overwhelm, the crunchy buttery pecans.

BUTTERED PECANS

Makes: 145 grams/1¼ cups

unsalted butter	21 grams	1½ tablespoons
pecan halves	125 grams	1¼ cups
fine sea salt	.	⅛ teaspoon

✣ About 30 minutes ahead, set the butter on the counter at room temperature (65° to 75°F/18° to 24°C).

PREHEAT THE OVEN

✣ Twenty minutes or longer before baking, set an oven rack at the middle level. Set the oven at 325°F/160°C.

1) Break or chop the pecans into medium-coarse pieces. Spread the pecans in an even layer on a rimmed baking sheet. Bake for 5 minutes, without browning, to enhance the flavor. Stir once or twice to ensure even baking.

2) Empty the hot pecans into a medium bowl. Add the butter and toss to coat evenly. Sprinkle with the salt and toss again. Cool completely.

Continued

ICE CREAM BASE

light brown sugar, preferably Muscovado	122 grams	½ cup plus 1 tablespoon, firmly packed
heavy cream	348 grams	1½ cups (355 ml)
5 (to 8) large egg yolks (see page xxxii)	93 grams	¼ cup plus 2 tablespoons (89 ml)
glucose or reduced corn syrup (see page xxi)	28 grams	4 teaspoons (20 ml)
fine sea salt	.	a pinch
milk	121 grams	½ cup (118 ml)
pure vanilla extract	.	1 teaspoon (5 ml)
Buttered Pecans	145 grams	1¼ cups

SCOOPS

❊ The brown sugar is added to the cream instead of to the milk because the milk proteins would curdle if the brown sugar were added directly to it.

❊ If desired, top each serving with bourbon to taste.

❊ Have ready a fine-mesh strainer suspended over a medium bowl.

1) In a medium saucepan, place the sugar. With a silicone spatula, stir in the cream and then the egg yolks. Stir in the glucose and salt until well blended.

2) Heat the mixture on medium-low, stirring constantly, until slightly thicker than heavy cream. When a finger is run across the back of the spatula, it will leave a well-defined track. An instant-read thermometer should read 170° to 180°F/77° to 82°C.

3) Immediately pour the mixture into the strainer, scraping up the thickened mixture that has settled on the bottom of the pan. Press it through the strainer and scrape any mixture clinging to the underside into the bowl.

4) Stir in the milk and vanilla. Cover and refrigerate for a minimum of 8 hours or until no warmer than 43°F/6°C. (Alternatively, cool in an ice water bath.) Set a covered storage container in the freezer.

5) Churn the brown sugar custard in a prechilled ice cream maker. Add the pecans during churning when the ice cream has reached the consistency of soft serve and begins to ball up around the dasher. Transfer the ice cream to the chilled container. Press a piece of plastic wrap on the surface of the ice cream, cover the container, and allow the ice cream to firm in the freezer for at least 4 hours before serving.

STORE Covered storage container: frozen, 3 days

MAPLE CANDIED WALNUT ICE CREAM

Makes: A generous 5 cups/1.2 liters

My first taste of real maple syrup was as a freshman at the University of Vermont when my Vermont boyfriend had me taste the sap from the tree. He also took me to a sugaring house to watch the syrup being boiled and thickened. I loved the flavor of maple so much, we would carry a little can of it into ice cream parlors to top our ice cream.

The Candied Walnuts can be made up to 1 week ahead.

MAPLE CANDIED WALNUTS

Makes: 150 grams/1 cup

walnut halves or pieces	100 grams	1 cup
dark amber grade B maple syrup	56 grams	2 tablespoons plus 2 teaspoons (40 ml)

✿ Set a piece of parchment on the counter.

1) Chop the walnuts coarsely.

2) In a small sauté pan or saucepan, over low heat, combine the maple syrup and walnuts. Use a silicone spatula to stir and coat the walnuts with the maple syrup. Heat the mixture until the maple syrup starts to bubble, stirring constantly. Allow it to simmer for about 2 minutes, continuing to stir, until the nuts absorb all of the maple syrup.

3) Transfer the walnuts to the parchment, separating them into a single layer. Allow them to air dry for about 1 hour. Separate any of the nuts that stick together.

The maple candied walnuts will keep, airtight, for 1 week at room temperature.

Continued

ICE CREAM BASE

dark amber grade B maple syrup	168 grams	½ cup (118 ml)
7 (to 11) large egg yolks (see page xxxii)	130 grams	½ cup (118 ml)
milk	242 grams	1 cup (237 ml)
sugar	50 grams	¼ cup
glucose or reduced corn syrup (see page xxi)	42 grams	2 tablespoons (30 ml)
fine sea salt	.	a pinch
heavy cream	290 grams	1¼ cups (296 ml)
Maple Candied Walnuts	138 grams	¾ cup plus 2 tablespoons

✣ Have ready a fine-mesh strainer suspended over a medium bowl containing the maple syrup.

1) In a medium saucepan, with a silicone spatula, stir together the egg yolks and milk until well blended. Stir in the sugar, glucose, and salt until the sugar has dissolved.

2) Heat the mixture on medium-low, stirring, until slightly thicker than heavy cream. When a finger is run across the back of the spatula, it will leave a well-defined track. An instant-read thermometer should read 170° to 180°F/77° to 82°C.

3) Immediately pour the mixture into the strainer, scraping up the thickened mixture that has settled on the bottom of the pan. Press it through the strainer and scrape any mixture clinging to the underside into the bowl.

4) Stir the maple syrup into the custard mixture until well blended. Then stir in the cream. Cover and refrigerate for a minimum of 8 hours or until no warmer than 43°F/6°C. (Alternatively, cool in an ice water bath.) Set a covered storage container in the freezer.

5) Churn the maple custard in a prechilled ice cream maker. During churning, when the ice cream has reached the consistency of soft serve and begins to ball up around the dasher, remove the dasher and use a large spoon or spatula to fold in the nuts. Transfer the ice cream to the chilled container. Press a piece of plastic wrap on the surface of the ice cream, cover the container, and allow the ice cream to firm in the freezer for at least 4 hours before serving.

STORE

Covered storage container: frozen, 3 days

SCOOPS

✣ If desired, top each serving with extra maple syrup to taste.

PISTACHIO ICE CREAM

Makes: About 5 cups/1.2 liters

Pistachio nuts and paste vary widely in quality, so the flavor can be very elusive. It is, therefore, only worth making with the best pistachio paste from Sicily. The pistachios are blanched so the color of the ice cream will be a lovely pale green. The oil contained in the pistachios contributes to the ice cream's voluptuous creaminess.

My favorite pistachio paste is from Agrimontana, which is made from 100% Sicilian pistachios. If using another product, if no percentage is listed on the label, it is likely to be lower, so add it to taste.

ICE CREAM BASE

100% pistachio paste (see Scoops)	112 grams	½ cup
6 (to 9) large egg yolks (see page xxxii)	112 grams	¼ cup plus 3 tablespoons (104 ml)
milk	242 grams	1 cup (237 ml)
heavy cream	464 grams	2 cups (473 ml), *divided*
sugar	150 grams	¾ cup
glucose or reduced corn syrup (see page xxi)	42 grams	2 tablespoons (30 ml)
fine sea salt	.	a pinch

✣ Have ready a fine-mesh strainer suspended over a medium bowl containing the pistachio paste.

1) In a medium saucepan, with a silicone spatula, stir together the egg yolks, milk, and 116 grams/½ cup/118 ml of the cream until well blended. Stir in the sugar, glucose, and salt until the sugar has dissolved.

2) Heat the mixture on medium-low, stirring constantly, until slightly thicker than heavy cream; when a finger is run across the back of the spatula, it will

Continued

leave a well-defined track. An instant read thermometer should read 170° to 180°F/77° to 82°C.

3) Immediately remove the pan from the heat and pour the mixture into the strainer, scraping up the thickened mixture that has settled on the bottom of the pan. Press it through the strainer and scrape any mixture clinging to the underside into the bowl. Wipe out the strainer and set it on top of another medium bowl.

4) Whisk the pistachio paste into the custard mixture until well blended. Then press it through the strainer and scrape any mixture clinging to the underside into the bowl.

5) Pour the remaining cream (348 grams/1½ cups/355 ml) through the strainer and stir it into the custard mixture. Cover and refrigerate for a minimum of 8 hours or until no warmer than 43°F/6°C. (Alternatively, cool in an ice water bath.) Set a covered storage container in the freezer.

6) Churn the pistachio custard in a prechilled ice cream maker. Transfer the ice cream to the chilled container. Press a piece of plastic wrap on top, cover it, and allow it to firm in the freezer for about 4 hours before serving.

STORE Covered storage container: frozen, 3 days

SCOOPS

❋ Be sure to stir the pistachio paste before weighing or measuring it to integrate the oil that separates and comes to the top.

❋ For extra texture and flavor, add about 75 grams/½ cup of unsalted pistachio nuts, chopped medium-coarse, during churning when the ice cream has reached the consistency of soft serve and begins to ball up around the dasher.

FLUFFY NOUGAT ICE CREAM

Makes: About 1.7 quarts/1.6 liters

Like the Lemon Ginger Ice Cream on page 117, this is another amazing ice cream that is easy to make, doesn't require an ice cream maker, and has a billowy, creamy, and never icy texture. The flavors of toasted almonds and your favorite honey are satisfying on their own, but a sprinkling of grated chocolate or a drizzle of chocolate ganache can add a pleasing extra dimension. I also like to add pistachios for their softer texture, subtle flavor, and beautiful color.

ICE CREAM BASE

2 large egg whites	60 grams	¼ cup (59 ml)
cream of tartar	.	¼ teaspoon
slivered almonds	60 grams	½ cup
blanched pistachio nuts (optional)	28 grams	3 tablespoons
heavy cream	348 grams	1½ cups (355 ml)
pure vanilla extract	.	½ teaspoon (2.5 ml)
pure almond extract	.	¼ teaspoon (1.2 ml)
superfine sugar	175 grams	¾ cup plus 2 tablespoons
honey	112 grams	⅓ cup (79 ml)
water	59 grams	¼ cup (59 ml)

PREHEAT THE OVEN

✲ Twenty minutes or longer before baking, set an oven rack at the middle level. Set the oven at 350°F/175°C.

✲ At least 30 minutes and up to 1 hour ahead, weigh or measure the egg whites and cream of tartar into a stand mixer bowl. Cover the bowl.

✲ Toast the Almonds: Set the almonds on a baking sheet and bake for about 7 minutes, or until light to medium brown. Stir once or twice to ensure even toasting. Allow them to cool completely. Then coarsely chop the almonds and the pistachios, if using.

❊ In a chilled metal bowl, pour the cream and the extracts and refrigerate, covered, for at least 15 minutes. Chill a handheld mixer's beaters alongside the bowl.

1) In a medium saucepan, with a silicone spatula, stir together the sugar, honey, and water. Continue stirring, on medium heat, until it comes to a boil. Then lower the heat and simmer for 2 minutes. An instant-read thermometer should read 230°F/110°C.

2) While the syrup is simmering, attach the whisk beater to the stand mixer. Beat the egg whites and cream of tartar until stiff peaks form when the beater is raised.

3) On low speed, add the hot syrup to the egg whites, avoiding the whisk. Then turn the mixer to high, and beat until very thick, 7 to 10 minutes.

4) Using the chilled hand mixer, whip the cream to soft peaks.

5) Scrape the whipped cream into the meringue. Add the nuts and fold the mixture until evenly incorporated. Then use a large silicone spatula to reach to the bottom of the bowl.

6) Transfer the ice cream to a covered storage container. Press a piece of plastic wrap on the surface of the ice cream, cover the container, and allow the ice cream to firm in the freezer for about 6 hours before serving (or 3 hours if you like it semifreddo, or soft serve).

STORE Covered storage container: frozen, 1 week

NOCCIOLA ICE CREAM

Makes: About 5 cups/1.2 liters

Nocciola is the word for hazelnut in Italian. Nocciola ice cream is made with praline paste, which is hazelnut and sometimes part almond, processed with caramelized sugar. Commercial praline pastes vary in the percentage of sugar, between 20% and 50%, depending on whether the sugar is caramelized and whether the nuts used are all hazelnut or part almond, which gives a more subtle flavor. The best praline paste I've found is the Agrimontana brand from Italy, which is 60% Piedmontese hazelnuts with 40% caramelized sugar. You can also make your own praline paste, using the recipe that follows. It will have a slightly crunchy texture and will be just as delicious, especially if you use the most flavorful hazelnuts, which are from the Piedmont region of Italy. They are available from Gustiamo. (For Agrimontana praline paste and Gustiamo, see Ingredients, page xxxiv.)

This is a creamy, dense, and delicious ice cream. It freezes very hard but has a terrific texture if allowed to soften before serving. A hot fudge topping would enhance the praline flavor.

ICE CREAM BASE

Praline Paste (recipe follows; see Scoops)	200 grams	¾ cup
7 (to 11) large egg yolks (see page xxxii)	130 grams	½ cup (118 ml)
milk	242 grams	1 cup (237 ml)
heavy cream	464 grams	2 cups (473 ml), *divided*
sugar	150 grams	¾ cup
glucose or reduced corn syrup (see page xxi)	42 grams	2 tablespoons (30 ml)
fine sea salt	.	a pinch
pure vanilla extract	.	1 teaspoon (5 ml)

✽ Have ready a fine-mesh strainer suspended over a medium bowl containing the praline paste.

Continued

1) In a small saucepan, with a silicone spatula, stir together the egg yolks, milk, 116 grams/½ cup/118 ml of the cream, and the sugar until well blended. Stir in the glucose and salt until the sugar has dissolved.

2) Heat the mixture on medium-low, stirring constantly, until slightly thicker than heavy cream. When a finger is run across the back of the spatula, it will leave a well-defined track. An instant-read thermometer should read 170° to 180°F/77° to 82°C.

3) Immediately pour the mixture into the strainer, scraping up the thickened mixture that has settled on the bottom of the pan. Press it through the strainer and scrape any mixture clinging to the underside into the bowl.

4) Whisk the praline paste into the custard mixture until well blended. Then whisk in the remaining cream (348 grams/1½ cups/355 ml) and the vanilla. Cover and refrigerate for a minimum of 8 hours or until no warmer than 43°F/6°C. (Alternatively, cool in an ice water bath.) Set a covered storage container in the freezer.

5) Churn the praline custard in a prechilled ice cream maker. Transfer the ice cream to the chilled container. Press a piece of plastic wrap on the surface of the ice cream, cover the container, and allow the ice cream to firm in the freezer for at least 4 hours before serving.

STORE Covered storage container: frozen, 3 days

SCOOPS

✣ Hazelnuts are very high in oil and can become rancid, so be sure to taste before using them and store them in the refrigerator or freezer.

✣ My homemade praline paste is 77% hazelnut and 23% sugar, compared to the 60% hazelnut and 40% sugar in the Agrimontana praline paste, so if using the Agrimontana in the base, you will need to use 260 to 272 grams/about 1 cup, and only 90 grams/about 7 tablespoons of sugar.

PRALINE PASTE

Makes: About 274 grams/1 cup plus 1 tablespoon

water	710 grams	3 cups (710 ml)
baking soda	60 grams	¼ cup
hazelnuts	213 grams	1½ cups
sugar	67 grams	⅓ cup
canola or safflower oil	11 grams	2½ teaspoons (12.5 ml)

PREHEAT THE OVEN

❋ Twenty minutes or longer before baking, set an oven rack at the middle level. Set the oven to 350°F/175°C.

❋ Have ready a colander placed in the sink, and a large bowl filled halfway with cold water.

REMOVE THE HAZELNUT SKINS

1) In a 3 quart/3 liter saucepan, bring the water to a boil. Remove it from the heat and stir in the baking soda. The water will bubble vigorously. Add the hazelnuts and return the pan to the heat. Boil the nuts for 3 minutes. The water will turn a deep maroon from the color of the skins. Test a nut by running it under cold water. The skin should slip off easily. If not, boil for a couple of minutes longer.

2) Pour the nuts into the colander and rinse them under cold running water. Transfer the nuts to the bowl of cold water. Use both your hands to slide off the skins underwater, scraping lightly in places if necessary. As each one is peeled, set it on a clean towel to dry.

TOAST THE HAZELNUTS

3) Set the hazelnuts on the baking sheet and bake for 15 to 20 minutes, or until the oil rises to the surface and they become slightly shiny and golden brown. Shake the pan once or twice to ensure even toasting. Set the baking sheet on a wire rack. If not using the Silpat, transfer the nuts to the second baking sheet.

Continued

SPECIAL EQUIPMENT

One baking sheet, no preparation needed or topped with Silpat (if not using the Silpat, a second baking sheet topped with aluminum foil and lightly coated with nonstick cooking spray)

MAKE THE PRALINE POWDER

4) To ensure complete removal of the caramel, lightly coat the sides of a small saucepan, preferably nonstick, with nonstick cooking spray. Also coat a silicone spatula and wipe off any excess with a paper towel. Add the sugar and heat on medium-low, stirring constantly, until the sugar melts and starts to darken. Lower the heat to low and continue stirring until the syrup starts to caramelize to deep amber. Take it off the heat before it gets too dark as it will continue to darken very quickly.

5) Immediately pour the caramel over the nuts on the sheet; use the spatula, if necessary, to scrape it all out of the pan. Let it harden completely, 15 to 30 minutes.

6) Remove the praline from the sheet and break it into several pieces. Process the praline in a food processor until it is as fine as possible. Add the oil and process until the praline begins to come together and form a paste, scraping down the sides of the bowl as needed.

7) Weigh or measure out 200 grams/¾ cup of the praline.

STORE Airtight: refrigerated, up to 6 months; frozen, over 1 year

SCOOPS

✻ Coating the saucepan and spatula with nonstick cooking spray helps greatly to ensure getting all of the caramel onto the nuts. Without it you will lose quite a bit that sticks to the sides of the pan and spatula.

✻ The caramel is poured over the nuts to make a thinner layer, which is easier to process.

TRUE COCONUT ICE CREAM

Makes: 1 generous quart/1 generous liter

I came really close to giving up on this ice cream because the flavor was too subtle. Then I remembered that cream of coconut, produced from the pulp of the coconut, has a much deeper coconut flavor than coconut milk because it has much less added water. It also has quite a bit of sugar and coconut oil, so I used unsweetened coconut to steep in the milk, and added more milk in proportion to cream to lower the fat content. The lovely creamy consistency is in good part due to the guar gum contained in the cream of coconut. Only a whisper of vanilla is needed to heighten the flavor without overpowering it. An optional sprinkle of toasted coconut adds a delightful crunch.

ICE CREAM BASE

milk	363 grams	1½ cups (355 ml)
nonfat dry milk	21 grams	3 tablespoons
unsweetened shredded coconut	100 grams	1¼ cups
cream of coconut, well stirred	288 grams	½ cup (118 ml)
6 (to 9) large egg yolks (see page xxxii)	112 grams	¼ cup plus 3 tablespoons (104 ml)
glucose or reduced corn syrup (see page xxi)	42 grams	2 tablespoons (30 ml)
fine sea salt	.	a pinch
heavy cream	348 grams	1½ cups (355 ml)
pure vanilla extract	.	¼ teaspoon (1.2 ml)

1) In a medium saucepan, with a silicone spatula, stir together the milk and dry milk. Bring it to a boil, stirring constantly, and simmer for 2 minutes. Remove it from the heat and add the shredded coconut. Cover and let it steep at room temperature for 1 to 1½ hours.

2) Scrape the cream of coconut into a medium saucepan. With a silicone spatula, stir in the egg yolks. Then stir in the glucose and salt. Set a fine-mesh

Continued

strainer over the pan and pour the shredded coconut and milk mixture into it. Squeeze all the liquid from the coconut and discard the coconut. Set the strainer over a medium bowl. Stir the coconut mixture until well blended.

3) Heat the mixture on medium-low, stirring constantly, until slightly thicker than heavy cream. When a finger is run across the back of the spatula, it will leave a well-defined track. An instant-read thermometer should read 170° to 180°F/77° to 82°C.

4) Immediately pour the mixture into the strainer, scraping up the thickened mixture that has settled on the bottom of the pan. Press it through the strainer and scrape any mixture clinging to the underside into the bowl.

5) Stir in the heavy cream and vanilla. Cover and refrigerate for a minimum of 8 hours or until no warmer than 43°F/6°C. (Alternatively, cool in an ice water bath.) Set a covered storage container in the freezer.

6) Churn the coconut custard in a prechilled ice cream maker. Transfer the ice cream to the chilled container. Press a piece of plastic wrap on the surface of the ice cream, cover the container, and allow the ice cream to firm in the freezer for at least 4 hours before serving.

STORE Covered storage container: frozen, 3 days

TOASTED COCONUT TOPPING

Makes: 68 grams/rounded ¾ cup

sweetened flaked coconut	84 grams	1 cup

✢ Spread the coconut in a thin layer on a baking sheet. In a preheated 350°F/175°C oven, toast the coconut for 7 to 10 minutes, stirring often, until lightly browned.

STORE Airtight: room temperature, 3 weeks

TOPPINGS, ADORNMENTS, AND ADD-INS FOR ICE CREAM

These are all my favorite additions and toppings for ice cream, but most can also be used to top cakes or pastries. They range from chocolate butterscotch toffee add-ins to fruit toppings, hot fudge, and citrus stardust. Mix and match to your heart's content.

My preference is to use ¾ to 1 cup of add-ins per quart/liter of ice cream. And when adding fluid ingredients such as dulce de leche, pomegranate syrup, or melted jelly or jam, the ice cream needs to be churned fully but soft enough to spread. I like to add zigzag lines of a fluid add-in (as described on page 172) rather than swirling it into the ice cream so that it doesn't mix into the ice cream base. Then, when scooping it into serving bowls, the swirls are more distinct. When adding jelly or jam, such as in the Pure Peanut Butter Ice Cream (page 145), different brands will vary in consistency, so if it seems a bit thin, it may work best to boil it for a few minutes before straining it.

Any leftover add-ins can be passed in a pitcher or small bowl to use as a topping.

The technique of integrating add-ins varies according to the consistency and type. Some fluid add-ins are piped and others are spread. Delicate fruits such as brandied cherries are folded in, while nuts can be stirred into a fully churned base. The consistency of the churned base will sometimes be specified as soft serve, and other times as slightly firmer and beginning to ball up around the dasher. Other ice creams are described just as "churned," which means to a hard consistency.

Please Note: Since so many of these recipes are sauces, whipped cream, or chips, for the yield, I have listed the volume before the weight because it's easier to determine how many spoonfuls you might want to make.

ADDING SWIRLS

To add distinct swirls of fluid ingredients, use a 9 by 5 inch loaf pan, preferably Pyrex, to store the ice cream. (Set it in the freezer for a minimum of 30 minutes before adding the ice cream.) Put the swirl in a disposable piping bag or quart-size reclosable freezer bag. Cut off a semicircle from the point of the bag and close it with a binder clamp until ready to pipe. (Alternatively, you can use a spoon, but it's easier and faster with a piping bag.)

Pipe about one-third of the swirl in zigzags onto the bottom of the pan. Spread about one-third of the ice cream on top. Quickly pipe more zigzags on top, using about half of the remaining swirl. Repeat with another one-third of the ice cream and then the remaining swirl. Top with the remaining ice cream.

CRÈME FRAÎCHE

Makes: 2 cups plus 2 tablespoons/503 ml/494 grams

Crème fraîche can be used in place of heavy cream in ice creams where a subtle tang would be desirable. Commercial brands, such as Vermont Creamery, are an excellent choice, but you can easily make your own. It is, however, more difficult than ever to find cream that has not been ultra pasteurized, so it will take longer to thicken and the flavor will not be quite as lilting.

For the best results, use a high butterfat cream (see page xxxii for how to determine the fat content). Crème fraîche takes 12 to 14 hours for the cream to thicken when made with cream that is pasteurized. If ultra pasteurized it can take as long as 36 hours.

| heavy cream | 464 grams | 2 cups (473 ml) |
| buttermilk | 30 grams | 2 tablespoons (30 ml) |

1) In a canning jar or jar with a tight fitting lid, stir together the cream and buttermilk.

2) Place the jar in a warm spot, such as the top of the refrigerator or near the cooktop, and allow it to sit undisturbed until thickened but still pourable. It will continue to thicken on chilling.

STORE Airtight: refrigerated, 3 weeks

CHOCOLATE "CHIPS"

Chocolate curls or thickly grated chocolate flakes provide the ideal texture for using in ice cream and are a great complement to many different flavors. When stirred in, they break up into smaller pieces to form delicate chips that won't overwhelm the flavor of the ice cream.

For 1 quart/1 liter of ice cream, add up to 128 grams/1½ cups of the chips.

1) To produce thick enough curls or pieces, the chocolate needs to be softened slightly. Set a block of chocolate, about 3 inches square, in a warm place, such as under a lamp, or heat it in a microwave using 3-second bursts, turning it over several times. Hold the chocolate block in a towel when curling or grating it to help keep it from melting in your hand.

2) To make chocolate curls, use a sharp vegetable peeler. Hold it against the upper edge of the chocolate block. Dig the upper edge of the peeler into the chocolate and pull it toward you. To grate the chocolate, use the large holes of a box grater.

3) In either case, allow the chocolate to fall onto a parchment-lined baking sheet. Refrigerate the chocolate, covered, until it is firm. Then transfer it to a covered container and keep it chilled until ready to add it to the ice cream.

4) Add the chocolate during churning when the ice cream mixture has reached the consistency of soft serve and begins to ball up around the dasher. If using chocolate curls, add them to the mixture and continue spinning just until they are mixed in. If using grated chocolate, remove the dasher and mix them in gently with a spatula.

STORE Airtight: cool room temperature, several weeks (If there is a wide fluctuation in temperature, it is best to freeze them to avoid "bloom," the grayish color that results from cocoa butter rising to the surface.)

BUTTERSCOTCH CHOCOLATE TOFFEE

Makes: 454 grams/1 pound

OVEN TEMPERATURE:
350°F/175°C

BAKING TIME:
7 to 9 minutes

SPECIAL EQUIPMENT

One 17¼ by 12¼ by 1 inch half sheet pan topped with Silpat, or a nonstick or buttered cookie sheet

An instant-read thermometer

Toffee is my favorite candy, so how could I resist not offering my favorite version for adding to ice cream? Heath bars make a fine substitute.

I find that the toffee contrasts best with vanilla or coffee ice cream. This recipe makes a lot more than is needed for a quart/liter of ice cream, but it stores well in an airtight container for as long as a month if you can manage not to polish it off well before then!

unsalted butter	113 grams	8 tablespoons (1 stick)
dark chocolate, 53% to 70% cacao, coarsely chopped	170 grams (6 ounces)	about 1 cup
sliced almonds, preferably blanched	175 grams	1¾ cups, *divided*
light brown Muscovado sugar or dark brown sugar	270 grams	1¼ cups, firmly packed
corn syrup	82 grams	¼ cup (59 ml)
water	30 grams	2 tablespoons (30 ml)
pure vanilla extract	.	1 teaspoon (5 ml)
baking soda	2.7 grams	½ teaspoon

PREHEAT THE OVEN

✳ Twenty minutes or longer before baking, set an oven rack at the middle level. Set the oven at 350°F/175°C.

✳ About 1 hour ahead, set the butter on the counter at room temperature (65° to 75°F/18° to 24°C).

✳ In a food processor, finely process the chocolate (or finely chop it by hand) and transfer it to a bowl.

✳ Toast the Almonds: Spread the almonds evenly on a baking sheet and bake for 7 to 9 minutes, or until medium-gold. Stir a few times to ensure even toasting and avoid overbrowning. Allow them to cool completely.

In the food processor, process the almonds until medium-fine. Remove the blade and sprinkle half of the ground almonds over a roughly 10 by 12 inch oval on the prepared sheet pan. Set it near the cooktop.

MAKE THE TOFFEE

1) In a medium heavy saucepan, preferably nonstick, lightly coated with nonstick cooking spray, using a wooden spatula or spoon, stir together the brown sugar, corn syrup, butter, and water. (Do not use a silicone spatula unless it has a wooden handle.) Over medium heat, bring the mixture to a boil, stirring constantly. Continue boiling, stirring gently, until an instant-read thermometer reaches 285°F/140°C. Immediately remove the saucepan from the heat. The temperature should continue to rise to 290°F/143°C, which is the ideal temperature.

2) Immediately stir in the vanilla and baking soda. Stir well to distribute the baking soda. The mixture will be lighter in color.

COAT THE TOFFEE

3) Pour the toffee mixture over the almonds. If needed, spread it with the back of a silicone spatula to cover the almonds and to make it even.

4) Immediately scatter the chocolate over the hot toffee.

5) As soon as the chocolate starts to melt, use a long metal spatula, preferably offset, to spread the chocolate in an even layer over the surface of the toffee.

6) Sprinkle the remaining almonds on top of the melted chocolate and use a small offset spatula to move them gently into an even layer.

7) Refrigerate for 40 minutes to 1 hour, or until cool and the chocolate is set.

8) Break or cut about one-third of the toffee into small (about ¼ inch) irregular pieces to yield 140 grams/1 cup. During churning, when the ice cream mixture reaches the consistency of soft serve and begins to ball up around the dasher, gradually add the toffee. (Alternatively, remove the dasher and fold in the toffee.) Break or cut the remaining toffee into larger pieces for munching, or into small pieces for future batches of ice cream.

STORE Airtight: room temperature, 1 month (After 1 month it is still delicious, but the sugar may start to crystallize.)

SCOOPS

❋ An instant-read thermometer is essential for this recipe because the correct temperature is critical to achieve the ideal texture.

❋ The higher the temperature of the finished toffee mixture, the crunchier the texture, but too high and it will taste burnt and have a crumbly texture. The purpose of the corn syrup is to help ensure a smooth texture.

CHOCOLATE WAFERS

Makes: Twenty-six 2 inch square wafers

OVEN TEMPERATURE:
350°F/175°C

BAKING TIME:
16 to 20 minutes for each of two batches

SPECIAL EQUIPMENT

Two 16 by 12 inch cookie sheets, lined with parchment

These cookies are crunchy around the edges with fudgy centers. They are wonderful to use for Cookies 'n' Cream Ice Cream (see page 180), where they stay crunchy and chewy in the ice cream even after storing in the freezer. They are also fantastic for making into bourbon balls for Bust My Bourbon Balls Ice Cream (page 7). They make more than double what you will need but are delicious to eat on their own and will also keep frozen for many months for future batches of ice cream. (A smaller batch of dough is difficult to mix.)

Plan Ahead Make the dough a minimum of 4 hours before rolling it.

DOUGH

Makes: 370 grams (322 grams baked)

unsalted butter	43 grams	3 tablespoons
1½ large egg whites	44 grams	3 tablespoons (45 ml)
bleached all-purpose flour	86 grams	⅔ cup (lightly spooned into the cup and leveled off) plus 2 teaspoons
unsweetened alkalized cocoa powder	42 grams	½ cup plus 1 tablespoon (sifted before measuring)
fine sea salt	.	⅛ teaspoon
light brown sugar, preferably Muscovado	81 grams	¼ cup plus 2 tablespoons, firmly packed
granulated sugar	75 grams	¼ cup plus 2 tablespoons
pure vanilla extract	.	1 teaspoon (5 ml)

✴ About 1 hour ahead, set the butter on the counter at room temperature (65° to 75°F/18° to 24°C), and into a 1 cup/237 ml glass measure with a spout, weigh or measure the egg whites.

MAKE THE DOUGH

1) In a medium bowl, whisk together the flour, cocoa, and salt.

2) In the bowl of a stand mixer fitted with the flat beater, beat the sugars, butter, and vanilla on medium speed until well mixed and lightened in color, about 5 minutes, scraping the bowl occasionally.

3) Gradually add the egg whites and beat until smoothly incorporated, about 30 seconds. Scrape down the sides of the bowl.

4) Add the flour mixture. Mix on low speed for 30 seconds, or until incorporated.

5) Scrape the dough onto a piece of plastic wrap and overlap both ends loosely to cover the dough, then press it into a rectangle. Divide the dough in half (185 grams each). Wrap each piece of dough in plastic wrap and set them on a small baking sheet.

6) Refrigerate the dough until it is firm, about 4 hours or overnight. The dough should be firm enough to roll but still pliant.

PREHEAT THE OVEN

✲ Twenty minutes or longer before baking, set an oven rack at the middle level. Set the oven at 350°F/175°C.

ROLL THE DOUGH

7) Set one piece of the dough on a lightly floured sheet of plastic wrap. Lightly flour the dough and cover it with a second sheet of plastic wrap. Roll the dough into a ¼ inch thick rectangle 10 inches by 6 inches, using a bench scraper butted up against the edges to keep the sides even. To make cutting easier, slide the shaped dough on the plastic wrap onto a baking sheet and set it in the freezer for about 5 minutes.

8) With a pizza wheel or chef's knife, cut the dough into roughly 2 inch squares. Any irregular shapes can be baked alongside the squares.

9) Use a thin pancake turner to set the dough squares a minimum of 1 inch apart on a cookie sheet. With a fork, pierce each one several times to prevent excess puffing.

Continued

BAKE THE WAFERS

10) Bake the wafers for 8 minutes. Rotate the cookie sheet halfway around. Continue baking for 8 to 12 minutes, or until the wafers are firm and slightly puffed, but still a little soft.

11) While the first batch is baking, roll and cut the wafers for the second batch.

COOL THE WAFERS

12) Set the cookie sheet on a wire rack and let the wafers cool completely.

13) Bake and cool the second batch of wafers.

STORE Airtight: room temperature, 7 days; refrigerated, 2 weeks; frozen, 3 months

COOKIES 'N' CREAM ICE CREAM

These wafer cookies are a great addition to many ice creams including vanilla, chocolate, coffee, cherry, nocciola—you choose!

Break up the wafers into no larger than ½ inch pieces. You will need about 100 grams/1 cup. Store them in the freezer and add them to the ice cream during churning, when it has reached the consistency of soft serve and begins to ball up around the dasher.

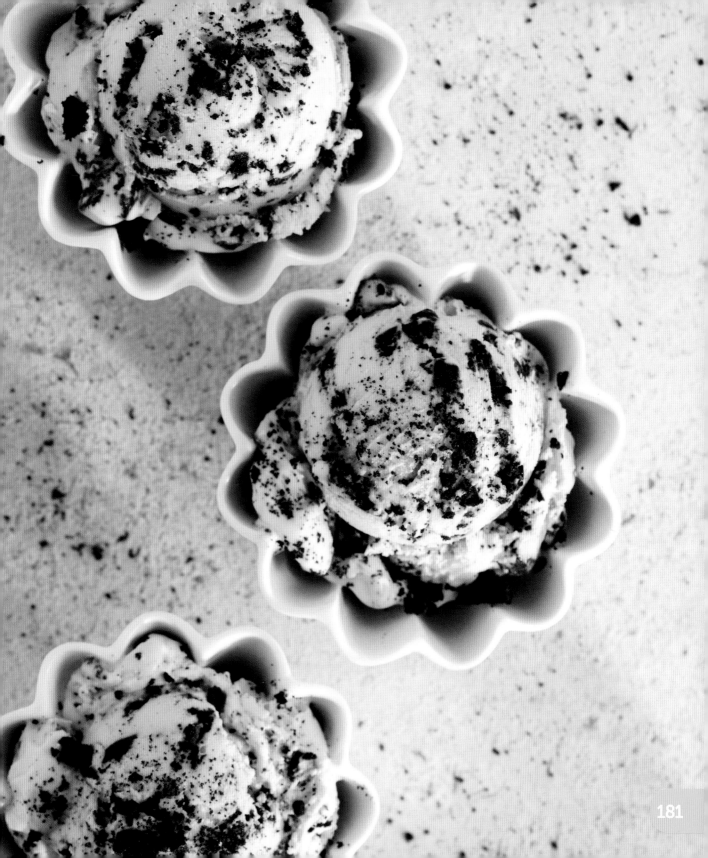

BOURBON BALLS

Makes: Eleven 1¼ inch balls

These no-bake cookies are one of my most requested recipes around the holidays and make a splendid ice cream add-in. The combination of chocolate, pecans, and bourbon marries magnificently with pumpkin, vanilla, caramel, and chocolate ice creams. The balls break up readily into fudgy little morsels as they are stirred into the ice cream base. You will need about 8 bourbon balls/160 grams for 1 quart/1 liter ice cream.

Plan Ahead Make a minimum of 1 day or up to 6 weeks ahead.

DOUGH

Makes: 225 grams

chocolate wafers, preferably homemade (page 178)	100 grams	1 cup broken into pieces or ¾ cup loosely packed crumbs
pecan halves	37 grams	¼ cup plus 2 tablespoons
powdered sugar	35 grams	¼ cup (lightly spooned into the cup and leveled off) plus 1 tablespoon
unsweetened alkalized cocoa powder	12 grams	2 tablespoons plus 2 teaspoons (sifted before measuring)
unsalted butter, cold	14 grams	1 tablespoon
corn syrup	21 grams	1 tablespoon (15 ml)
bourbon, preferably Maker's Mark	15 grams	1 tablespoon (15 ml)

MAKE THE DOUGH

FOOD PROCESSOR METHOD

1) In a food processor or blender (in several batches), pulverize the cookies into fine crumbs. Empty them into a medium bowl.

2) Process the pecans with the powdered sugar and cocoa until finely ground.

3) Cut the butter into 2 pieces and add it and the corn syrup. Process until combined.

4) Add this mixture to the cookie crumbs and, with your fingers or a wooden spoon, mix until evenly incorporated.

HAND METHOD

1) Smash the wafers into crumbs by placing them in a plastic bag and rolling with a rolling pin. Transfer them to a medium bowl.

2) Using a nut grater, finely grate the pecans.

3) Sift the powdered sugar and cocoa into the bowl with the cookie crumbs. Add the butter, nuts, and corn syrup.

4) With a wooden spoon, stir the mixture until uniform in consistency.

BOTH METHODS

MIX IN THE BOURBON

5) Add the bourbon to the cookie crumb mixture. With a wooden spoon, stir the mixture until it is uniform in consistency and begins to clean the bowl. Add a teaspoon at a time of extra bourbon if the mixture is too dry to hold together.

6) Let the mixture sit for 30 minutes to absorb evenly. Add more bourbon if needed.

ROLL THE BOURBON BALLS

7) Scoop out level tablespoons (20 grams each) of the mixture, then press and roll them between the palms of your hands to shape into 1¼ inch balls.

8) Place the bourbon balls in an airtight container lined with a paper towel or crumpled parchment.

STORE Airtight: room temperature, 6 weeks

FRESH FRUIT AS AN ADORNMENT

In summer, when fresh berries and fruit abound, I love to serve them with ice cream. The first of the season is rhubarb, which I make into a compote. Of course it makes a perfect complement to strawberry or raspberry ice cream. Cherries, both sweet and sour, I poach and brandy to fold into vanilla or chocolate ice cream. Strawberries are best cut in half or quarters or even slices and sprinkled lightly with sugar, a simple process known as maceration that heightens the flavor of the fruit. Peaches are a dream, sliced and sprinkled with sugar and sometimes a little brandy.

Redcap, aka thimble, berries, which I find on the back roads near my home, I sprinkle lightly with sugar, then let sit for 30 minutes to an hour. I drain the juices into a glass measure with a spout that has been lightly coated with nonstick cooking spray, and reduce the juices in a microwave until thickened. I spoon the juice and the fruit into ice cream bowls and top them with ice cream.

SOFT CANDIED GRAPEFRUIT PEEL CHANTERELLE

Makes: About 30 slices

When I lived within walking distance of David and Karen Waltuck's exquisite New York City restaurant Chanterelle, I fell in love with these candied peels and was overjoyed that they shared the recipe. What makes them so special is that Chef Waltuck leaves a thin layer of pulp on each strip of skin, so that they are moist and flavorful. They are also easy to make and will keep up to two days, but the flavor is best on the day they are made.

1 large grapefruit, preferably ruby red	340 grams	12 ounces
fine sea salt	3 grams	½ teaspoon
sugar	200 grams	1 cup, *divided*

1) Scrub the grapefruit with a little liquid dishwashing detergent and rinse well.

2) Cut the grapefruit into 8 wedges. With a grapefruit knife or sharp paring knife, cut away the peel, leaving ⅛ inch of pulp attached.

3) Cut the wedges of peel lengthwise into ½ inch slices.

4) In a medium saucepan, place the slices and cover them with cold water. Bring the water to a boil. Add the salt and continue boiling for 5 minutes.

5) Drain and rinse the grapefruit peels. Add fresh cold unsalted water again to cover and bring to a second boil. Boil for 5 minutes. Drain, rinse, and repeat boiling with fresh unsalted water. Drain well.

6) In a large skillet, place the grapefruit peels in a single layer and sprinkle with 100 grams/½ cup of the sugar. Cook over very low heat, uncovered, for 30 minutes, stirring occasionally, until translucent and all of the syrup has been absorbed.

Continued

7) Dry the grapefruit peels on a metal rack for 1 to 1½ hours. They should be quite dry so that they will absorb less sugar and retain a crunchy surface but still be succulent.

8) Roll each peel in the remaining 100 grams/½ cup of sugar until coated on all sides. Serve at once or layer between wax paper and refrigerate.

STORE Lightly covered: room temperature, 1 day; refrigerated, 2 days

SCOOPS

❊ Select grapefruits with thick rinds. The lighter the weight of the fruit, the thicker the rind. Fruit with pointier ends as opposed to rounded ends tend to have a thicker peel.

❊ Boiling the peels in several changes of water removes the bitterness.

❊ Thick-skinned oranges or lemons may be substituted for grapefruit.

❊ A few drops of liquid food color appropriate to the fruit, added during the third boil, will enhance the color.

CANDIED ORANGE PEEL

Makes: About 150 grams/About 1 cup chopped

The best candied orange peel I've ever encountered was when I went to Lyon, France, to translate Maurice and Jean-Jacques Bernachon's *La Passion du Chocolat*. The secret to the bright orange color and true orange flavor with a touch of bitterness is the process, which took 10 days of about 5 minutes work each day, and required a densimeter to determine the consistency of the syrup. The only time-consuming part was peeling the oranges and removing the bitter white pith beneath. Confectioner Jean-Jacques Bernachon liked to leave a little of the pith, but I prefer to remove as much as possible.

It took me 30 years to return to this recipe with a eureka moment: Instead of using a densimeter, why not use an instant-read thermometer, because surely temperature has a direct correlation to density/concentration. Yes! What is more, taking the temperature is a lot faster and easier than using the densimeter. After two tests I discovered that the final density of 1310 Baumé (a unit of relative density) is exactly 220°F/104°C! And that 8 to 9 days work just fine, bringing up the temperature by 1°F/0.5°C each day. The slow process enables the orange peel to absorb the syrup completely into its structure. The resulting candied peel is slightly chewy and totally superior to any commercial brand I have ever tasted. The strips make a delightful garnish for lemon or orange ice cream (page 119 or 121).

SPECIAL EQUIPMENT

One 17¼ by 12¼ by 1 inch half sheet pan

A large rack, lightly coated with nonstick cooking spray

An instant-read thermometer

2 large thick-skinned oranges	about 500 grams	about 1¼ pounds
water	500 grams	2 cups plus 2 tablespoons (500 ml)
sugar	375 grams	1¾ cups plus 2 tablespoons
1 vanilla bean, split lengthwise	.	.
glucose or reduced corn syrup (see page xxi)	21 grams	1 tablespoon (15 ml)

✤ Prepare an ice water bath (see page xvii).

1) Scrub the oranges with a little liquid dishwashing detergent and rinse them well.

2) Score the peel of each orange into six vertical pieces and remove the ovals of peel. Use a sharp paring knife to cut and scrape off as much of the white pith as possible.

3) Fill a medium nonreactive saucepan with water and bring to a boil. Add the orange peels and boil for 5 minutes.

4) Drain the orange peels and immediately add them to the ice water bath to set their color. Then drain them again.

5) In the same saucepan, stir together the 500 grams/2 cups plus 2 tablespoons/ 500 ml of water, the sugar, and vanilla bean. Over medium heat, bring it to a boil, stirring constantly.

6) Add the orange peels, swirling the pan without stirring, and boil for 5 minutes. Remove the pan from the heat, cover tightly, and set it aside for 3 to 4 hours.

7) Over medium-low heat, cook the orange peels, uncovered, for about 5 minutes, or until the instant-read thermometer registers 212°F/100°C. Remove the pan from the heat, cover tightly, and set it aside until the next day. When removing the cover, allow any condensation to fall back into the pot.

8) Continue cooking the orange peels over the next 7 or 8 days, each day bringing the temperature 1°F/0.5°C higher. This usually takes 1 to 2 minutes after the syrup reaches a boil. When the temperature reaches 218°F/103°C, add the glucose and swirl it in.

9) When the temperature reaches 220°F/104°C, remove the pan from the heat and cover tightly. Allow it to sit for 2 to 3 hours before draining the peels. Reserve the syrup to use for the Pomegranate Bourbon Sour (page 268) or to mix with a little triple sec or Grand Marnier and sprinkle on cakes.

10) Use tongs to arrange the peels in a single layer on the rack set over the sheet pan to catch any falling syrup. Set the pan in a warm area for several hours until the peels are barely sticky. A dehydrator set at 110° to 125°F/43° to 52°C or a warm oven (heated only by the pilot light or viewing light) will speed the process.

11) Use sharp kitchen scissors, lightly coated with nonstick cooking spray or oil, to cut the candied peel into long strips, about ¼ inch wide. Set them back

Continued

on the rack and continue to dry them for several hours until no longer sticky. They will still be flexible.

12) Transfer the dried candied peels to a canning jar or container with a tight fitting lid. On storage, a fine layer of sugar crystals will form on the outside of the peels, which adds a pleasant texture.

STORE Airtight: cool room temperature, 1 month; frozen, 6 months

SCOOPS

❊ Use a stainless steel, enamel, glass, or nonstick saucepan.

❊ When the syrup has reached 220°F/104°C, the density will be exactly the required 1310.

❊ Glucose helps prevent crystallization.

CITRUS STARDUST

Makes: 2 teaspoons/5 grams

This magical and delicious zest makes a lovely garnish for fruit ice creams, and also for plated desserts.

SPECIAL EQUIPMENT

A mortar and pestle or spice mill

A dehydrator (or oven with a pilot light or viewing light on)

superfine sugar		1 teaspoon
citrus zest, finely grated (from 1 to 5 medium lemons, limes, or oranges)	12 grams	2 tablespoons, loosely packed

1) In a small bowl, rub the sugar into the citrus zest. Spread the sugared zest in a thin layer on a plate. Place the plate in the dehydrator with its temperature set at 110° to 125°F/43° to 52°C (or in the oven, with the light on). Let the zest dry to the touch, about 4 hours, scraping the plate every hour to dislodge any zest stuck to the plate. (Alternatively, the zest can be dried at room temperature, which can take 12 to 16 hours.)

✲ Have ready a medium-mesh strainer suspended over a medium bowl.

2) Place the dried zest in the mortar and grind it, as much as possible, to a powder. Sift it into the medium bowl. Grind and sift the zest remaining in the strainer two more times. Pour the powdered zest into an airtight container. Save any larger flakes of zest in a separate container.

STORE Airtight: room temperature, 2 weeks; frozen, 6 months

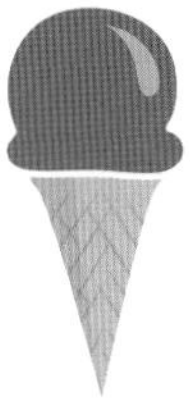

SCOOPS

✲ Be sure to scrub the fruit with a little liquid dishwashing detergent, rinse well, and dry before zesting.

AFFOGATO

My great-uncle Nat (inventor of the Movado Museum Watch), one day at a Friendly's Ice Cream Parlor in the Berkshires, introduced me to the concept of coffee poured over vanilla ice cream. Years later, when I saw the movie *Five Easy Pieces*, I was reminded of that afternoon when my uncle argued with the server that he did not want a whole cup of coffee—just a spoonful to pour over the ice cream. He had me try the result, explaining that just that little bit of coffee did amazing things to the ice cream. It was true. It wasn't until a few years ago that I discovered affogato—a shot of hot espresso poured over vanilla ice cream—when I was offered it as a dessert in an Italian restaurant. *Affogato* means "drowned," which was a far cry from Uncle Nat's more restrained concept.

And here is my still more deeply drowned version: I add a scoop of Dulce de Leche Ice Cream (page 17) to a glass of iced coffee.

This brings to mind my best ice cream soda: We had a major power outage that lasted for so many days that everything in my freezer thawed, including a container of commercial dulce de leche ice cream. I had several bottles of Perrier water left from another project. Inspiration struck and yes—the combination of melted ice cream and sparkling water was divine!

CARAMEL SAUCE

Makes: 1⅔ cups/394 ml/466 grams

Caramel sauce is a delicious topping for many ice creams, such as vanilla, banana, chocolate, and coffee, and, of course, is a classic topping for a sundae.

unsalted butter	43 grams	3 tablespoons
heavy cream	232 grams	1 cup (237 ml)
sugar	200 grams	1 cup
water	45 grams	3 tablespoons (45 ml)
corn syrup	62 grams	3 tablespoons (45 ml)
cream of tartar	.	⅜ teaspoon
pure vanilla extract	.	1 teaspoon (5 ml)

✣ About 30 minutes ahead, cut the butter into a few pieces and set it on the counter at room temperature (65° to 75°F/18° to 24°C).

✣ Have ready a 2 cup/473 ml glass measure with a spout, lightly coated with nonstick cooking spray.

1) Into a 1 cup/237 ml glass measure with a spout, weigh or measure the cream. Heat it in a microwave until hot and then cover it.

2) In a medium heavy saucepan, preferably nonstick, with a silicone spatula, stir together the sugar, water, corn syrup, and cream of tartar until all the sugar is moistened. Heat, stirring constantly, until the sugar has dissolved and the syrup is bubbling.

3) Stop stirring completely and allow the syrup to boil undisturbed until it turns a deep amber. (An instant-read thermometer should read 370°F/188°C.) Remove it immediately from the heat, or even slightly before it reaches that temperature, as the temperature will continue to rise, and just as soon as it reaches the correct temperature, pour in the hot cream. The mixture will bubble up furiously.

4) Use a clean silicone spatula to stir the mixture gently, scraping the thicker part that has settled on the bottom of the pan. If necessary, return it to very low heat, continuing to stir gently for 1 minute, until the mixture is uniform in color and the caramel has fully dissolved.

5) Remove the caramel from the heat and gently stir in the butter until incorporated. The mixture will be a little streaky but will become uniform once cooled and stirred.

6) Pour the caramel into the prepared glass measure and let it cool for 3 minutes. Gently stir in the vanilla and let it cool until room temperature, stirring it gently once or twice.

STORE Airtight: room temperature, 2 days; refrigerated, 2 weeks (Bring to room temperature before using.)

CHOCOLATE COLD SNAP TOPPING

Makes: Almost 1 cup/222 ml/232 grams

A crisp, paper-thin shell of bittersweet chocolate can be an enticing adornment to many flavors of ice cream, from dulce de leche to chocolate to black raspberry. There is something very pleasing about cracking through the fine coating and into the creamy ice cream.

| dark chocolate, preferably 62% cacao, coarsely chopped | 128 grams (4.5 ounces) | about ¾ cup |
| coconut oil or neutral-tasting vegetable oil (see Scoops) | 104 grams | ½ cup (118 ml) |

SCOOPS

❖ Expeller-pressed (chemical-free) refined coconut oil, designated for high heat cooking, is the best choice. It will harden on top of the ice cream a lot faster than vegetable oils.

1) In a 2 cup/473 ml glass measure with a spout, combine the chopped chocolate and coconut oil. In a microwave, stirring with a silicone spatula every 15 seconds, heat the chocolate and coconut oil until completely melted and smoothly combined. (Alternatively, heat the chocolate in the top of a double boiler set over hot, not simmering, water, stirring often—do not let the bottom of the upper container touch the water.)

2) Allow the chocolate to cool until no longer warm to the touch (an instant-read thermometer should read no higher than 90°F/32°C). Pour it into a plastic squeeze bottle or pour directly from the cup. The coating will take just a few seconds to harden and the color will go from shiny to dull.

3) For a sundae-style serving, pour a thin coat over the scoops of ice cream. You can do this for an ice cream cone too; alternatively, make sure the exposed ice cream scoop is securely attached to the cone, then carefully dip the ice cream scoop into the cooled chocolate until the chocolate meets the cone.

STORE Airtight: room temperature or refrigerated, several weeks

❖ After several hours, the coconut oil will crystallize and the texture will thicken. Heat it in the microwave with several 3-second bursts, stirring to restore its smooth and liquid consistency.

HOT FUDGE TOPPING AND DIPPING SAUCE

Makes: 2½ cups/592 ml/850 grams

STORE

Airtight: room temperature, 3 days; refrigerated, 3 weeks; frozen, 3 months (Bring to room temperature or heat before using.)

I thought that my hot fudge was the best ever until I tasted pastry chef Letty Flatt's, at Snowball on the slopes of the Deer Valley ski resort. The secret of its deliciously fudgy texture is using unsweetened chocolate, with its high percentage of cocoa butter. When the hot chocolate hits the cold ice cream, the cocoa butter hardens instantly to the perfect consistency: smooth, sticky, and fudgy.

fine quality unsweetened or 99% cacao chocolate, coarsely chopped	113 grams (4 ounces)	about ⅔ cup
unsalted butter	85 grams	6 tablespoons (¾ stick)
unsweetened alkalized cocoa powder	19 grams	¼ cup (sifted before measuring)
sugar	267 grams	1⅓ cups
heavy cream	232 grams	1 cup (237 ml)
pure vanilla extract	.	1 teaspoon (5 ml)

1) In the top of a double boiler set over hot, not simmering, water, heat the chocolate and butter. (Do not let the bottom of the upper container touch the water.) Stir often with a silicone spatula until completely melted. Whisk in the cocoa and set aside.

2) In a small heavy saucepan, heat the sugar and cream over medium heat, stirring, until the sugar has dissolved. Bring the mixture to the boiling point and then whisk it into the chocolate mixture. Add the vanilla and whisk until smooth.

3) Transfer the hot fudge to a heatproof pitcher. Cover and keep it warm for up to an hour. It can be hot or room temperature when poured onto the ice cream; reheat it in a microwave or double boiler when ready to use.

RASPBERRY BUTTERSCOTCH SAUCE

Makes: About 1 cup/230 ml/280 grams

This rosy tinged, lilting raspberry butterscotch sauce is divine with so many ice creams, from fruity to chocolate. Butterscotch is caramel made with brown sugar. I use Muscovado sugar to give it extra flavor dimension, but brown sugar is also delicious. The sauce would also be lovely laced through the ice cream after spinning.

Plan Ahead The frozen raspberries will take several hours to thaw.

RASPBERRY PURÉE

Makes: ½ cup minus 2 teaspoons/108 ml/112 grams

frozen raspberries with no added sugar	228 grams (8 ounces)	2 cups
pure vanilla extract	.	1 teaspoon (5 ml)
fine sea salt	.	a pinch
lemon juice, freshly squeezed and strained	10 grams	2 teaspoons (10 ml)

MAKE THE RASPBERRY PURÉE

1) In a strainer suspended over a medium bowl, thaw the raspberries completely. This will take several hours. (To speed thawing, place the strainer and bowl in an oven with a pilot light or viewing light on.) Press and stir the berries to force out all the juice. There should be almost ⅓ cup/79 ml of juice. Cover the berries and set aside.

2) Transfer the juice to a small saucepan and bring to a boil, stirring constantly. Lower the heat and simmer, stirring constantly, until it becomes very syrupy and is reduced to 4 teaspoons/20 ml. Watch carefully toward the end as it goes really quickly and could scorch. (Alternatively, you can do this in the

SCOOPS

❊ Do not use the microwave for melting the chocolate and butter. It risks scorching the chocolate because fat in the butter reacts to the microwave more quickly.

Continued

microwave, in a 4 cup/1 liter glass measure with a spout, lightly coated with nonstick cooking spray, swirling or stirring every 20 to 30 seconds.)

3) Press the berries through a fine-mesh strainer, using the back of a spoon. You should have about ⅓ cup/79 ml of pulp. (This will take about 20 minutes.) Stir in the vanilla and salt.

4) Stir the raspberry syrup and lemon juice into the purée. Into a 1 cup/237 ml glass measure with a spout, pour ⅓ cup/79 ml/72 grams of the raspberry purée. (Reserve any remaining purée to add to the completed raspberry butterscotch to taste.)

STORE Airtight: room temperature, 1 day; refrigerated, 1 week; frozen, 3 months (Bring to room temperature before using.)

RASPBERRY BUTTERSCOTCH SAUCE

unsalted butter	57 grams	4 tablespoons (½ stick)
light brown Muscovado sugar or dark brown sugar	108 grams	½ cup, firmly packed
corn syrup	21 grams	1 tablespoon (15 ml)
heavy cream	58 grams	¼ cup (59 ml)
Raspberry Purée	72 grams	⅓ cup (79 ml)

❖ About 30 minutes ahead, cut the butter into a few pieces and set it on the counter at room temperature (65° to 75°F/18° to 24°C).

MAKE THE BUTTERSCOTCH

1) In a small saucepan, using a silicone spatula, stir together the butter, brown sugar, corn syrup, and cream until the sugar has dissolved. Bring it to a boil over medium-low heat, stirring constantly. Simmer for about 8 minutes, stirring gently, until very thickly bubbling. (An instant-read thermometer should read 240° to 244°F/116° to 118°C.)

2) Remove the pan from the heat and pour the butterscotch into the glass measure containing the raspberry purée. Stir until uniform in consistency. Cover tightly with plastic wrap.

Continued

3) Allow the raspberry butterscotch to cool to room temperature, about 1 hour. If desired, add more of the reserved raspberry purée to taste.

TO ADD TO ICE CREAMS

To use as a swirl, while the ice cream is churning, set a 9 by 5 inch loaf pan, preferably Pyrex, in the freezer.

1) Pour about 155 grams/½ cup/118 ml of the sauce into a disposable piping bag or quart-size reclosable freezer bag, and cut a very small semicircle from one corner.

2) Spread about half of the ice cream evenly into the cold pan. Quickly pipe loops of the sauce over the top. With a small metal spatula or spoon, lightly swirl the raspberry butterscotch into the ice cream.

3) Repeat with the remaining ice cream and sauce.

4) Set the pan in the freezer for 30 minutes. Then use a large spoon to scoop the ice cream into a storage container or leave it in the pan. Press a piece of plastic wrap on the surface of the ice cream and allow it to firm for at least 4 hours in the freezer before serving.

STORE Airtight: room temperature, 1 day; refrigerated, 1 week; frozen, 3 months.

If the sauce crystallizes slightly on storage, reheat in the microwave for a few seconds, or in a small saucepan on low heat, stirring often, until melted and smooth.

BUTTERSCOTCH TOFFEE SAUCE

Makes: 2¼ cups/532 ml/572 grams

This rich, flavorful, tangy sauce is a fabulous topping for my Sticky Toffee "Pudding" Cake Sundaes (page 259). It would also be delicious drizzled over ice creams such as chocolate, pumpkin, and peanut butter. Lightly toasted pecans make a perfect garnish.

unsalted butter	227 grams	16 tablespoons (2 sticks)
dark brown sugar, preferably Muscovado	227 grams	1 cup minus 1 tablespoon, firmly packed
1 vanilla bean, split lengthwise	.	.
heavy cream	116 grams	½ cup (118 ml)
salt	.	⅛ teaspoon
lemon juice, freshly squeezed and strained (1 to 2 lemons)	32 grams	2 tablespoons (30 ml)

✤ About 30 minutes ahead, cut the butter into a few pieces and set it on the counter at room temperature (65° to 75°F/18° to 24°C).

1) In a small saucepan, place the sugar and vanilla bean. Scrape the vanilla bean seeds into the sugar and rub them in with your fingers. Remove and reserve the pod. With a silicone spatula, stir in the butter.

2) Over medium heat, stirring constantly, bring the mixture to a boil. Remove it from the heat and stir in the cream, salt, lemon juice, and reserved vanilla pod. The sauce will be slightly grainy but will become totally smooth on standing for a few minutes. Reheat if necessary, then remove the vanilla pod and pour the sauce into a pitcher for serving.

STORE Airtight: room temperature, 1 day; refrigerated, 6 months; frozen, 1 year

CRANBERRY TOPPING FOR LEMON, ORANGE, AND RASPBERRY ICE CREAMS

Makes: About 1 cup/237 ml/266 grams

Cranberry is an intense flavor, so a little goes a long way. Brief cooking, just until the berries burst, maintains their shape and makes an appealing flavor and textural addition to citrus or raspberry ice cream.

cranberries, fresh or frozen	133 grams	1⅓ cups
water	79 grams	⅓ cup (79 ml)
sugar	100 grams	½ cup
cornstarch	9 grams	1 tablespoon
fine sea salt	.	a small pinch
lemon juice, freshly squeezed and strained	.	1 teaspoon (5 ml)

1) In a medium saucepan, stir together the cranberries, water, sugar, cornstarch, and salt. Bring the mixture to a boil over medium heat, stirring constantly. Stop stirring, reduce the heat, and simmer for 5 minutes, swirling the pan occasionally. The mixture will be thickened but pourable. Stir in the lemon juice.

2) Allow the sauce to cool until warm or reheat it before serving. Scrape the cranberry topping into a pitcher or spoon heaping tablespoons on top of the ice cream.

STORE Airtight: refrigerated, 1 month; frozen, 6 months

RHUBARB COMPOTE

Makes: About 2 cups/473 ml (6 servings)

This rhubarb compote is also wonderful in savory preparations, such as served with duck. But the bright, tart deliciousness of rhubarb is sensational as a dessert, especially with strawberry and lavender ice creams.

rhubarb, preferably red	567 grams	1¼ pounds
sugar	113 grams	½ cup plus 1 tablespoon
fine sea salt	.	a pinch

1) Trim off and discard the leaves and the wider part of the base of the rhubarb and cut the stalks into ½ inch pieces. Stalks that are wider than ¾ inch should be sliced in half. You should have about 454 grams/1 pound/ 4 cups.

2) Set the rhubarb in a skillet large enough to hold the slices in a single layer. Sprinkle with the sugar and salt, and allow the rhubarb to sit for about 15 minutes, or until the sugar is moistened and mostly dissolved.

3) Cover and simmer the rhubarb on low heat for about 6 minutes, or until a skewer inserted into one of the pieces goes in with little resistance. Raise the heat to medium-high and continue cooking, uncovered, for about 2 minutes more to evaporate most of the juices. This will deepen and intensify the red color of the rhubarb.

4) Remove the pan from the heat and allow the rhubarb to cool completely without stirring. Then slide it into a bowl to avoid breaking up the pieces, cover, and refrigerate for up to 5 days.

To serve with ice cream, gently spoon the rhubarb compote into each bowl and top with a scoop or two of ice cream.

STORE Airtight: refrigerated, 5 days; frozen, 6 months

SCOOPS

✳ Rhubarb freezes well. To keep its color and texture, it is best to sprinkle the cut rhubarb with about 25 grams/ 2 tablespoons of sugar for 454 grams/1 pound of rhubarb (5% by weight). Allow it to thaw until the rhubarb pieces can be separated easily before cooking so that it keeps its shape. Remember to remove the extra sugar from the recipe!

BRANDIED CHERRIES

Makes: About 4¼ cups/684 grams

Brandied cherries are not only delicious, they do not harden when frozen. And they will keep indefinitely in the refrigerator. Luxardo cherries are an excellent alternative because the heavily concentrated syrup also prevents them from freezing hard.

sugar	100 grams	½ cup
water	59 grams	¼ cup (59 ml)
Bing cherries, fresh (pitted) or frozen and thawed	684 grams	3¾ cups
cherry brandy (see Scoops)	119 grams	½ cup (118 ml)

SCOOPS

✳ Cherry brandy intensifies the cherry flavor, but if you're planning to store it for more than a few weeks, use plain brandy because the cherry brandy causes the cherries to disintegrate on long standing.

✳ Have ready a 4 cup/1 liter glass measure with a spout, lightly coated with nonstick cooking spray.

1) In a medium saucepan, stir together the sugar and water. Add the cherries and bring the mixture to a full boil, stirring gently. Boil for 1 minute.

2) Transfer the cherries to canning jars and pour the liquid into the prepared glass measure. There will be about 1 cup/237 ml. Reduce this liquid in a microwave, stirring every 20 to 30 seconds (or in a saucepan on medium heat) to ½ cup/118 ml. (This will take about 10 minutes in the microwave.)

3) Pour the reduced liquid over the cherries and add the cherry brandy. Swirl to mix.

STORE Airtight: refrigerated, up to 1 year.

SOUR CHERRY TOPPING

Makes: About 1 cup/237 ml/175 grams

This topping, based on my favorite cherry pie filling, is a glorious accompaniment to my Cordon Rose Cheesecake Ice Cream (page 10). It is also a lovely accompaniment to vanilla, sour cream, or chocolate ice cream.

CHERRY TOPPING

sugar	50 grams	¼ cup
cornstarch	9 grams	1 tablespoon
salt	.	a pinch
sour cherries	142 grams pitted (227 grams before pitting)	¾ cup pitted (about 1 cup before pitting)
pure almond extract	.	1/16 teaspoon

SCOOPS

❊ Almond extract greatly enhances the flavor of cherries.

1) In a medium saucepan, stir together the sugar, cornstarch, and salt. Gently stir in the cherries along with any juices. Allow the mixture to sit for at least 10 minutes to liquefy the sugar mixture.

2) Over medium heat, stirring constantly, bring the cherry mixture to a boil and simmer for 2 to 3 minutes, until thickened and syrupy. Scrape the mixture into a wide bowl and allow it to cool completely.

3) Stir in the almond extract and transfer it to a serving bowl or airtight container.

STORE Airtight: refrigerated, 5 days; frozen, 6 months

WHIPPED CREAM TOPPING

Makes: 2 cups/473 ml/244 grams

Lightly sweetened whipped cream is classic and wonderful as a sundae topping.

heavy cream	232 grams	1 cup (237 ml)
superfine sugar	13 grams	1 tablespoon
pure vanilla extract	.	1 teaspoon (5 ml)

1) In a chilled metal bowl, or the bowl of a stand mixer (see Scoops), combine the cream, sugar, and vanilla and refrigerate it, covered, for at least 15 minutes. (Chill a handheld mixer's beaters or stand mixer's whisk beater alongside the bowl.)

2) Whip the mixture, starting on low speed and gradually raising the speed to medium-high as it thickens, just until stiff peaks form when the beater is raised.

STORE Airtight: refrigerated, 3 hours (Whisk lightly before using.)

SCOOPS

✻ If you are whipping 2 cups/473 ml or less of cream, a handheld mixer works better than a stand mixer.

✻ Cream whips best if it is as cold as possible, so it helps to refrigerate the cream in the mixing bowl, along with the beaters.

✻ The ideal bowl is one that is tall, with a diameter just slightly wider than the handheld mixer's beaters.

ICE CREAM SOCIALS

Ice cream is wonderful on its own, but with so many other compatible sweets it is also a marriage made in heaven.

This chapter includes vanilla and chocolate waffle ice cream cones, ice cream sandwiches, meringues, and even spun sugar nests. A few are some of my longtime favorites, adapted to join with ice cream into irresistible new desserts.

You'll also find some new favorites, such as an ice cream angel food cake made with caramelized sugar, which I call the Golden Angel, Sticky Toffee "Pudding" Cake Sundaes, and two special drinks: the Frozen Mango Lassi and the Pomegranate Bourbon Sour.

WAFFLE ICE CREAM CONES

Makes: 6 cones

Wafer cones, aka cake cones, were always my favorite, but lacking the machinery to make them at home, I tried my hand at homemade waffle cones and now there's no going back! Thin, flavorful, crunchy, and crispy, once you taste a homemade waffle cone you will be spoiled for life. Whether you make vanilla or chocolate, the batter is very quick to make and because it has no leavening, it can be made up to 3 days ahead and refrigerated.

I enjoy the texture produced by the waffle maker, but you can also use the same batter to bake smooth textured cones in an oven. Most waffle makers suggest 3 tablespoons of batter per cone, but I find 2 tablespoons, which yield 5 inch discs, to be the ideal size. The exact amount and size of the cone is up to you.

The cooked batter can be shaped into cones or cups, or even left flat and crumbled over the ice cream. To make cones, you will need a cone-shaped form (which is often included with an electric waffle cone maker); you can make your own using file folders and aluminum foil (see page 217).

VANILLA BATTER

unsalted butter	21 grams	1½ tablespoons
1 large egg	50 grams	3 tablespoons plus ½ teaspoon (47.5 ml)
fine sea salt	.	⅛ teaspoon
sugar	50 grams	¼ cup
pure vanilla extract	.	½ teaspoon (2.5 ml)
bleached cake flour (or bleached all-purpose flour; see Note, page 216)	57 grams	½ cup (lightly spooned into the cup and leveled off)

Continued

CHOCOLATE BATTER

unsalted butter	21 grams	1½ tablespoons
bleached cake flour (or bleached all-purpose flour; see Note, page 216)	38 grams	⅓ cup (lightly spooned into the cup and leveled off)
unsweetened alkalized cocoa powder	14 grams	3 tablespoons (sifted before measuring)
1 large egg	50 grams	3 tablespoons plus ½ teaspoon (47.5 ml)
fine sea salt	.	⅛ teaspoon
sugar	67 grams	⅓ cup
pure vanilla extract	.	1 teaspoon (5 ml)

MAKE THE VANILLA BATTER

1) In a 1 cup/237 ml glass measure with a spout in the microwave, or in a small saucepan over low heat, melt the butter. Allow it to cool until no longer hot.

2) In a medium bowl, lightly whisk together the egg and salt. Add the sugar and whisk for about a minute, until light and foamy. Whisk in the melted butter and vanilla.

3) Add the flour and use the whisk to stir it in. When all the flour is moistened, whisk for 15 seconds, or until smooth.

MAKE THE CHOCOLATE BATTER

1) In a 1 cup/237 ml glass measure with a spout in the microwave, or in a small saucepan over low heat, melt the butter. Allow it to cool until no longer hot.

2) In a small bowl, whisk together the flour and cocoa.

3) In a medium bowl, lightly whisk together the egg and salt. Add the sugar and whisk for about a minute, until light and foamy. Whisk in the melted butter and vanilla.

4) Add the flour mixture and use the whisk to stir it in. When all the flour mixture is moistened, whisk for 15 seconds, or until smooth.

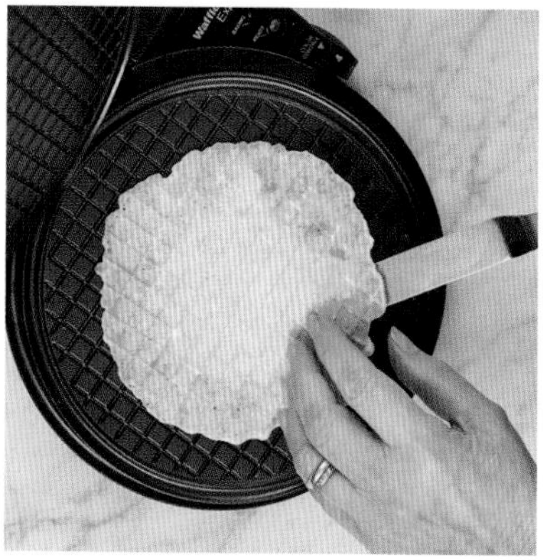

Use an offset spatula to lift the waffle.

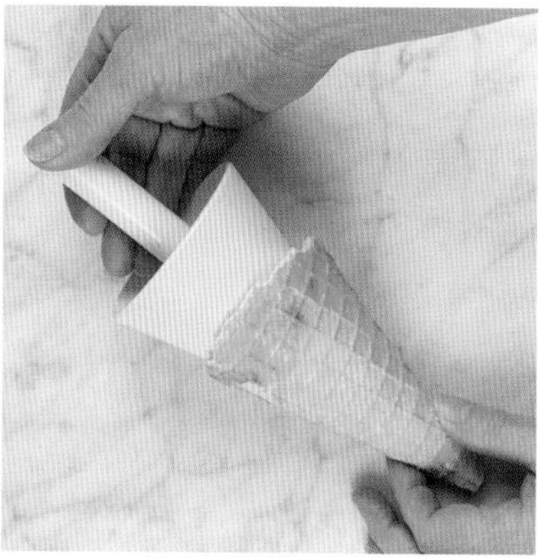

Roll the disc into a cone shape and press down on the seam.

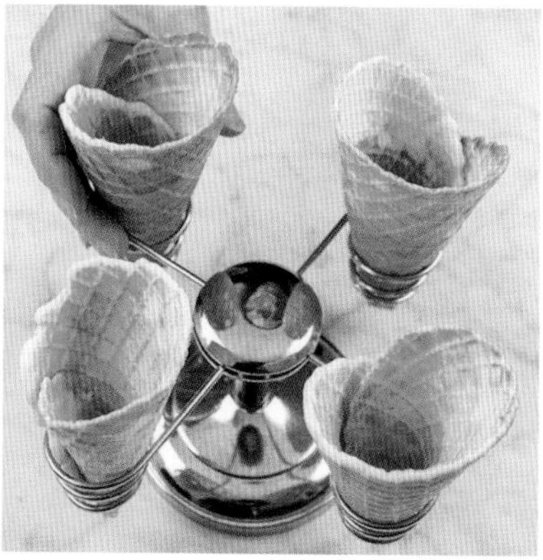

Set the cone in a cone holder or glass until cool and firm.

COOK THE BATTER

WAFFLE MAKER METHOD

5) Follow the instructions on your waffle cone maker. Mine takes about 1 minute and 20 seconds for the vanilla and only 1 minute for the chocolate. I like to use a rounded 1¾ inch diameter/2 tablespoon/30 ml ice cream scoop for each waffle cone.

6) Roll each hot disc into a cone shape using the cone form. It will firm up within seconds so that you can continue with the remaining cones. Set the cone in a glass to help it keep its shape while firming completely, which will happen in just a few minutes.

OVEN METHOD

If baking in the oven instead of a waffle cone maker, you will need one or two baking sheets, lined with parchment.

PREHEAT THE OVEN

✲ Twenty minutes or longer before baking, set an oven rack at the middle level. Set the oven at 325°F/160°C.

5) Bake only two rounds of batter at a time so that they remain flexible enough to roll into cones. Use an offset spatula to spread the batter onto the baking sheet to form 5 inch discs.

Continued

6) Bake for 10 to 15 minutes, or until set and no longer shiny.

7) Use a pancake turner to flip each disc onto a dish towel.

8) Roll each hot disc into a cone shape using a cone form. Set the cone in a glass to help keep its shape while firming. If the second disc becomes too firm to roll, return it to the oven for a few seconds.

9) Repeat with the remaining batter in two batches. If using only one baking sheet, allow it to cool between batches, and reline it with parchment.

NOTE If using bleached all-purpose flour, use the same weight but slightly less volume, as follows:

For 57 grams, use ½ cup (lightly spooned into the cup and leveled off) minus 2 teaspoons.

For 38 grams, use ⅓ cup (lightly spooned into the cup and leveled off) minus 1 teaspoon.

Increase the butter to 28 grams/2 tablespoons, which will give the same tenderness as when using cake flour.

STORE Airtight: room temperature, 1 week (If the weather is humid and the cones soften slightly, they can be recrisped in a preheated 325°F/160°C oven for a few minutes.)

TO MAKE YOUR OWN WAFFLE CONE SHAPER

Draw a 12 inch circle on a file folder. Draw lines to divide the circle into 4 equal wedges. Cut out the wedges. Curve a wedge to form a cone shape. Overlap the two sides of the wedge by ¼ inch and tape the edges together to secure the cone's shape. Repeat with the other three wedges.

Cut four 9 inch squares of aluminum foil. Wrap each cone with foil, taping the edges to seal. Fold the excess foil over the open top of the cone to secure the foil to the cone. Encase each cone in foil, taping the edges and folding the excess foil over the open edge of the cone. (If necessary, staple the foil near the edge of the open end of the cone.)

Lightly coat each foil-encased cone with nonstick cooking spray. Set the inverted cones on a countertop.

SCOOPS

✳ My favorite waffle cone maker is made by Chef's Choice.

✳ If the batter starts to thicken as it stands, it's fine to stir in a few tablespoons of water.

✳ If a cone has a small opening at the bottom, to seal it you can drop in a complementary component such as a berry, nut, or some melted chocolate.

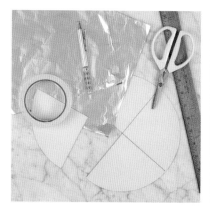

Cut out 4 wedges from a file folder.

Make a cone shape from each wedge and secure it with tape.

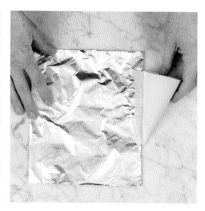

Cut four 9 inch squares of aluminum foil.

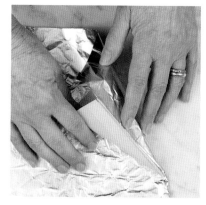

Position a cone 1 inch from a corner of the foil.

Roll the cone to encase it in foil.

Fold over the tip and fold excess at the top into the inside of the cone.

MAKING COOKIE ICE CREAM SANDWICHES

Cookies are an excellent and classic component for making ice cream sandwiches. Along with their added flavor, you also get their firmer texture to contrast with the soft and creamy texture of the ice cream. The assembled sandwiches hold their shape beautifully and can be individually wrapped and frozen for impulse treats.

COMPOSING ICE CREAM SANDWICHES

You will need about 1½ quarts/1½ liters of homemade ice cream or 2 quarts/2 liters of commercial ice cream for the recipes. (Commercial ice cream usually contains more air—this is called overrun—so, when softened, it will have less volume and you will thus need a little more.)

1) Refrigerate the ice cream for 20 minutes before sandwiching the cookies to soften it slightly. Set baking sheets or cookie sheets in the freezer to chill.

2) Assemble only half of the ice cream sandwiches at a time to keep the ice cream from melting. Return the ice cream to the freezer until ready to do the second batch of sandwiches. Set half of the cookies, bottom sides up, on one of the chilled baking sheets. Set a scoop of ice cream, about ¼ cup, on top of each cookie.

3) Place a second cookie, bottom side down, on top. When the ice cream is soft enough to press down easily, evenly press the top of each cookie until the ice cream comes almost to the edges. The ice cream should be about ½ inch thick.

4) Cover the sandwiches with a sheet of plastic wrap and set them in the freezer until firm. If desired, serve with Hot Fudge Dipping Sauce (page 198).

5) If not serving the same day, wrap each sandwich in plastic wrap and store in an airtight container in the freezer. Repeat with the remaining cookies.

STORE The completed ice cream sandwiches: frozen, up to 3 days

MY FAVORITE CHOCOLATE CHIP COOKIE ICE CREAM SANDWICHES

Makes: Eleven 2¾ inch sandwich cookies

OVEN TEMPERATURE:
325°F/160°C for the walnuts; 350°F/175°C for the cookies

BAKING TIME:
7 minutes for the walnuts; 8 to 10 minutes for the cookies for each of two batches

SPECIAL EQUIPMENT
Two 16 by 12 inch cookie sheets, lined with parchment

I brown the butter for these cookies to add flavor and remove the water. Adding golden or corn syrup helps keep them moist and chewy. Golden syrup adds a delicious butterscotch element. Unbleached all-purpose flour gives a slightly chewier texture than bleached flour. I also like to add walnuts; lightly toasting them brings out their flavor. Removing as much peel as possible also removes any bitterness. I like my cookies moist and chewy on the inside, so it is best to bake them just until the centers are still soft. My favorite ice cream pairings for this cookie are Vanilla (page 3) and Back Road Wild Mint Chip (page 30).

DOUGH

Makes: 690 grams

unsalted butter (see Scoops)	113 grams	8 tablespoons (1 stick)
1 large egg	50 grams	3 tablespoons plus ½ teaspoon (47.5 ml)
walnut halves	75 grams	¾ cup
all-purpose flour, preferably unbleached	161 grams	1⅓ cups (lightly spooned into the cup and leveled off)
baking soda	2.7 grams	½ teaspoon
fine sea salt	.	¼ teaspoon
light brown sugar, preferably Muscovado	81 grams	¼ cup plus 2 tablespoons, firmly packed
granulated sugar	25 grams	2 tablespoons
golden syrup or corn syrup	42 grams	2 tablespoons (30 ml)
pure vanilla extract	.	1 teaspoon (5 ml)
dark chocolate chips, 52% to 63% cacao (see Scoops)	170 grams (6 ounces)	1 cup

Continued

❉ Twenty minutes or longer before baking, set an oven rack at the middle level. Set the oven at 325°F/160°C.

MISE EN PLACE

❉ About 1 hour ahead, set the butter and egg on the counter at room temperature (65° to 75°F/18° to 24°C).

❉ Clarify and Brown the Butter: Have ready, by the cooktop, a 1 cup/237 ml glass measure with a spout.

In a small heavy saucepan, on very low heat, melt the butter, stirring often with a light-colored silicone spatula. Raise the heat to low and boil, stirring constantly, until the milk solids on the spatula become little brown specks. Immediately pour the butter into the glass measure, scraping in the browned solids as well. Allow the browned butter to cool to no higher than 80°F/27°C.

❉ Toast the Walnuts: Spread the walnuts evenly on a baking sheet and bake for about 7 minutes. Stir once or twice to ensure even toasting and avoid overbrowning. Turn the walnuts onto a dish towel, then roll and rub them around to loosen the skins. Discard any loose skin and cool completely. Chop into coarse pieces.

❉ In a medium mixing bowl, whisk together the flour, baking soda, and salt.

❉ Into the bowl of a stand mixer, weigh or measure the egg.

MAKE THE DOUGH

1) Into the bowl of the stand mixer fitted with the flat beater, add the browned butter with the solids, the sugars, golden syrup, and vanilla, and mix on low speed for 1 minute.

2) Add the flour mixture. Starting on the lowest speed, beat just until the flour is moistened. On low speed, continue beating for 30 seconds. Add the chocolate chips and walnuts and continue beating only until evenly incorporated.

Continued

3) Divide the dough in half, about 345 grams each. Wrap each piece in plastic wrap. If the dough is very sticky, refrigerate for about 30 minutes.

PREHEAT THE OVEN

✻ Twenty minutes or longer before baking, set an oven rack at the middle level. Set the oven at 350°F/175°C.

ROLL THE DOUGH INTO BALLS

4) Divide the dough into 11 walnut-size pieces (31 grams). Roll each piece of dough between the palms of your hands to form 1½ inch balls. Place the balls on the cookie sheet a minimum of 2 inches apart.

5) Flatten the cookies to about 2 inches wide by ½ inch high. (If desired, freeze the shaped cookie dough to bake at a later time. Baking time will be about 2 minutes longer when baked from frozen. For the ideal texture, preheat the oven to 325°F/160°C and raise the temperature to 350°F/175°C once the cookies are in the oven.)

BAKE THE COOKIES

6) Bake for 4 minutes. Rotate the cookie sheet halfway around. Continue baking for 4 to 6 minutes, or until the cookies are just beginning to brown on the tops. When gently pressed with a fingertip, they should still feel soft in the middle.

COOL THE COOKIES

7) Set the cookie sheet on a wire rack and let the cookies cool for 1 minute to be firm enough to transfer to another wire rack for cooling. Use a thin pancake turner to transfer the cookies to the wire rack.

8) Repeat with the second batch.

9) To assemble the ice cream sandwiches, see page 218.

STORE The cookies: Airtight: room temperature, 2 weeks; refrigerated, 1 month; frozen, 3 months

SCOOPS

❈ Use an AA butter as lower quality will result in a lesser amount of clarified butter. You will need a total of 84 grams/7 tablespoons/104 ml to 90 grams/7½ tablespoons/110 ml. It's also fine to use butter that is softened and not clarified, but it will result in a less flavorful and puffier cookie.

❈ Use your favorite chocolate. My favorites are Valrhona dark chocolate chips 52% and 60%, Ghirardelli bittersweet chips 60%, and Scharffen Berger bittersweet chunks 61%.

❈ Many variations work for this cookie base. You can use a mix of white, milk, and dark chocolate. You can use butterscotch chips instead of chocolate. You can use pecans or your favorite nuts instead of walnuts, or no nuts at all. Also, you can add dried fruit such as cranberries or raisins.

FUDGY CHOCOLATE SANDWICH COOKIES

Makes: Twenty-three 2¾ inch cookie sandwiches

OVEN TEMPERATURE:
350°F/175°C

BAKING TIME:
8 to 10 minutes
for each of
four batches

SPECIAL EQUIPMENT

Two 16 by 12 inch
cookie sheets,
nonstick or lined
with parchment

Two 12 by 1⅝ inch
(measured from the
inside) cardboard
tubes from paper
towel rolls, each
cut in quarters

A sharp knife with
a 1½ to 2 inch tall
blade

A 2 inch ice cream
scoop or ¼ cup
solid measure

This cookie stays fudgy even when frozen. The edges of the cookies are crisp, which provides a charming contrast to the fudgy interior of the cookie and the creamy ice cream filling.

My favorite ice cream pairings for these cookies are Cherry Vanilla, Caramel, and Nocciola.

Plan Ahead The dough requires 1½ hours to chill before shaping and 3 hours to freeze before baking, or can be frozen for 3 months.

DOUGH

Makes: 600 grams

unsalted butter	142 grams	10 tablespoons (1¼ sticks)
1 large egg	50 grams	3 tablespoons plus ½ teaspoon (47.5 ml)
bittersweet chocolate, 60% to 62% cacao, chopped	42 grams (1.5 ounces)	about ¼ cup
bleached all-purpose flour	144 grams	1 cup (lightly spooned into the cup and leveled off) plus 3 tablespoons
unsweetened alkalized cocoa powder	37 grams	½ cup (sifted before measuring)
baking soda	2.7 grams	½ teaspoon
fine sea salt	.	⅛ teaspoon
heavy cream	43 grams	3 tablespoons (45 ml)
corn syrup	14 grams	2 teaspoons (10 ml)
pure vanilla extract	.	1 teaspoon (5 ml)
superfine sugar	150 grams	¾ cup

✣ About 1 hour ahead, set the butter and egg on the counter at room temperature (65° to 75°F/18° to 24°C).

MELT THE CHOCOLATE

1) In a small microwavable bowl, stirring with a silicone spatula every 15 seconds, heat the chocolate until almost completely melted. (Alternatively, heat the chocolate in the top of a double boiler set over hot, not simmering, water, stirring often—do not let the bottom of the container touch the water.)

2) Remove the chocolate from the heat and stir until fully melted. Let it cool for about 10 minutes, or until it is no longer warm to the touch but is still fluid.

MIX THE DRY INGREDIENTS

3) In a small bowl, whisk together the flour, cocoa, baking soda, and salt. Sift the mixture onto a sheet of parchment.

MIX THE LIQUID INGREDIENTS

4) In a small bowl, whisk the egg, cream, corn syrup, and vanilla just until lightly combined.

MAKE THE DOUGH

5) In the bowl of a stand mixer fitted with the flat beater, beat the sugar and butter on medium speed until well mixed, about 1 minute. Scrape down the sides of the bowl.

6) Gradually beat in the egg mixture. It should take about 15 seconds. Scrape in the cooled melted chocolate and beat until thoroughly incorporated, about 1 minute.

7) Scrape down the sides of the bowl.

8) Detach the flat beater and add the dry ingredients. Stir in the flour mixture until moistened. Reattach the flat beater and beat on low speed until incorporated, about 15 seconds. The dough will be like a thick, fluffy butter cake batter.

Continued

9) Scrape the dough onto a piece of plastic wrap. Use the plastic wrap to flatten it into a 6 by 5 inch rectangle and refrigerate it for at least 1½ hours, until firm enough to shape. (An instant-read thermometer should read below 63°F/17°C.)

SHAPE FOUR DOUGH LOGS

10) Divide the dough into quarters, about 150 grams each. Work with one piece at a time and refrigerate the rest.

11) Set the dough on a piece of plastic wrap and wrap the plastic wrap around the entire piece of dough. Roll the dough into a log, about 1½ inches in diameter and about 5½ inches long. Slide the plastic-wrapped log into one of the cardboard tubes and set it upright in the freezer. Repeat with the remaining dough logs. (If not using the cardboard tubes, lay the dough logs on their sides and turn them a few times until frozen to keep them round.)

12) Freeze the dough logs for at least 2 hours, or until an instant-read thermometer reads below 32°F/0°C, to firm it for even cutting. The dough can be frozen for up to 3 months.

PREHEAT THE OVEN

✣ Twenty minutes or longer before baking, set an oven rack at the middle level. Set the oven at 350°F/175°C.

CUT THE DOUGH INTO COOKIES

13) The dough cuts most easily when not frozen solid, so it helps to let it soften for a few minutes at room temperature before slicing. It is best to bake one sheet at a time to ensure that the cookies can be removed from the cookie sheet as soon after baking as possible so that they stay soft. Remove one of the frozen dough logs from the freezer and cut 12 (⅜ inch thick) slices. Set them 2 inches apart on the cookie sheet and bake at once.

BAKE THE COOKIES

14) Bake for 4 minutes. Rotate the cookie sheet halfway around. Continue baking for 4 to 6 minutes, or just until set but still soft to the touch.

COOL THE COOKIES

15) Set the cookie sheet on a wire rack and let the cookies cool for about 1 minute, or just until they can be lifted. (Do not leave them on the cookie sheet, as they will continue to bake and become brittle.) Use a thin pancake turner to transfer the cookies directly to another wire rack. They will bend slightly but become flat when set on the wire rack to cool.

16) As soon as the cookies are cool, sandwich them with the ice cream (see page 218) or store them airtight. While each batch of cookies is baking, shape the dough for the next batch.

STORE The cookies: Airtight: room temperature, 1 week; refrigerated, 2 weeks; frozen, 1 month

PRALINE PECAN MERINGUE ICE CREAM SANDWICHES

Makes: Twenty 2½ inch sandwich cookies

OVEN TEMPERATURE:
350°F/175°C

BAKING TIME:
10 to 15 minutes for each of two batches

SPECIAL EQUIPMENT

Four 16 by 12 inch cookie sheets, lined with parchment

A 2 inch/ 3 tablespoon/43 ml ice cream scoop or two tablespoons

This is my top favorite ice cream sandwich. The meringue cookie is airy, slightly chewy, and extra flavorful from the brown sugar and pecans. With or without ice cream, it is one great cookie.

My favorite ice cream pairings for these meringues are Espresso (page 28) and Dulce de Leche (page 17).

PRALINE PECAN MERINGUE COOKIES

Makes: 700 grams

4 large egg whites, at room temperature	120 grams	½ cup (118 ml)
pecan halves	300 grams	3 cups, *divided*
light brown Muscovado sugar or dark brown sugar	300 grams	1¼ cups plus 2 tablespoons, firmly packed

PREHEAT THE OVEN

❊ Twenty minutes or longer before baking, set the oven racks in the upper and lower thirds of the oven. Set the oven at 350°F/175°C.

MISE EN PLACE

❊ About 30 minutes ahead, set the egg whites on the counter at room temperature (65° to 75°F/18° to 24°C).

❊ Toast and Prepare the Pecans: Spread the pecans evenly on a baking sheet, set the pan on the upper rack, and bake for about 5 minutes, or just until light brown to enhance their flavor. Stir once or twice to ensure even toasting and avoid overbrowning. Cool completely.

❊ Divide the pecans into two equal parts. Leave one part whole and chop the other part into medium-fine pieces.

MAKE THE PRALINE PECAN MERINGUE

1) In the bowl of a stand mixer fitted with the whisk beater, beat the egg whites and the brown sugar on medium speed until well mixed, about 1 minute. Scrape down the sides of the bowl. Raise the speed to medium-high and beat for about 5 minutes, or until very thick and light in color.

2) Remove the bowl from the mixer stand. Add all of the pecans and, using a silicone spatula, fold them into the meringue.

SHAPE THE MERINGUES

3) Use the ice cream scoop to drop 10 dollops (about 17 grams) of the pecan meringue onto each prepared cookie sheet a minimum of 1½ inches apart. Using a small offset spatula, shape the dollops into ½ inch high by 2¼ inch wide discs. They will spread to about 2½ inches but will not widen any more on baking. Stir the meringue mixture from time to time to ensure that each spoonful includes some of the nuts. If necessary, use a small metal spatula to coax each meringue into a more even disc.

BAKE THE COOKIES

4) Bake for 10 to 15 minutes. The meringues will crack slightly in an appealing way. Check for doneness by inserting a metal cake tester into one of the cracks. It should come out sticky and the cookies should give slightly to pressure. (An instant-read thermometer should read about 190°F/88°C.) If more baking is required, rotate the cookie sheets halfway around, reverse their positions from top to bottom, and continue baking for a few more minutes.

While the first batch of meringues is baking, shape the second batch of meringues.

COOL THE COOKIES

5) Set the cookie sheets on wire racks and let the cookies cool completely on the sheets. They will firm on sitting and become easy to lift off the parchment using a small pancake turner.

6) To assemble the ice cream sandwiches, see page 218.

STORE The cookies: Airtight: room temperature, 2 months

SCOOPS

✳ You can also make these as open-face sandwich cookies by making a half batch of the cookies and just topping them with ice cream.

CHOCOLATE ICE CREAM SANDWICH CAKE

Serves: 8 to 10

OVEN TEMPERATURE:
350°F/175°C

BAKING TIME:
25 to 35 minutes

SPECIAL EQUIPMENT

A 10 by 2 inch cake pan, encircled with a cake strip (see Scoops), bottom coated with shortening, topped with a parchment round that has been coated with baking spray with flour (leave the sides uncoated)

One 9½ or 9 inch springform pan or expandable flan ring in which to mold the sandwich cake

This is the perfect chocolate cake for an ice cream cake. It is deliciously chocolaty, light, and velvety. Because it is made with oil rather than butter, it stays soft and tender when sandwiched with ice cream and frozen.

BATTER

2 to 3 large eggs, separated, plus 1 additional white		
2 (to 3) yolks	37 grams	2 tablespoons plus 1 teaspoon (35 ml)
3 whites	90 grams	¼ cup plus 2 tablespoons (89 ml)
unsweetened alkalized cocoa powder	33 grams	¼ cup plus 3 tablespoons (sifted before measuring)
boiling water	59 grams	¼ cup (59 ml)
flavorless vegetable oil, such as canola or safflower	54 grams	¼ cup (59 ml)
pure vanilla extract	.	½ teaspoon (2.5 ml)
bleached all-purpose flour	75 grams	½ cup (lightly spooned into the cup and leveled off) plus 2 tablespoons
sugar	150 grams	¾ cup
salt	.	⅛ teaspoon
baking powder	4.5 grams	1 teaspoon
baking soda	2.7 grams	½ teaspoon

PREHEAT THE OVEN

✲ Twenty minutes or longer before baking, set an oven rack at the middle level. Set the oven at 350°F/175°C.

Continued

MISE EN PLACE

✣ About 30 minutes ahead, into separate bowls, weigh or measure the egg yolks and egg whites. Spray the yolks with nonstick cooking spray and cover the bowls tightly with plastic wrap. Set on the counter at room temperature (65° to 75°F/18° to 24°C).

MIX THE COCOA AND LIQUID INGREDIENTS

1) In the bowl of a stand mixer, whisk together the cocoa and boiling water until smooth. Add the oil and egg yolks to the cocoa mixture. Cover with plastic wrap to prevent evaporation and cool to room temperature (about 20 minutes). To speed cooling, place it in the refrigerator. Bring it to room temperature if necessary before proceeding.

2) Attach the whisk beater. Start beating on low speed, gradually raising the speed to medium. Beat for about 1 minute, or until smooth and shiny. The mixture will resemble buttercream. Scrape down the sides of the bowl and beat in the vanilla.

MIX THE DRY INGREDIENTS AND MAKE THE BATTER

3) In a medium bowl, whisk together the flour, sugar, salt, baking powder, and baking soda.

4) Add half of the flour mixture to the chocolate mixture. Start beating on low speed until the dry ingredients are moistened. Scrape down the sides of the bowl and repeat with the remaining flour mixture.

5) Raise the speed to medium-high and beat for 1 minute. Scrape down the sides of the bowl, reaching to the bottom. The mixture will be very thick.

6) On low speed, add the egg whites. Gradually raise the speed to medium-high and beat for 2 minutes. The batter will be the consistency of a thick soup. Scrape the batter into the prepared pan. It will be about one-quarter full.

BAKE THE CAKE

7) To prevent collapse of the delicate foam structure while still hot, the cake must be unmolded as soon as it is baked. Have ready a small metal spatula and two wire racks lightly coated with nonstick cooking spray. (The top of the cake will have decorative markings from the rack.)

8) Bake for 25 to 35 minutes, or until the cake begins to shrink away from the sides of the pan. During baking the batter will rise almost to the top of the pan and a little higher in the middle. It will start to lower just before the end of baking.

COOL AND UNMOLD THE CAKE

9) Run a small metal spatula between the sides of the pan and the cake and invert it onto a prepared wire rack. Remove the parchment and immediately reinvert it onto the second rack to keep it from sinking, and let it cool completely.

ICE CREAM FILLING AND DIPPING SAUCE

Ice cream of your choice	.	1 quart/1 liter (see Scoops)
Hot Fudge Topping and Dipping Sauce (page 198), optional	680 grams	2 cups (473 ml)

10) Transfer the ice cream to the refrigerator to soften until it is a spreadable consistency (the exact time depends on the temperature of your freezer and refrigerator). You can also use a microwave, with 4-second bursts, to speed softening, but empty the softened ice cream into a larger bowl and stir it to equalize the consistency.

COMPOSE THE SANDWICH CAKE

11) Cut two 30 inch long pieces of plastic wrap.

If using the springform pan, crisscross the bottom of the pan with the plastic wrap and drape the excess over the sides.

If using the expandable flan ring, cut a cardboard round the exact dimension of the baked cake. Place the expandable flan ring on top of a 15 by 12 inch cookie sheet. Set the cardboard round into the ring. Crisscross the cardboard round with the plastic wrap and drape the excess over the sides.

12) Using a long serrated knife, cut the cake horizontally into two even layers. Use the loose bottom of a tart pan, a cardboard round, or open-sided baking sheet to lift the layers.

13) Set the bottom layer into the prepared pan or flan ring. If it is slightly larger than the pan, it will compress to fit or, if necessary, you can trim it with small scissors. To keep the ice cream from melting, set the pan into a slightly larger

Continued

silicone pan or wrap the bottom of the pan with foil and set it in a large pan surrounded by ice cubes.

14) With a small offset spatula, spread the ice cream in an even layer on top of the cake. Set the top cake layer on top of the ice cream and press down firmly on it.

15) Fold the excess plastic wrap to cover the cake tightly and set it in the freezer for a minimum of 8 hours or until frozen through.

UNMOLD THE CAKE

16) Use a hot damp towel to wipe the sides of the springform pan or flan ring and remove the sides. Remove the plastic wrap.

17) If you are serving the whole cake, allow it to soften for about 10 minutes before cutting. If you want to serve only a few pieces, cut them right away with a chef's knife dipped in very hot water between each slice. Return the rest of the cake to the freezer, wrapped in plastic wrap and set in a freezer-weight plastic bag. Allow the slices to soften for 10 to 15 minutes before serving. Top with the hot fudge and pass any extra for dipping.

SCOOPS

✼ Commercial ice cream has what is called overrun. This refers to the amount of air that gets incorporated during the freezing process. When the ice cream is softened to make it possible to spread it into the cake-lined mold, it loses the air, and the volume can decrease by as much as two-thirds. If using homemade ice cream, you will need only about 1 quart/1 liter. If using commercial ice cream, start with 2 quarts/2 liters.

✼ I recommend encircling pans with cake strips, such as my silicone Rose's Heavenly Cake Strips, to ensure even baking. These slow down the baking at the sides of the pan, which otherwise would set sooner than the center, resulting in doming in the middle and dryness at the edges of the cake. You can make your own using a strip of aluminum foil: Cut it long enough to encircle the pan with a little overlap, triple the height of the pan. Wet some paper towels, fold them to the height of the pan, and lay them along the middle of the foil strip. Fold the top, bottom, and ends of the foil over to encase the paper towels. Wrap the strip around the pan and secure it with a metal paper clip or binder clamp.

FUDGY PUDGY BROWNIES

Makes: Nine 2½ inch squares with scraps, for ice cream bases; or 1 cup of ½ inch cubes for 1 quart of ice cream.

OVEN
TEMPERATURE:
350°F/175°C

BAKING TIME:
7 minutes for the
walnuts; 30 to 40
minutes for the
brownies

SPECIAL
EQUIPMENT

One 8 by 2 inch
square baking
pan, coated with
shortening, lined
with two pieces of
crisscrossed heavy-
duty aluminum
foil or parchment
(bottom and sides),
extending a few
inches past the edge
of the pan, attached
to each other by
a thin coating of
shortening, then
lightly coated with
baking spray with
flour

I have many brownie recipes, but these dense, moist, and fudgy ones are my top choice to add to ice cream. They can be mixed into the ice cream or used as a base for a scoop of ice cream topped with hot fudge sauce.

Plan Ahead Make the brownies a day ahead. When adding them to the ice cream, the cubes need to be cold.

BATTER

ingredient	weight	measure
unsalted butter	170 grams	12 tablespoons (1½ sticks)
3 large eggs	150 grams	½ cup plus 1½ tablespoons (140 ml)
walnut halves	100 grams	1 cup
fine quality unsweetened or 99% cacao chocolate, coarsely chopped	142 grams (5 ounces)	about ¾ cup plus 1½ tablespoons
white chocolate containing cocoa butter, coarsely chopped	85 grams (3 ounces)	about ½ cup
unsweetened alkalized cocoa powder	16 grams	3½ tablespoons (sifted before measuring)
sugar	267 grams	1⅓ cups
pure vanilla extract	.	½ tablespoon (7.5 ml)
all-purpose flour, either bleached or unbleached	91 grams	¾ cup (lightly spooned into the cup and leveled off)
fine sea salt	.	a pinch

PREHEAT THE OVEN

❧ Twenty minutes or longer before baking, set an oven rack at the middle level. Set the oven at 350°F/175°C.

Continued

MISE EN PLACE

✣ About 1 hour ahead, set the butter and eggs on the counter at room temperature (65° to 75°F/18° to 24°C).

✣ Into a 1 cup/237 ml glass measure with a spout, weigh or measure the eggs and cover them.

✣ Toast the Walnuts: Spread the walnuts evenly on a baking sheet and bake for about 5 minutes. Stir once or twice to ensure even toasting and avoid overbrowning. Turn the walnuts onto a dish towel and roll and rub them around to loosen the skins. Discard any loose skin and cool completely. Chop into coarse pieces.

MAKE THE BATTER

1) In a double boiler over hot, not simmering, water, melt the butter and the chocolates, stirring often—do not let the bottom of the container touch the water. Scrape the melted chocolate mixture into a large mixing bowl.

2) Whisk the cocoa into the melted chocolate mixture and then the sugar, until incorporated.

3) Whisk in the eggs and vanilla until the mixture becomes thick and glossy.

4) Stir in the flour and salt, just until the flour is moistened.

5) Stir in the walnuts, reaching to the bottom of the bowl, until evenly incorporated.

6) Scrape the batter into the prepared pan and smooth the surface evenly, but mound it slightly in the center, which tends to dip on baking.

BAKE THE BROWNIE

7) Bake for 30 to 40 minutes, or until a toothpick inserted 1 inch from the edge comes out almost clean. (An instant-read thermometer inserted in the center should read about 190°F/88°C.)

COOL AND UNMOLD THE BROWNIE

8) Set the pan on a wire rack and let the brownie cool for 10 minutes. Run a small metal spatula between the pan and the foil to ensure that no batter has leaked through and stuck to the sides.

9) Invert the brownie onto a wire rack lined with plastic wrap and lift off the pan. Carefully peel off the foil. If the brownie's bottom is slightly oily, pat off the oil with a paper towel before reinverting the brownie onto another rack. Cool completely. Refrigerate, covered, for about 1 hour, until firm enough to cut.

CUT THE BROWNIE

10) Transfer the brownie to a cutting board.

To use as a base for a scoop of ice cream: Use a long serrated knife to cut the brownie into nine 2½ inch squares (or four 3 inch squares) with scraps to enjoy on the side or crumbled on top of the ice cream.

To use to add to the ice cream: Cut nine 1 inch cubes and then cut or break each cube into roughly ½ inch cubes or chunks. You will need about 140 grams/1 cup of brownie cubes for 1 quart/1 liter of ice cream. Refrigerate the cubes until ready to add them to the ice cream. Set a large bowl in the freezer for mixing together the ice cream and the brownies. When the ice cream mixture has reached the consistency of soft serve and begins to ball up around the dasher, scrape it into the cold bowl and fold in the cubes with a silicone spatula. (You can set the bowl in an ice water bath or, if the ice cream softens too quickly, set the bowl in the freezer until firm enough to add the brownies.) Set the ice cream in the freezer for about 1 hour to firm up before transferring it to the storage container.

STORE Airtight: room temperature, 1 week; refrigerated, 1 month; frozen, 3 months

SCOOPS

✲ Do not use the microwave for melting the chocolate and butter. It risks scorching the chocolate because fat in the butter reacts to the microwave more quickly.

BLACK FOREST ICE CREAM CAKE ROLL

Serves: 12

OVEN TEMPERATURE:
450°F/230°C

BAKING TIME:
7 to 10 minutes

SPECIAL EQUIPMENT

One 17¼ by 12¼ by 1 inch half-sheet pan, bottom coated with shortening, then lined with parchment (cut the parchment to extend 1 inch past one of the long sides of the pan) coated with baking spray with flour

Two large uncoated wire racks

A clean dish towel that is slightly larger than the half sheet pan

My first taste of Black Forest cake, with its chocolate cake, whipped cream, and cherry filling, was at Café Geiger, which had been in the German section of New York City known as Yorkville. It immediately became my favorite cake and I returned often to order it. When I found it in bakeries in Switzerland many years later, I preferred their interpretation, with its lofty layer of whipped cream and thinner layer of cake. I included it in *The Cake Bible*, where I also created it as this ice cream cake roll. You will need to have a wide freezer to accommodate the long roll.

COMPONENTS

Vanilla Ice Cream (page 3), about 2½ cups/590 ml
Brandied Cherries (page 206), about 1 cup, plus ⅓ cup/79ml of the syrup
Hot Fudge Topping and Dipping Sauce (page 198)

CHOCOLATE BISCUIT ROULADE BATTER

5 (to 8) large eggs (see page xxxii), separated, at room temperature		
5 (to 8) yolks	93 grams	¼ cup plus 2 tablespoons (89 ml)
about 4 whites	120 grams	½ cup (118 ml), *divided*
unsweetened alkalized cocoa powder	23 grams	¼ cup plus 1 tablespoon (sifted before measuring)
boiling water	45 grams	3 tablespoons (45 ml)
pure vanilla extract	.	¾ teaspoon (3.7 ml)
sugar, preferably superfine	113 grams	½ cup plus 1 tablespoon, *divided*
bleached cake flour (or bleached all-purpose flour)	33 grams	⅓ cup (or ¼ cup plus 2 teaspoons), sifted into the cup and leveled off
cream of tartar	.	¼ teaspoon

PREHEAT THE OVEN

❊ Twenty minutes or longer before baking, set an oven rack at the middle level. Set the oven at 450°F/230°C.

MISE EN PLACE

❊ About 1 hour ahead, set the eggs on the counter at room temperature (65° to 75°F/18° to 24°C).

❊ Into separate bowls, weigh or measure the egg yolks and egg whites. Spray the yolks with nonstick cooking spray and cover the bowls tightly with plastic wrap.

MAKE THE BATTER

1) In a small bowl, weigh or measure the cocoa and stir in the boiling water until smooth. Then stir in the vanilla. Cover tightly to prevent evaporation and allow it to cool until no longer hot.

2) In the bowl of a stand mixer fitted with the whisk beater, place the egg yolks, half of the egg whites (60 grams/¼ cup/59 ml) and 100 grams/½ cup of the sugar. Beat on high speed until thick, fluffy, and tripled in volume, about 5 minutes. Lower the speed and beat in the chocolate mixture. If you do not have a second mixer bowl, scrape this mixture into a large bowl and thoroughly wash, rinse, and dry the mixer bowl and whisk beater to remove any trace of oil.

3) Sift half of the flour over the egg mixture and, using a large balloon whisk, slotted skimmer, or silicone spatula, fold it in gently but rapidly until almost all of the flour has disappeared. Repeat with the remaining flour until all traces of the flour have disappeared.

BEAT THE EGG WHITES INTO A STIFF MERINGUE

4) In the bowl of a stand mixer fitted with the whisk beater, beat the remaining half of the egg whites and the cream of tartar on medium-low speed until foamy. Gradually raise the speed to medium-high and beat until soft peaks form when the beater is raised. Gradually beat in the remaining 13 grams/1 tablespoon of sugar and continue beating until stiff peaks form when the beater is raised slowly.

Continued

ADD THE MERINGUE TO THE BATTER

5) Using a large balloon whisk, slotted skimmer, or large silicone spatula, gently fold the meringue into the batter. Scrape the batter into the prepared pan and, using a small offset spatula, smooth it as evenly as possible.

BAKE THE CAKE

6) Bake for 7 to 10 minutes, or until set and the cake springs back when pressed lightly in the center. Have ready a small sharp knife.

UNMOLD AND COOL THE CAKE

7) If necessary, loosen the sides of the cake with the tip of the sharp knife. Immediately slip a small offset spatula under the narrow edge of the parchment to loosen it. Grasp the parchment and gently slide the cake onto a large uncoated wire rack.

8) Place the towel on top of the cake. Position the other wire rack on top of the towel. Invert the cake and carefully peel off the parchment. Sprinkle the cake lightly with cocoa and roll it up while still hot, towel and all. Set it on the wire rack to cool completely, about 20 minutes.

9) Wash and dry the half sheet pan and set it in the freezer.

COMPOSE THE CAKE ROLL

10) Set the ice cream in the refrigerator to soften to a spreadable consistency.

11) Cut the cherries in half and set them on paper towels to dry.

12) Unroll the cake onto the back of the chilled half sheet pan, leaving the towel underneath the cake.

13) Brush the cake evenly with the brandied cherry syrup.

14) With an offset spatula, quickly spread the softened ice cream over the cake, leaving one inch uncovered along one long side. If the ice cream begins to melt, set the pan in the freezer for 5 to 10 minutes, or until firm.

15) Scatter the cherries over the ice cream.

16) Starting from the long side that is covered with ice cream, use the towel to assist with rolling the cake, removing it as you roll up the cake. Set it seam side down on the pan, cover it lightly with plastic wrap, and return it to the freezer.

17) When the cake roll is very firm, after a minimum of 2 hours, wrap it tightly with two layers of plastic wrap and freeze it for at least 12 hours before serving.

18) Use a sharp knife dipped in hot water to slice the roll. Set each slice on a plate and drizzle with the hot fudge sauce. If the ice cream is still very solid, allow the slices to sit on the plates for 5 to 10 minutes before serving.

STORE Filled cake: Airtight: frozen, minimum 12 hours and up to 3 days (about 1 week if using commercial ice cream with stabilizer)

Unfilled cake: Airtight: room temperature, 3 days; refrigerated, 5 days; frozen, 2 months

SCOOPS

❊ The ice cream can be softened with 7-second bursts in the microwave or by beating it in the chilled bowl of a stand mixer with the chilled flat beater.

❊ Commercial ice cream usually has more overrun than homemade. (This refers to the amount of air that gets incorporated during the freezing process.) When the ice cream is softened to make it possible to spread it into the cake-lined mold, it loses much of the air, and the volume can decrease by as much as one-third. If using commercial ice cream, you will need extra to achieve the desired thickness. A quart/liter will be more than enough.

GOLDEN ANGEL CAKE

Serves: 12 to 16

OVEN
TEMPERATURE:
350°F/175°C

BAKING TIME:
25 to 35 minutes

SPECIAL
EQUIPMENT

**FOR THE
CARAMELIZED
SUGAR:**

One 17¼ by 12¼
by 1 inch half sheet
pan, lined with
a large sheet of
uncoated heavy-
duty foil (be sure it
comes up the sides
of the pan)

A coarse strainer

Caramelized sugar is the sweetener for this cake, which also lends it a lovely golden color. The flavor has a subtle edge of caramel with a soft, moist crumb. Angel food cake and ice cream are a marriage made in heaven. The ideal foil to the cake's caramelized sweetness is a big scoop of coffee or vanilla ice cream. Alternatively, I like to cut 1 inch cubes of cake to add to each serving bowl—they act like little sponges to sop up some of the ice cream as it slowly melts.

Plan Ahead Combine the egg whites and caramelized sugar at least 1 and up to 4 hours ahead, for most of the sugar to dissolve.

CARAMELIZED SUGAR

Makes: 350 grams/1¾ cups

sugar, preferably superfine	350 grams	1¾ cups
water	79 grams	⅓ cup (79 ml)

MAKE THE CARAMELIZED SUGAR

1) In a small saucepan, preferably nonstick, stir together the sugar and water until the sugar is moistened. Be careful to avoid getting sugar crystals on the sides of the pan above the syrup. Heat, stirring constantly, until the sugar has dissolved and comes to a boil. (If any sugar crystals form on the sides of the pan, either wash them down with a clean, wet pastry brush or set a lid on top of the pan for a minute and the steam will dissolve them.) Continue boiling, without stirring, until the syrup caramelizes to deep amber, about 370° to 375°F/188° to 190°C. (Do not let it go above 375°F/190°C or it will be bitter.)

2) Immediately remove the pan from the heat and pour the caramel (do not scrape the bottom) onto the prepared pan, tilting to spread it thinly.

SPECIAL EQUIPMENT

FOR THE GOLDEN ANGEL CAKE:

One uncoated 10 inch (16 cup) two-piece metal tube pan (if your pan has feet, a wire rack elevated at least 4 inches above the work surface by 3 or 4 cans, coffee mugs, or glasses of equal height OR a long-necked glass bottle weighted with sugar or marbles to keep it from tipping OR a large inverted metal funnel that will fit into the opening at the top of the pan)

3) When the caramel is completely cool, carefully break it into pieces and process in a food processor until most of it is fairly fine. Do not make all of it powder fine, because it will have a tendency to clump.

4) Weigh out or measure 300 grams/1½ cups into the bowl of a stand mixer.

BATTER

Caramelized Sugar	300 grams	1½ cups
16 large egg whites	480 grams	2 cups (473 ml)
cream of tartar	.	2 teaspoons
salt	.	¼ teaspoon
bleached cake flour	125 grams	1¼ cups (sifted into the cup and leveled off)
pure vanilla extract	20 grams	4 teaspoons (20 ml)

PREHEAT THE OVEN

✲ Twenty minutes or longer before baking, set an oven rack in the lower third of the oven. Set the oven at 350°F/175°C.

MISE EN PLACE

✲ Into the bowl of the stand mixer containing the caramelized sugar, weigh or measure the egg whites, cream of tartar, and salt and, with the whisk beater held in your hand, whisk them together until blended. Cover and allow it to sit at room temperature for at least 1 and up to 4 hours, or until most of the sugar has dissolved.

✲ In a small bowl, weigh or measure the flour and have a medium-mesh strainer or sifter ready.

BEAT THE EGG WHITE MIXTURE INTO A STIFF MERINGUE

1) Attach the whisk beater. Beat the egg white mixture on medium-low speed until foamy. Gradually raise the speed to high and beat for a full 10 minutes. When the beater is raised slowly, the meringue will have very stiff peaks. Beat in the vanilla until combined.

Continued

COMPLETE THE BATTER

2) Sift the flour over the meringue, about ¼ cup at a time. With a large balloon whisk, slotted skimmer, or large silicone spatula, fold in the flour mixture quickly but gently. It is not necessary to incorporate every speck until the last addition. Use a large silicone spatula to reach to the bottom of the bowl.

3) Use a long narrow metal spatula to spread a thin layer of batter onto the sides of the pan (this will ensure smooth sides). With a large spoon, gently scoop in the rest of the batter, distributing it evenly into the pan. In a 16-cup pan, it will be ½ inch from the top of the rim.

4) Run the metal spatula or a knife through the batter to prevent air pockets and smooth the surface evenly.

BAKE THE CAKE

5) Bake for 25 to 35 minutes. The cake will rise about 1 inch above the sides of the pan, and will be done when it just starts lowering in the pan. It will be golden brown, with no moist spots visible in the cracks, and a wooden skewer inserted between the tube and the side will come out clean. An instant-read thermometer should read 202°F/94°C.

COOL AND UNMOLD THE CAKE

6) Immediately invert the pan onto the prepared wire rack or invert the center tube opening of the pan onto the neck of the bottle to suspend it well above the countertop. Cool completely in the pan, about 1½ hours.

7) To loosen the sides of the cake from the pan, use a rigid sharp knife or stiff metal spatula, preferably with a squared-off end. Scrape firmly against the pan's sides and slowly and carefully circle the pan. In order to ensure that you are scraping against the sides of the pan to remove the crust from the pan and leave it on the cake, begin by angling the knife or spatula about 20 degrees away from the cake and toward the pan, pushing the cake inward a bit. It is best to use a knife blade that is at least 4 inches long and no wider than 1 inch.

8) Grasp the center core and lift out the cake. Run a wire cake tester or wooden skewer around the center core. Dislodge the cake from the bottom with a metal spatula or thin, sharp knife.

STORE
Loosely
covered: room
temperature,
3 days;
refrigerated,
1 week

9) Invert the cake onto a flat plate covered with plastic wrap that has been coated lightly with nonstick cooking spray and then reinvert it onto a cardboard round or serving platter. Allow the cake to sit for 1 hour, or until the top is no longer tacky. Then cover it with a cake dome or wrap it airtight.

SCOOPS

✢ Do not spray or oil the foil for the caramel as it would prevent the egg whites from beating.

✢ If it's a humid day and the powdered caramel clumps after pulverizing, it will still dissolve in the egg white.

✢ The beater bowl and whisk must be free of any grease to enable the whites to beat to stiff peaks.

✢ This cake is unique to angel food cakes. Caramelized sugar is always slightly sticky and therefore requires 25 grams/¼ cup more flour than my other angel food cakes. It also takes a little less time to bake.

✢ My recipe uses 1 egg white per cup capacity of the pan. (To determine the volume of your pan, line it with a clean plastic bag and pour in water up to the top, counting the cups as you go.) If your pan is smaller, simply decrease the recipe or bake any extra batter as cupcakes. Be sure to cool the cupcakes upside down on a wire rack to ensure maximum volume. Sixteen beaten whites will rise to the very top of a 5 quart/5 liter mixer.

✢ To prevent cake batter from spilling inside the center core when filling the pan, wrap a piece of aluminum foil to cover the opening and about ½ inch down the outside of the tube to secure it. Remove it before baking the cake.

✢ To serve the cake à la mode, cut the cake using two forks back to back (for the fluffiest texture). Alternatively, use an electric knife or a serrated knife, but hold the cake gently without compressing it as you cut.

Continued

VARIATION

ANGEL FOOD TUNNEL CAKE

Angel food cake does not freeze as hard as most cakes, which makes it an ideal ice cream cake! Here the ice cream hides inside a tunnel cut inside the cake.

Espresso (page 28) or Vanilla (page 3) Ice Cream, 3 to 4 cups/710 ml to 1 liter
You may need the higher amount of ice cream if using commercial ice cream because when softened, it loses more volume (due to higher overrun—or more air—in the ice cream). It is best to have 1½ quarts/1½ liters on hand.

Composing the Ice Cream Tunnel Cake

1) Measure down 1 inch from the top (wider end) of the cake, and score the cake with a serrated knife. Using the scored line as a guide, cut through the cake. With two large spatulas or a removable bottom from a tart pan, lift the cut cake ring off the cake and set it aside.

2) Measure 1½ inches from the tip of a sharp paring knife and apply a piece of masking tape to the knife as a guide marker for depth. Cut the outer and inner sides of the tunnel, angled with the sides of the cake, so that the tunnel is about 1¾ inches wide and 1½ inches deep.

3) To remove the cake from the tunnel, first cut across the width of the tunnel at every inch to make sections. Use a fork to remove each sliced section. Once all of the sections are removed, you can use the fork or a spoon to scrape the bottom of the tunnel to make a somewhat even surface. (Save the scraps to make a trifle or parfait.)

4) Freeze the cake for 20 to 30 minutes. While the cake is freezing, soften the ice cream in the refrigerator. Fill the cake's tunnel with softened ice cream and replace the cake top.

5) Set a serving plate or 10 inch cake round covered with plastic wrap on top, and invert the cake. Cover with two layers of plastic wrap and freeze for a minimum of 6 hours.

Serving the Cake

6) Set the cake in the refrigerator for 20 to 30 minutes to soften the ice cream. Use a sharp serrated knife, dipped in hot water and wiped dry, to slice through the cake. If the ice cream is still very solid, allow the slices to sit on the plates for 5 to 10 minutes before serving.

STORE Airtight: frozen, 3 days (about 1 week if using commercial ice cream with stabilizers)

Powdered caramel for making the cake.

Cut the cake horizontally 1 inch down from the top on scored lines.

Cut the outer and inner sides of the tunnel.

Use forks to remove sections of the tunnel.

Fill the tunnel with softened ice cream.

The inside of the cake.

SPUN SUGAR NESTS

Makes: About 6 nests

Spun sugar is so magical and fun to make. Golden nests of spun sugar provide one of the most exquisite presentations for ice cream. Beeswax works effectively to keep the sugar strands flexible, but if you're not using it, it is advisable to make the spun sugar in two batches and work quickly to shape it into nests.

SPECIAL EQUIPMENT

Six large custard cups or shallow containers, lightly coated with nonstick cooking spray

A long wire whisk with the looped ends cut off with a wire cutter so that all the extending wires are straight and even in length (or two forks held back to back)

sugar	150 grams	¾ cup
corn syrup	164 grams	½ cup (118 ml)
beeswax, grated (optional)	.	½ tablespoon

MISE EN PLACE

✤ Cover the floor and counter with parchment or newspaper to catch stray strands of the spun sugar. Oil the handles of two long wooden spoons or dowels and tape them to the counter about 12 inches apart, with the handles extending well beyond the edge of the counter.

✤ Have ready a 2 cup/473 ml glass measure with a spout and the prepared wire whisk.

MAKE THE SPUN SUGAR

1) In a small heavy saucepan, stir together the sugar and corn syrup. Over medium heat, bring it to a boil, stirring constantly. Raise the heat slightly and continue boiling until medium amber. An instant-read thermometer should read 360°F/180°C. Immediately remove it from the heat and pour it into the glass measure. The temperature will continue to rise to 370°F/188°C.

2) Allow the caramel to cool for a few minutes and then add the beeswax, if using. When the smoking stops, use a fork to lift the caramel to see if it forms strings rather than droplets. If not, let it cool a little more until it forms strings.

3) Dip the whisk or forks into the caramel and wave it quickly and continuously, in a whiplike motion, over the spoon handles, allowing it to fall in long, thin

Continued

Start to spin the sugar over the spoon handles.

Use a whiplike motion to spin the sugar.

Inspect the spun sugar strands.

A close-up of the spun sugar strands.

Shape the spun sugar into a nest.

The happiness of having a beautiful spun sugar nest.

strands. If the caramel starts cooling and thickening, heat it with 3-second bursts in the microwave. Repeat with the remaining caramel.

4) Form the strands into small nests, molding them into the custard cups, and set them in airtight containers. Store them at room temperature or in the freezer.

5) To serve, use a small ice cream scoop, preferably oval, to set scoops of ice cream, or one large scoop, into the nests.

STORE Airtight: room temperature (at low humidity), 2 to 3 weeks; frozen, 3 months

SCOOPS

❊ Beeswax can be found in stores that sell sewing and craft supplies or beeswax candles.

❊ Avoid making the caramel in humid weather because the spun sugar will be sticky and most of it will evaporate.

❊ If the caramel is too hot, it will form droplets instead of fine strands.

UPSIDE DOWN LEMON MERINGUE PIE

Serves: 6 to 8

OVEN TEMPERATURE:
200°F/93°C

BAKING TIME:
2 hours, plus 20 minutes with the oven off and door open

SPECIAL EQUIPMENT

One 9½ inch deep dish pie plate, preferably Pyrex, coated with nonstick cooking spray and then coated with cornstarch (invert the pie plate and tap it to knock out any excess cornstarch)

A large disposable piping bag fitted with a ½ inch star pastry tube or a quart-size reclosable freezer bag with a small semicircle cut from one corner and fitted with the star pastry tube

This is my top favorite "socials" recipe in the book! A sweet and crisp meringue shell is the perfect container for the tart and creamy True Lemon Ice Cream (page 119), but it works with your favorite ice cream as well. Piping the meringue makes it easier to spread evenly, but it will be every bit as beautiful if spread with a spatula instead. The secret to its easy unmolding is nonstick cooking spray and cornstarch. You can unmold the meringue shell from the pie plate and fill it with whipped cream and berries instead of ice cream, but if you are filling it with ice cream, it needs the support of the pie plate for cutting slices.

Plan Ahead Fill the meringue shell with ice cream a minimum of 2 hours and up to 5 days before serving.

COMPONENTS

True Lemon Ice Cream (page 119), about 3½ cups/about 830 ml (see Scoops)

Lemon Stardust (optional; page 191)

CRISP MERINGUE PIE SHELL

3 large egg whites	90 grams	¼ cup plus 2 tablespoons (89 ml)
cream of tartar	.	⅜ teaspoon
superfine sugar	175 grams	¾ cup plus 2 tablespoons

PREHEAT THE OVEN

✻ Twenty minutes or longer before baking, set an oven rack at the middle level. Set the oven at 200°F/93°C.

Continued

✣ Into the bowl of a stand mixer, weigh or measure the egg whites, cream of tartar, and sugar and whisk them together until blended. Cover and allow it to sit at room temperature for a minimum of 30 minutes and up to 6 hours.

MAKE THE MERINGUE

1) Attach the whisk beater. Starting on low speed and gradually raising the speed to high, beat for 12 minutes. The meringue will be very thick and glossy and form curved peaks when the beater is raised.

PIPE THE MERINGUE SHELL

2) Insert the star tube into the piping or freezer bag and fill it with half of the meringue. Hold the bag in a vertical position (straight up and down) with the tube at least 1½ inches above the pan. To achieve the full height, the meringue must be allowed to fall from the tube (not pressed against the pan).

3) Starting at the center of the pie plate, pipe a spiral coil to cover the bottom and sides of the plate. To prevent gaps, let the spirals of meringue fall against the side, almost on top of the previous spirals. The weight of the meringue will cause them to fall perfectly into place. Continue piping until the coil has reached the sides of the plate.

4) Refill the bag with the remaining meringue. For the sides, pipe single rings of meringue until the last ring is just above the rim. Smooth the top edge of the meringue to form a level, ½ inch wide top edge. To reinforce where the sides and bottom coils meet, in order to prevent cracking, pipe a coil of meringue against the bottom side coil and smooth it with a spoon. Fill in any gaps in the meringue coils and smooth the surfaces of the bottom and sides with a spoon or small offset spatula. If desired, pipe a decorative border (see Scoops).

BAKE AND COOL THE MERINGUE SHELL

5) Bake for 2 hours without opening the oven door. The meringue should not be brown. To check the meringue for doneness, without removing it from the oven, use the tip of a small, sharp knife to dig out a little from the bottom's center. It can still be slightly sticky, as it will continue to dry while cooling. If it is stickier, continue to bake it, checking every 10 minutes until it is done. (A slight stickiness in the meringue shell bottom can be extra pleasing!)

6) To prevent cracking, turn off the oven and prop the door open slightly with a wooden spoon handle. Let the meringue sit for 10 minutes. Then open the oven door completely and let the meringue sit for another 10 minutes. Remove it from the oven and place it on a counter. Place a cake dome or large bowl over the pie plate and cool the meringue for another 30 minutes.

COMPOSE THE PIE

7) Soften the ice cream until spreadable, then fill the meringue shell. Set a piece of plastic wrap on top of the ice cream surface and freeze the completed pie for a minimum of 4 hours. Depending on the temperature of your freezer and refrigerator, you will need to allow it to soften in the refrigerator for 30 minutes to an hour before serving.

8) To cut slices, first slip the tip of a small knife between the top edge and the pie plate to dislodge it. The meringue will unmold easily from the pie plate but will crumble slightly on serving.

Garnish if desired with the lemon stardust.

SCOOPS

❄ Commercial ice cream usually has more overrun than homemade. (This refers to the amount of air that gets incorporated during the freezing process.) When the ice cream is softened to make it possible to spread it into the meringue shell, it loses much of the air and the volume can decrease by as much as one-third. If using commercial ice cream, you will need extra to fill the meringue shell to the desired thickness. Have at least 1½ quarts/1½ liters on hand.

❄ If piping a large decorative border, you will need to increase the meringue by 1⅓ times (4 egg whites/120 grams, ½ teaspoon cream of tartar, and 1 cup plus 2 tablespoons and 2 teaspoons/233 grams sugar).

❄ You can create a decorative swirl on the top of the ice cream by using a small offset spatula. Allow the ice cream to freeze for about 30 minutes before setting the plastic wrap on top.

MINI PAVLOVAS

Makes: 8 servings (4 inches by ⅞ inch high)

OVEN TEMPERATURE:
200°F/93°C

BAKING TIME:
1 hour and 35 to 45 minutes

SPECIAL EQUIPMENT

Two 16 by 12 inch cookie sheets, lined with parchment

These little pavlovas serve as lovely crunchy containers for ice cream. They're filled and frozen until shortly before serving, then adorned with the topping of your choice. I especially like strawberry ice cream and then a topping of macerated strawberries (see page 184).

MERINGUE

4 large egg whites	120 grams	½ cup (118 ml)
cream of tartar	.	½ teaspoon
superfine sugar	240 grams	1 cup plus 3 tablespoons

PREHEAT THE OVEN

✢ Twenty minutes or longer before baking, set the oven racks in the upper and lower thirds of the oven. Set the oven at 200°F/93°C.

MISE EN PLACE

✢ Into the bowl of a stand mixer, weigh or measure the egg whites, cream of tartar, and sugar and whisk them together until blended. Cover and allow it to sit at room temperature for a minimum of 30 minutes and up to 6 hours.

✢ Draw four 4 inch circles on each parchment sheet and invert them onto the cookie sheets. With masking tape, secure the edges of the parchment to the cookie sheets in two or three places.

MAKE THE MERINGUE

1) Attach the whisk beater. Starting on low speed and gradually raising the speed to high, beat for 12 minutes. The meringue will be very thick and glossy and form curved peaks when the beater is raised.

2) With a large spoon, spread the meringue within the 4 inch circles. With the back of the spoon, form a 2 inch hollow in the middle of each to create a 1 inch border that is about ¾ inch high. Remove the tape.

BAKE AND COOL THE MERINGUES

3) Bake without opening the oven door for 1½ hours, at which point it's fine to check the interior of one of the pavlovas. With the tip of a small, sharp knife, dig out a little of the meringue from the inside border. It should be a little soft and sticky. Set the cookie sheet on a wire rack to cool to room temperature.

FILL THE PAVLOVAS

4) Fill each pavlova with a large scoop of your favorite ice cream.

STORE Filled ice cream pavlovas: Airtight: frozen, 3 days (about 1 week if using commercial ice cream with stabilizer)

Unfilled pavlovas: Airtight: room temperature (at low humidity), 5 days; frozen, 3 months

STICKY TOFFEE "PUDDING" CAKE SUNDAES

Makes: 12 servings

OVEN TEMPERATURE:
350°F/175°C

BAKING TIME:
20 to 30 minutes

SPECIAL EQUIPMENT

One 9 by 13 by 2 inch high pan, coated with solid shortening, bottom lined with parchment

A baking sheet, lined with plastic wrap and lightly coated with nonstick cooking spray

A second baking sheet or a cutting board

This sundae came about by pure serendipity. I had invited friends for afternoon tea and wanted to treat them to one of my favorite desserts—Sticky Toffee Pudding—but I knew that their daughter loved chocolate ice cream, so I made that as well. The unique recipe for this pudding cake comes from Jenn Giblin, pastry chef of Blue Smoke, in New York City. The addition of stout beer as the liquid for the batter gives it the most delicious flavor of any I have tasted.

COMPONENTS

Butterscotch Toffee Sauce, makes enough for 3 tablespoons per serving (page 203)

Ice Cream, about 2 quarts/2 liters, chocolate or vanilla

Lightly toasted pecans, coarsely broken, 120 grams/1 rounded cup

BATTER

unsalted butter	85 grams	6 tablespoons (¾ stick)
3 large eggs	150 grams	½ cup plus 1½ tablespoons (140 ml)
stout beer, preferably Guinness extra stout	227 grams	1 cup (237 ml)
baking soda	5.5 grams	1 teaspoon
dates (pitted)	170 grams	about 6 large dates
sugar	225 grams	1 cup plus 2 tablespoons
pure vanilla extract	.	½ tablespoon (7.5 ml)
bleached all-purpose flour	227 grams	2 cups (sifted into the cup and leveled off)
baking powder	4.5 grams	1 teaspoon
salt	.	¼ teaspoon
ground cinnamon	.	1 teaspoon
nutmeg, freshly grated	.	½ teaspoon

Continued

PREHEAT THE OVEN

✣ Twenty minutes or longer before baking, set an oven rack in the lower third of the oven. Set the oven at 350°F/175°C.

MISE EN PLACE

✣ About 1 hour ahead, set the butter and eggs on the counter at room temperature (65° to 75°F/18° to 24°C).

SOFTEN AND PROCESS THE DATES

1) In a small saucepan, bring the stout beer to the boiling point. Remove it from the heat and add the baking soda. It will fizz up a lot. Set the pitted dates in a small bowl and pour the beer over them. Cover tightly with plastic wrap and allow it to cool to room temperature.

2) When cool, place the dates in a food processor along with a little of the beer. Process until a paste is formed and then gradually add the rest of the beer through the feed tube. The mixture will be very smooth, dark, and glossy. Scrape it into a bowl and cover it tightly with plastic wrap until ready to use.

MIX THE BATTER

3) In the bowl of a stand mixer fitted with the whisk beater, beat the butter, sugar, and vanilla on medium speed until light and fluffy.

4) In a small bowl, lightly whisk the eggs. Gradually add the eggs to the batter in three parts, beating on medium speed for about 15 seconds after each addition. Scrape down the sides of the bowl after each addition. (The mixture may appear curdled, but after adding the flour it will be smooth.)

MIX IN THE FLOUR MIXTURE AND DATES

5) In a medium bowl, whisk together the flour, baking powder, salt, cinnamon, and nutmeg.

6) Add one-third of the flour mixture to the batter and mix on low speed for 10 to 15 seconds, just until incorporated. Scrape down the sides of the bowl.

7) Add half of the date mixture and mix just until incorporated, about 15 seconds. Repeat with another third of the flour mixture, then the remaining date mixture, and finally the remaining flour mixture. Mix just until the batter is uniform in color and no streaks remain. Scrape down the sides of the bowl as needed.

8) Scrape the batter into the prepared pan and smooth the surface evenly with a small offset spatula. It will be about one-third full.

BAKE THE CAKE

9) Bake for 20 to 30 minutes, or until a cake tester comes out clean when inserted in the center and the cake springs back when pressed lightly in the center.

10) While the cake is baking, make the toffee sauce (see page 203).

COOL AND UNMOLD THE CAKE

11) Set the pan on a wire rack and let the cake cool for 10 minutes. Run a small metal spatula between the sides of the pan and the cake, pressing firmly against the pan. Place the plastic-wrapped baking sheet on top and invert the cake. Remove the parchment. Reinvert it onto a second sheet and cool completely.

COMPOSE THE SUNDAES

12) Cut the pudding cake into 12 squares and set each slice on a serving plate. Top with 1 or 2 scoops of ice cream. Pass the toffee sauce and pecans.

STORE Untopped pudding cake: Airtight: room temperature, 2 days; refrigerated, 1 week; frozen, 3 months

SCOOPS

✲ If using a Pyrex pan, lower the baking temperature to 325°F/160°C.

✲ If measuring by volume rather than weighing, pour the beer carefully against the side of the measuring cup to prevent foaming. If there is some foam, allow it to settle so you can get an accurate measure.

WATERMELON ICE CREAM BOMBE

Makes: 6 to 8 servings

SPECIAL EQUIPMENT

One 6 cup/1.5 liter watermelon mold (or deep round bowl lined with plastic wrap long enough to extend over the sides of the bowl), placed in the freezer

Two baking sheets lined with parchment

This is one of the most delicious and stunning composed ice creams I know. I first experienced it as a child in the home of my great-aunt Polly. Her housekeeper Hannah was a gifted cook and had been a pastry chef in Vienna before moving to New York City. The concept of ice cream shaped to resemble a watermelon was hers, but the components offered in this version are mine. Hannah's version used raspberry sorbet, where I prefer the bombe to be ice cream through and through, except of course for the ganache seeds.

dark chocolate, 60% to 62% cacao, finely chopped	56 grams (2 ounces)	about ⅓ cup
heavy cream	14 grams	1 tablespoon (15 ml)
Pistachio Ice Cream (page 157)	.	2½ cups (600 ml)
Raspberry Ice Cream (page 58)	.	2¼ cups (500 ml)

MAKE THE GANACHE SEEDS

1) In a 1 cup/237 ml glass measure with a spout, or small microwavable bowl, stirring every 15 seconds, heat the chocolate until almost completely melted. (Alternatively, heat the chocolate in the top of a double boiler set over hot, not simmering, water, stirring often—do not let the bottom of the upper container touch the water.)

2) Remove the chocolate from the heat source and stir in the cream until smooth and uniform.

3) Use a small offset spatula to spread the ganache in a thin layer on one of the lined baking sheets. Allow it to harden at room temperature for several hours or set the baking sheet in the freezer just until the chocolate is firm, about 20 minutes.

Continued

4) Use the tip of a small, sharp knife or an elliptical canapé cutter about ⅞ inch long to form the "seeds." Place the sheet of seeds in the freezer until very hard.

5) Separate the seeds from the chocolate sheet by sliding a knife or metal spatula under the chocolate. The seeds will pop out. Place them on the second lined baking sheet and return them to the freezer until very hard.

COMPOSE THE BOMBE

6) Set the pistachio ice cream in the refrigerator to soften to a spreadable consistency.

7) Spread the pistachio ice cream into the bottom and up the sides of the chilled mold, just up to the edge of the decorative ridged part if using a watermelon mold. Cover with plastic wrap and set it in the freezer for about 30 minutes or until firm. To achieve an even layer of pistachio ice cream on the sides and bottom, use a toothpick inserted into the ice cream as a gauge. If necessary, with the back of a tablespoon, spread some of the ice cream from the bottom, where it usually will be thicker, onto the sides. Re-cover with plastic wrap and return it to the freezer until very firm.

8) Soften the raspberry ice cream and fold about half of the ganache seeds into it.

9) Fill the center of the mold with the raspberry ice cream. Press a piece of plastic wrap on top, wrap tightly with plastic wrap, and freeze for at least 6 hours and up to 3 days.

SERVE THE BOMBE

10) Remove the plastic wrap and invert the mold onto a serving plate. Run a towel under warm water and wring it out. Drape it evenly over the mold and let it sit for about 30 seconds. Repeat as necessary until you can lift away the mold. (If using the bowl, use the ends of the plastic wrap to help pull out the ice cream.)

11) Use a sharp knife dipped in hot water to slice the bombe. Set each slice on a plate and place the remaining chocolate seeds on the raspberry ice cream, pressing them in slightly. If the ice cream is still very solid, allow the slices to sit on the plates for 5 to 10 minutes before serving.

STORE In its mold: frozen, 3 days

SCOOPS

✻ The ice cream can be softened with 7-second bursts in the microwave or by beating it in the chilled bowl of a stand mixer with the chilled flat beater.

✻ Commercial ice cream usually has more overrun than homemade. (This refers to the amount of air that gets incorporated during the freezing process.) When the ice cream is softened to make it possible to spread it into the mold, it loses much of the air, and the volume can decrease by as much as one-third. If using commercial ice cream, you will need a little extra of each ice cream to fill the mold to the desired thickness. It's best to have 1 quart/1 liter of each on hand.

FROZEN MANGO LASSI

Makes: 8 to 10 servings (about 3½ quarts/3.3 liters)

I had tried for years to create a recipe for this luscious drink that had the full rich flavor of the mango and then, while working on this book, inspiration struck: Add mango ice cream! This indulgent version has the consistency of a thick milkshake. If you prefer it thinner, simply add more water.

Mango Ice Cream (page 79)	800 grams	1 quart/1 liter (see Scoops)
Alphonso mango pulp, preferably Ratna brand	600 grams	3 cups (710 ml)
plain whole milk yogurt (regular, not Greek)	300 grams	1¼ cups
cold water	532 grams	2¼ cups (532 ml)

MAKE IN 2 BATCHES

1) Allow the ice cream to soften until scoopable.

2) In a blender, combine half of the ice cream (400 grams/2 cups/473 ml), mango pulp, yogurt, and water until well mixed. Scrape down the sides as needed.

3) Pour the lassi into glasses and, if desired, top each with a little scoop of the leftover ice cream.

4) Repeat with the remaining ingredients (400 grams/2 cups/473 ml of the ice cream) to make the second batch.

The mango lassi will keep refrigerated for up to 24 hours but will be a little less thick as the ice cream softens.

SCOOPS

✴ The Mango Ice Cream recipe makes slightly more than 1 quart/1 liter, so you will have a little left over, which you can use to top the lassis.

✴ You will need a total of 935 grams/33 ounces of mango pulp to make both the ice cream and the lassi if making 8 servings. Mango pulp is usually only in 850 gram/20 ounce cans; it's fine to decrease the amount of pulp in the lassi and add all of the ice cream instead.

✴ A marigold makes a gorgeous garnish.

POMEGRANATE BOURBON SOUR

Makes: 2 servings

This isn't an ice cream recipe, but if you've bought Pama pomegranate liqueur for topping the Pomegranate Pride Ice Cream (page 110), this is a perfect use for it! I've always loved bourbon sours, but when I discovered a pomegranate version in Kentucky, the land of bourbon, I was determined to recreate it. It turns out, as with so many things, that making the sour mix from scratch is a world apart from the bottled variety in freshness of flavor.

If the wonderful pomegranate liqueur is not available, simply double the bourbon.

I like drinking my sour from a brandy snifter, but if you prefer a more traditional tumbler, it will taste just as good.

granulated sugar	25 grams	2 tablespoons
water	30 grams	2 tablespoons (30 ml)
bourbon, preferably Woodhall Reserve or Gentleman Jack	60 grams	¼ cup (59 ml)
Pama pomegranate liqueur	60 grams	¼ cup (59 ml)
lemon juice, freshly squeezed and strained (2 lemons)	84 grams	⅓ cup (79 ml)
1 large, thick-skinned orange	.	.
2 maraschino cherries, preferably Luxardo	.	.

MAKE A SIMPLE SYRUP

1) In a small saucepan, stir together the sugar and water. Over medium heat, bring it to a boil. Pour the syrup into a small glass measure with a spout and set it aside to cool completely.

MIX THE LIQUID INGREDIENTS

2) A minimum of 30 minutes and up to 8 hours ahead, in a pitcher, stir together the bourbon, pomegranate liqueur, lemon juice, and simple syrup.

3) Cut the orange in half and cut two slices from the center. Squeeze the juice from the rest of the orange. Strain it and stir it into the juices in the pitcher.

4) Place the two orange slices and the two maraschino cherries in the pitcher. If some extra sweetness is desired, add a little of the maraschino juice. Cover and refrigerate until well chilled.

To serve: Fill two glasses with ice cubes. Stir the sour and pour it over the ice cubes. Garnish each with an orange slice and a cherry.

ACKNOWLEDGMENTS

This is the book of my heart because of all sweet things, ice cream is my favorite to eat. My first thanks goes to my dear editor, Stephanie Fletcher, who loves ice cream as I do and who believed that there are many others out there who will value the ability to make delicious creamy ice cream at home.

I have been graced by the best of all possible production teams: As always, Woody Wolston of team "RoseWood," who has aptly been named by *Publishers Weekly* my "partner in crème"; the incredibly talented, organized, and generous Erin Jeanne McDowell and her invaluable assistant, Kaitlin Wayne, who are responsible for the beauty of all the photos in this book, rising to the greatest challenge of scooping and arranging ice cream at its most appealing moment before melting; and Matthew Septimus, genius photographer, who joyfully goes the extra mile, capturing all that Erin created with brilliant lighting and focus. Never has "labor of love" been more appropriate. Deep bow, hugs, and kisses to all of them and also to my brilliant friend Marissa Rothkopf Bates, who graced this book with a foreword that brings tears to my eyes every time I read it.

Great gratitude to the HMH production team: Tai Blanche, art director, for her stunning cover and both gorgeous and useful book design; Marina Padakis Lowry, dedicated managing editor, baker, and kindred spirit; Jamie Selzer, production editor; Karen Wise, copy editor; Sarah Vostok and my dear friend and colleague Zach Townsend, proofreaders; Elizabeth Parson, indexer; Samantha Simon, marketing manager; and Sari Kamin, publicity manager.

SPECIAL MENTIONS:

Dan O'Malley, American Products Group, producer of "Rose's Signature Series"; Organic Valley, producers of the best cultured butter, cream, and milk, so important for these dairy-centric recipes; India Tree, for the most transformative Muscovado sugars; Valrhona and Guittard, for their fabulous chocolates; Breville and Cuisinart for their stellar ice cream machines; ThermoWorks for producing the reliably accurate Thermapen thermometer; and Jim Baldwin of Stretch-Tite, who produces the indispensable plastic wrap used for every ice cream.

Infinite appreciation always goes to my husband, Elliott, who is an equally enthusiastic ice cream eater, and to the blessing of having my avocation also be my vocation, enabling me to do the work I love every day.

INDEX

Note: Page references in *italics* indicate photographs.